THE THEATRE OF RUPERT GOOLD

Sarah Grochala leads the MFA/MA Writing for Stage and Broadcast Media programme at the Royal Central School of Speech and Drama, London, UK. Her previous publications include *The Contemporary Political Play: Rethinking Dramaturgical Structure* (Methuen Drama, 2017) and her plays include *S-27* (Amnesty International/iceandfire Protect the Human Award 2007). Between 2012 and 2016, she was an associate artist with the theatre company Headlong and worked with Rupert Goold during the final year of his tenure as artistic director.

Related titles

THE CONTEMPORARY POLITICAL PLAY: RETHINKING
DRAMATURGICAL STRUCTURE
Sarah Grochala
ISBN 978-1-4725-8846-3

GOOD NIGHTS OUT: A HISTORY OF POPULAR BRITISH THEATRE
1940–2015
Aleks Sierz
ISBN 978-1-3500-4621-4

IVO VAN HOVE: FROM SHAKESPEARE TO DAVID BOWIE
Susan Bennett and Sonia Massai
ISBN 978-1-3500-3154-8

STAGING AMERICA: TWENTY-FIRST-CENTURY DRAMATISTS
Christopher Bigsby
ISBN 978-1-3501-2754-8

THE THEATRE OF RUPERT GOOLD

RADICAL APPROACHES TO ADAPTATION AND NEW WRITING

Sarah Grochala

methuen | drama
LONDON • NEW YORK • OXFORD • NEW DELHI • SYDNEY

METHUEN DRAMA
Bloomsbury Publishing Plc
50 Bedford Square, London, WC1B 3DP, UK
1385 Broadway, New York, NY 10018, USA

BLOOMSBURY, METHUEN DRAMA and the Methuen Drama logo are trademarks of
Bloomsbury Publishing Plc

First published in Great Britain 2021

Copyright © Sarah Grochala, 2021

Sarah Grochala has asserted her right under the Copyright, Designs and Patents Act, 1988,
to be identified as the author of this work.

For legal purposes the Acknowledgements on p. xi constitute an extension of this copyright page.

Cover photograph by Ellie Kurttz © RSC

All rights reserved. No part of this publication may be reproduced or transmitted in any form
or by any means, electronic or mechanical, including photocopying, recording, or any
information storage or retrieval system, without prior permission in writing from
the publishers.

Bloomsbury Publishing Plc does not have any control over, or responsibility for, any third-party
websites referred to or in this book. All internet addresses given in this book were correct
at the time of going to press. The author and publisher regret any inconvenience caused if
addresses have changed or sites have ceased to exist, but can accept no
responsibility for any such changes.

A catalogue record for this book is available from the British Library.

Library of Congress Cataloging-in-Publication Data
Names: Grochala, Sarah, author.
Title: The theatre of Rupert Goold : radical approaches to adaptation and new writing / Sarah Grochala.
Description: London ; New York : Methuen Drama, 2021. | Includes bibliographical references and index. |
Summary: "Since the late 1990s, Rupert Goold has garnered a reputation as one of the UK's most exciting and
provocative theatre directors. His exhilarating, risk-taking productions of both classic texts and new plays have
travelled from regional stages to the National Theatre, the West End, Broadway and beyond. Through his artistic
directorship of Headlong and then London's Almeida theatre, he has radically transformed, not only the
companies themselves, but the landscape of British theatre. This is the first book to survey and analyse the full
range of Goold's work and is a vital resource for students, scholars and his fans on different continents. The
Theatre of Rupert Goold offers a backstage view of both Goold's work and the work of other major UK theatre
artists he has nurtured, including Robert Icke, Blanche McIntyre, Mike Bartlett and Lucy Prebble. It gives an
inside view of the processes behind some of Goold's most successful productions and explores in detail
Goold's approach to making work that asks provocative questions of the modern world in the most theatrical
ways imaginable. The book features detailed analyses of key productions including Six Characters in Search of
an Author, ENRON and 1984 for Headlong, besides productions of Macbeth (Chichester Festival Theatre;
Gielgud Theatre, London; BAM; Lyceum Theater Broadway), Time and the Conways (National Theatre) and The
Merchant of Venice (RSC) and his move into screen with Macbeth (BBC) and The Hollow Crown (BBC). Together
with insights from the playwrights, directors, actors and designers who have collaborated with Goold, it
provides an accessible and fascinating guide to Goold's approach to making theatre, placing
his work within the wider context of contemporary performance"– Provided by publisher.
Identifiers: LCCN 2020020664 (print) | LCCN 2020020665 (ebook) | ISBN 9781350090729 (paperback) |
ISBN 9781350090736 (hardback) | ISBN 9781350090743 (epub) | ISBN 9781350090750 (ebook)
Subjects: LCSH: Goold, Rupert–Criticism and interpretation. | Theatrical producers and directors–Great Britain.
Classification: LCC PR6107.O664 Z67 2021 (print) | LCC PR6107.O664 (ebook) | DDC 822/.9029—dc23
LC record available at https://lccn.loc.gov/2020020664
LC ebook record available at https://lccn.loc.gov/2020020665

ISBN:	HB:	978-1-3500-9073-6
	PB:	978-1-3500-9072-9
	Epdf:	978-1-4081-3451-2
	eBook:	978-1-3500-9075-0

Typeset by RefineCatch Limited, Bungay, Suffolk
Printed and bound in Great Britain

To find out more about our authors and books visit www.bloomsbury.com
and sign up for our newsletters.

For Alex

CONTENTS

List of Illustrations ... viii
Foreword *Rupert Goold* ... ix
Acknowledgements ... xii

Introduction ... 1

Part I The Work

1 Beginnings: 1972–2002 ... 9

2 Northampton: 2002–2005 ... 16

3 Headlong and the RSC – Early Years: 2005–2009 ... 31

4 Headlong and the RSC– Later Years: 2009–2013 ... 55

5 Almeida: 2013–2017 ... 79

Part II Approaches to Practice

6 Directing ... 99

7 Shakespeare ... 115

8 Adaptation ... 121

9 New Writing ... 125

10 Opera ... 131

11 Artistic Direction ... 136

12 Talent Development ... 139

Afterword ... 146

Bibliography ... 153
Index ... 166

ILLUSTRATIONS

1. Darrell D'Silva as Satan, Caroline Faber as Raphael and Jonjo O'Neill as the Son in *Paradise Lost* (Northampton Royal & Derngate 2002).   21
2. Jonjo O'Neill as Dinos, Scott Handy as Faustus and Stephen Noonan as Jake in *Faustus* (Hampstead Theatre 2006).   24
3. Tobias Menzies as Hamlet, Paul Shelley as Polonius, Tom Edden as the Player Queen, Dominic Colchester as the Player King, Michael Shaeffer as the Third Player, Aled Pugh as Guildenstern and Jamie de Courcey as Rosencrantz in *Hamlet*.   27
4. Martin Turner as Banquo with the company of *Macbeth* (CFT 2007).   40
5. Noma Dumezweni as the Producer and Freya Parker as the Girl in *Six Characters in Search of an Author* (CFT 2008).   49
6. Hattie Morahan as Kay and Paul Ready as Alan in *Time and the Conways*.   56
7. The company of *ENRON* (Royal Court 2009).   59
8. Sam Troughton as Romeo and Mariah Gale as Juliet with the company of *Romeo and Juliet* (RST 2010).   63
9. Tobias Menzies, Amy Lennox and Cat Simmons in *Decade*.   71
10. Cassandra Compton as Jean, Ben Aldridge as Paul, Katie Brayben as Courtney, Matt Smith as Patrick, Susannah Fielding as Evelyn, Jonathan Bailey as Tim, Gillian Kirkpatrick as Patrick's Mother and Tom Kay as Sean in *American Psycho* (Almeida 2013).   82
11. Richard Goulding, Tafline Steen, Nyasha Hatendi, Tom Robertson, Katie Brayben, Lydia Wilson, Miles Richardson, Nicholas Rowe, Margot Leicester, Tim Pigott-Smith and Adam James in *King Charles III* (Almeida 2014).   85
12. Georgina Lamb, Ruth Everett, Charlotte Randle, Sarah Belcher and Emily Mytton in *Medea*.   89
13. The company of *Ink* (Almeida 2017).   92
14. The company of *Albion* (Almeida 2017).   94
15. The company of *The Hunt* (Almeida 2019).   108
16. Design sketch for *The Hunt*.   109
17. Design sketch for *The Hunt*.   111
18. Design sketch for *The Hunt*.   113

FOREWORD

Looking back over this account I'm struck by how much of the work I've made in the first decades of this century has been a reflection of those times. I think we all hope that the furrow we plough is unique to our own creativity, but reading back it's clear I was bobbing along in currents of upbringing and social context that I was oblivious to at the time. There is a naïvety throughout the account that probably reflects a set of assumptions and educational influences that makes me cringe now! What I will say, though, is at the time, for all our blinkered thinking, we felt we were busy taking on other sacred monoliths. It is the function of revolutionaries to become subsequent dinosaurs but that doesn't mean those dinosaurs didn't roar in their moment.

The noughties were a time of relative prosperity in this country managed by a government more committed to the arts than any other in my lifetime. The internet felt like a new frontier rather than the echo chamber it has now become, cross-art-form practice was thriving, globalization meant for what felt like the first time we had access to artists and artistic influences from around the world, immigration was celebrated, and above all the right were in disarray. With hindsight we can see that those times were built on shaky foundations, an out-of-control banking sector, a narrow media, international oligarchs making Britain their plaything, and a complacency about who had access to genuine opportunity despite all of the Arts Council's initiatives around diversity. So there is a certain guilt in declaring it as the very best of times but the theatre I made probably reflected what back then felt like a world of bright new opportunities, playful, transgressive, limitless at its best – from and for my generation.

Of course there was the war that sat over it all, a fight on foreign soil that seemed at the time the inevitable consequence of the atrocities of 9/11 (and, whatever national shame has followed, it's really important to remember quite how appalling and seismic that day was). However, to my mind there is simply no argument about the defining political event of these years and it is, by a country mile, the crash of 2008. The inability of our governments to see the crippling effects of the rising wealth gap that would follow on from policies of austerity is an utter tragedy and yet I remember one of the most important theatre figures at that time crisply saying that 'theatre had to do its bit too' as we began to roll over in the face of a decade of funding cuts. The desperation that followed led to the radical progressive movements of the last five years, and everything has become harder edged, angrier, more fierce. Ambiguity, irony, internationalism, playfulness and all the other postmodern watchwords that informed the work I made back then have been swept aside in favour of conviction, change, identity and affirmation. It's a new world and a new theatre. One that I probably recognize less but that I am excited to see emerge, an evolving landscape that I hope I can help support in some way.

Foreword

The other great change in this past twenty years has been in higher education. I went to university with the huge privilege of no fees to pay and so while there I felt my job (frequently and guiltily neglected) was to make my teachers happy, proud even. We worked to please them and their critical scrutiny was, for better or worse, our rule book. If you have to pay for your education, and through the nose now, then how can you not expect your teachers to provide the best service in return for your accumulating debt. They are there for your improvement rather than you for theirs. Radically expanding the number of people able to go to university has been a wonderful thing but those debts have led to a graduating cohort who expect the same contract from the theatre; that it is for the canon to prove its worth to them rather than the other way round. That I even worry about that probably sounds perverse from someone who was once viewed as an arch iconoclast, but somehow we ought to be able to balance the right kind of scepticism towards writing and performance styles that may often have their roots in power systems that were designed to exclude many groups with recognition of the underlying structures and skills that have been the deep discoveries of thousands of years of theatre practice.

Equally I can see now in the way I talk about my time at Northampton in particular a Reithian fervour that comes across as didactic and patronizing. However, passion and conviction married to confidence of voice are too rarely found in theatre for one not to cherish them irrespective of their agenda. I wanted theatre to be extraordinary, I wanted it to escape the bounds of both decorum and political necessity, I wanted it to be thrilling and irritating and careless, to break things apart in order to see how they were made. I wanted no rules, no inhibitions, nothing organized and managed and heavy-legged. This was not useful work. It was not work at all. It was dreaming. Some will say that sort of stance could only come from huge privilege, others only from a total narcissist. Maybe. I hope, though, that it laid some groundwork for more careful artists to take a few sparks of inspiration and add it to that bag of tricks we all borrow from to forge their own creative identities. It was a time when I was finding out who I was, as an artist and as a person. Sometime around 2012 I began to journey inwards rather than out, to make more personal work, to seek out stories that spoke to my interior landscape as much as what I saw through the window or in the papers. Quite where that journey will lead I wait to see. I'm not really comfortable with even that rather portentous statement. Theatre is a game. Games can be very serious or very silly. We play them because they pull us together, they are how we structure our imagination, they pit us in playful opposition so we may better understand how we connect. They pass the time.

One of my earliest memories is sitting at my primary school table practising handwriting. The boy next to me was dutiful and concentrating. His writing was clear but lacked finesse, as did mine. Why were we just trying to make our work joined up? Why were we copying by rote? Why were we not in conversation or writing our own stories? Why was the room so quiet? I abruptly jogged his arm and his pencil smeared up the sheet in a big, strong streak. He immediately punched me hard on the arm, bringing tears to my eyes. Then we wordlessly settled down again.

Foreword

A man walks across this empty space whilst someone else is watching him, and this is all that is needed for an act of theatre to be engaged.

(Brook 1990: 11)

That may very well be true but when the walker stops and turns directly to the watcher, when the journey is interrupted, this is when theatre really engages me.

Rupert Goold
November 2019

ACKNOWLEDGEMENTS

With special thanks to Rupert Goold for taking the time to talk to me about his work. Special thanks also to Lindsey Alvis, Kym Bartlett, Mike Bartlett, Johnathan Church, Adam Cork, Carrie Cracknell, Es Devlin, Caroline Faber, Susannah Fielding, Henny Finch, Simon Godwin, Jenni Grainger, Victoria Hamilton, Ella Hickson, Scott Handy, Laura Hopkins, Robert Icke, Tobias Menzies, Jonjo O'Neill, Adam Pollock, Ben Power, Clióna Roberts, Tom Scutt, Botis Seva, Lorna Seymour and John Wyver for finding time to share their experiences of working with Goold. Also to Sarvat Hasin and Emma Pritchard at the Almeida for their support with logistics and sourcing research material, and to Alecia Marshall at Headlong for letting me raid the company archive. This project could not have been completed without all of your support, assistance and enthusiasm, for which I am very grateful.

With thanks to the Royal Central School of Speech and Drama for enabling me to take the time I needed to write this book. And particularly to Christina Albertson, Maria Delgado, Melissa Dunne, Tony Fisher, Elaine Henry, Dan Hetherington, Joe Parslow and Farokh Soltani.

Thanks also to Dan Ayling, Charlie Bath and SFP, Michael Brailey and Northampton Royal & Derngate Archives, Graham Michael, Arthur Millie and Wiltshire Creative Archives, Simon Sladen and the V&A Theatre and Performance Archive, the NT Archive, all at the RSC Archives, and to the cast and company of *The Hunt* for allowing me to spend time in their rehearsal room.

Also to Gile and Molly for bearing with my extended physical and mental absences during the completion of this project. My life may be too full but it would be empty without you.

INTRODUCTION

This book provides an account of the work of the director Rupert Goold, one of Britain's most important twenty-first-century theatre-makers, from the beginnings of his career to the present day. It both documents Goold's productions and gives an insight into the creative processes that went into creating them. It is a personal account, being primarily based on extensive interviews conducted with Goold and a range of his collaborators, as well as my own experience of working with Goold at Headlong between 2012 and 2013. It aims to provide a view of Goold's career from the inside, and in doing so challenge perceptions of it from the outside. The latter have tended to misunderstand the impulses driving Goold's work, and run counter to the way his collaborators have described working with him.

Goold's work has been a major influence on the character of early twenty-first-century British theatre. As the dramaturg Ben Power, who worked at Headlong as an associate director between 2006 and 2010, notes:

> when we think about where we are in terms of our relationship as a theatre community to the classics, a lot of credit goes to the influx of European directors and European dramaturgy since 2005, especially at the Barbican and the Young Vic. But in a quieter way I think some of that is down to what we did at Headlong. I think it's partly responsible for a freeing-up of the way we do old plays, that then led to an approach to new writing.
>
> (Power 2018)

In addition to this, Goold has shaped the current industry by his fast-tracking of new talent. Artists whose work Goold has supported include the writers Lucy Prebble, Mike Bartlett and Ella Hickson, the directors Rebecca Frecknall and Robert Icke, and the designer Tom Scutt, amongst many others. As Scutt argues: 'what he did for Headlong in that period was immeasurable in terms of pushing young artists though [...] he's responsible for a lot of what the industry looks like at the moment' (Scutt 2019).

Despite this, Goold has a reputation for being a tricksy and flashy director.[1] His use of 'head-turning spectacles' (Lukowski 2011) and his 'imaginative transplantations' of

---

[1] Examples of Goold's work that could be seen as employing tricksy or flashy directorial choices include a re-location of *The Merchant of Venice* (2011) to Las Vegas, a Stalinist *Macbeth* (2007), setting *The Tempest* in the Arctic (2006), and an intercutting of *Dr Faustus* (2004) with a narrative about the contemporary visual artists the Chapman Brothers.

classic plays (Clapp in John 2008), have led some critics to view him as 'a chancer whose best results could be attributed to the element of surprise' (Halliburton 2007: 36). The composer Adam Cork, who has collaborated with Goold on a regular basis since the beginning of both their careers, describes Goold as a director who 'imagines to the point of recklessness':

> On one level he won't let practical considerations ruin the imaginative journey he and we all are going on. And you end up in rehearsals going, 'What? We've got to get ten benches and fifteen people into a tiny little greenhouse-sized thing in the middle of the stage in fifteen seconds, silently and without the thing rocking, simply so that we can then clear the glass and see them magically? You're mad!'[2]
>
> (Cork 2019)

A humorous stage management note made during rehearsals for Goold's Arctic *Tempest* (RSC 2006) captures a sense of his impulse to stage the seemingly unstageable: 'Caliban enters on stilts, dragging the boat and carrying a dismembered killer shark. He then climbs up the back wall & swings into the audience where the whale [*sic*] explodes into a thousand wriggling eels and bounces on a hidden trampoline back onto the stage. Can we try this in reh [*sic*] with all the stuff tomorrow please?' ('The Tempest: Stage Management Notes' 2006: 94). Goold's reckless imaginings have led to some of the most memorable moments of twenty-first-century British theatre to date: a drowned girl floating face down in a tank for an impossible length of time in *Six Characters in Search of an Author* (Headlong/Chichester Festival Theatre (CFT) 2008); a light sabre dance illustrating the movement of the energy markets in *ENRON* (Headlong/CFT/Royal Court 2009); a Renaissance study suddenly transformed into a white cube gallery space in *Faustus* (Royal & Derngate 2004). While Goold's imaginings may seem unstageable, he has a 'track record of pulling off the near impossible', producing shows that thrill audiences with their radical re-envisaging of classic texts and electrifying approach to contemporary issues (Lukowski 2011).

Goold's detractors see his employment of spectacle and radical re-imaginings as superficial bells and whistles. His 'boldness', they claim, both exceeds his 'talent' (Halliburton 2007: 36) and leads to a tendency to 'ride roughshod' over the text (McNulty 2008). As previous studies have observed of the work of directors such as Peter Sellars and Calixto Bieito (Delgado and Rebellato 2010), this study will argue that there is method underlying Goold's use of both spectacle and re-imaginings. His approach to classic texts is, as Power observes, 'informed by a deep reading of the plays' and his stagings have often revolved around making these plays more accessible to a modern audience (Power 2018). The familiar social worlds or genre tropes he layers onto texts act as lenses enabling the audience to see the text more clearly. His use of recognizable

---

[2] Cork is referring to the staging of Act Two, Scene Five of *The Hunt*. For an image of this scene see p. 108.

parallels from contemporary culture enables easy access to classical narratives and their meanings. For example, the terrifying nature of the witches in *Macbeth* (CFT 2007) is conveyed through references to contemporary horror films, while the act of selling your soul to the devil in *Faustus* is paralleled by the act of desecrating a priceless work of art. At the heart of Goold's work is a desire to recapture some sense of how the original audience might have experienced the play in its original context by disrupting accumulated cultural clichés around how classic texts should be performed.

Goold is sometimes presented by critics as an 'auteur' (Gardner 2009a; Billington 2012), which, as the critic Andrew Haydon notes, is 'not a complimentary term in mainstream British critics' books' (Haydon 2013: 79). This book will argue that rather than enforcing his singular vision on a production, Goold works collaboratively with his cast and his creatives to produce his productions, integrating their ideas and contributions into the final show. As the designer Tom Scutt notes, the image of the director as a singular visionary is one derived from the way directors are written about critically and in the media. It's 'the way the narrative has to be sold: here's this singular person that is the next guiding force of the narrative in British theatre' but it's not 'how it actually works'. Goold, Scutt argues has never had 'any sense of being this figurehead'. Instead, 'he surrounds himself with the people he trusts but not necessarily agrees with' (Scutt 2019). Unlike some directors, the producer Jenni Grainger (née Kershaw) notes, he is 'not afraid to work with talented people' and instead thrives on the creative conversation that working with other artists offers him (Grainger 2018). While Goold's vision may stand as the guiding vision within the creative process, it is not a singular vision. Cork notes that Goold gives his collaborators 'absolute permission to imagine as strongly as you want to and try things out' (Cork 2019). This applies both to working with other creatives during the pre-production process and working with actors on the rehearsal room floor. As, the actor Jonjo O'Neill observes, even though 'people would associate [Goold] as having a loud presence within his productions', he wants 'everyone involved to be part of that presence' (O'Neill 2019).

While Goold is often classified as a more 'European' director within British theatre as a result of his interventionist style, I will argue that his theatrical influences are largely drawn from the work of British and North American theatre directors, including Bill Alexander, John Barton, Jonathan Miller, Robert Lepage and Simon McBurney. In addition to this, I will argue that he is as influenced by the language of film as he is by theatre. As the director Jonathan Church notes, Goold has a rare ability 'to make theatre filmic and still theatrical' (Church 2018). His productions are as infused with filmic models and references as they are with theatrical ones,[3] which often, as the actor Scott Handy observes, place 'the audience in the point of view of a camera' (Handy 2019). Cork sees Goold's body of work as an experiment in the 'ways in which the language of

---

[3] Examples of this include the influence of the aesthetic of Powell and Pressburger in his 2003 *Othello*, of Kubrick in *Faustus* (2004) and the recreation of filmic temporal effects inspired by the work of Muybridge and the Wachowski Sisters in *Time and the Conways* (2009).

film can be brought to theatre and remixed in a theatrical way to create a new mode of expression for that medium' (Cork 2019).

Much of Goold's work is infused with ideas around the nature of faith and a sense of the sacred. Productions such as *Paradise Lost* (Royal & Derngate 2004) and *The Last Days of Judas Iscariot* (Headlong/Almeida 2008) are explicitly rooted in Christian narratives. Other work, such as his RSC *Romeo and Juliet* (2010), explores the ways in which 'faith is an increasingly difficult thing for people to really grapple with now' (Goold in Neill 2011). Scutt notes that Goold has an innate 'sense of theatre as a ritual of some sort'. There is something 'holy' about his work. This, he argues, is derived from a simple sense of 'what can happen when you commune with a group of people that come and sit in a shared space where something is told to you' (Scutt 2019).

Goold's approach to the creative process will ultimately be positioned as a dialectical process. He sees argument as central to theatre: 'ultimately I go to theatre for the play of an argument held in suspension' (Goold 2018a). Goold's process will be defined as one in which an initial question or provocation generates a range of further positions and provocations. These are then woven into the text of a new play or, in the case of existing texts, illuminated through the dramaturgy of the resulting production. While his work may offer 'jazz hands' on the surface, I will argue this surface spectacle is supported by dialectical rigour.

This book is split into two main parts. The first section is an account of Goold's work to date both as a director and as an artistic director. The first chapter covers his early work as a freelance director (prior to 2002). The second looks at the ways in which his work at Northampton (2002–2005) laid the seeds for the methods he would apply to his work at Headlong. The third and fourth chapters explore Goold's work for Headlong (2005–2013) and the RSC (2005–2011), during which time his interventionist approach reached its apex. The final chapter of the first part will examine Goold's work at the Almeida (2013–2017), covering what I see as the quietening of his directing style.

The second part of the book examines Goold's approach to a range of different areas of his work. The sixth chapter explores Goold's approach to directing and offers an analysis of his approach to working with actors and creatives during the development of a specific production, *The Hunt* (Almeida 2019). The seventh chapter examines his approach to Shakespeare, outlining the method underlying his radical re-imaginings of Shakespeare's plays. The eighth chapter looks at his approach to adaptation, both in terms of adapting other mediums for the stage and adapting classic plays for a modern audience. The ninth chapter, on new writing, explores his approach to both developing and directing new work. The tenth chapter offers an account of Goold's work in opera. The eleventh chapter considers the role of the artistic director, differentiating it from the role of director. The final chapter investigates Goold's approach to talent development and surveys his legacy in this area.

Rather than providing a comprehensive analysis of Goold's work, this book documents both Goold's body of work to date and the major shifts in his approach to creating it over the years. It provides a stepping stone of sorts, allowing others to take a more analytical approach to both Goold's body of work and the thinking patterns that lie behind it. For researchers and theatre-makers, it offers a dissection and examination of the methods and processes underlying Goold's work, so foregrounding the 'work' of artistic creation and the methods that underlie it, work which is so often erased in the consideration of a finished artwork. For students, it provides a foundational resource to support their study of Goold's work, one which hopes to inspire both future artists and academics. For the theatre enthusiast, it aims to give access to the history and the creative processes that lie behind Goold's work.

PART I
THE WORK

CHAPTER 1
BEGINNINGS: 1972–2002

Goold's earliest memory is a theatrical one, performing in 'some Guy Fawkes-y play' as a small child. He was a 'very sensitive boy' and remembers feeling 'really shy but oddly comfortable under the lights being looked at; I lay in a pile with my friends pretending to be part of the bonfire and felt both hidden and seen'. There was something in that transaction between actor and audience he felt was 'reassuring'; he felt that it 'organized the random aggression of the playground into a story' and that 'the discipline of doing [something] as a group was pacifying' (Goold 2018b). Apart from pantomimes, his earliest memory of going to the theatre is seeing Michael Bogdanov's production of *Hiawatha* (1980) at the National Theatre (National/NT) when he was eight years old: 'I remember that feeling of seeing an actor move through the auditorium, the shock of them descending the stairs among us, the final funeral boat – it was electrifying to my love of the heroic. I was really young, but it did make a long-lasting impression on me' (Goold 2019a).

At school, Goold remembers being on the 'periphery' of the drama scene but 'desperate to join in'. When he was fifteen, he was cast in a school production of Pinter's *The Hothouse* (Hampstead Theatre 1980), in which he played Lobb, a 'tiny role at the end, in a ridiculous outsized suit' (Goold 2018b). Also in the production were the future novelist China Miéville and composer Thomas Adès as well as the actress Caroline Faber, who would become one of Goold's earliest collaborators. Goold's school, University College School (UCS), was a private all-boys school. As there were no girls to play the female parts in school productions, girls were cast from other local schools. Faber, who was a pupil at a nearby comprehensive, was cast as Miss Cutts. She found herself 'hurled into this very strange but disconcerting new world, working on this sinister Pinter play with this group of brilliantly talented, vivid, eccentric boys'. She remembers Goold as 'younger than the rest, a little quieter maybe, but acutely observant and fiercely intelligent'. She got to know him better when she was cast as Adelaide in a UCS production of *Guys and Dolls*. Goold was playing an old man, Arvide Abernathy, 'smothered in grey panstick and with talc sprinkled all over his lustrous hair'. Faber remembers him offering her a perceptive note on her performance during rehearsals: 'He came up to me after I had sung "Adelaide's Lament" saying, "It's good, Caz, but I wonder if you should hold back a bit, build into it gradually and not throw everything at us at once"'. She 'was a bit taken aback by this fifteen-year-old boy telling [her] what to do but it was a brilliant note' (Faber 2019).

By the time he left school, Goold knew there was something about theatre that resonated with him: 'I thought, "I really want to stay part of this but I don't really know what that means"'. His English teacher asked him if he had considered directing: 'I thought, "No, I want to be in plays, you just don't think I'm good enough."' Just after he finished his A-levels, Goold met the future actor Sacha Grunpeter at a party. They hit it off straight away. Grunpeter was incredibly ambitious: 'I couldn't believe someone could be so confident'. Goold absorbed some of Grunpeter's drive and chutzpah 'in his slipstream', helping him to overcome his shyness: 'I owe any assertiveness and self-belief I have to him'. In a strange twist of fate, both Goold and Grunpeter were offered places to study English at Trinity College, Cambridge. Between finishing at school and going to university, they spent a year together 'working in bars and trying to set up a theatre company to do a touring production of *Othello* for schools' (Goold 2018b).

Cambridge

At Cambridge, Goold become involved with the Marlowe Society, whose remit is to revive Elizabethan and Jacobean drama. The society produces an annual production in which student casts and production crews work with a professional director and design team ('The Marlowe Society' n.d.). Goold played small parts in these professionally directed productions as, initially, he felt he would learn more about directing by working with professional directors than by directing his own productions.

Goold positioned himself as a director within the university scene before he had done any actual directing: 'wandering around going "I would like to be in theatre. I think I might be a director" without any proof of it'. Despite this lack of proof, 'people seemed to accept I was a director'. Goold attributes this to his shyness, which meant he tended to listen very carefully, often in adulation of his fellow Cambridge thespians: 'I think they could tell that I would listen to them really hard and that probably appealed to their vanity. So at some level, I was vaguely taken seriously' (Goold 2018b). Towards the end of his first year, he directed his first show, Sam Shepard's *Fool for Love* (Corpus Playroom 1992). It was 'duck water, day one, this feels right'. After *Fool for Love*, he continued to direct, taking a couple of shows to the Edinburgh Fringe, but it was not until his third year that his practice really started to take form. In autumn 1993, he directed a gangsta rap version of *Othello* (Cambridge University European Theatre Group), which he now sees as 'embryonic of all the basic flaws of my abilities, but also the strengths'. The production was ridiculous: 'the idea a bunch of Cambridge kids could go around Europe with a gangsta rap production of *Othello* was every bit as risible as it sounds'. Through directing it, however, Goold 'really began to learn about holding an audience' (Goold 2018b). He managed to convey the story of the play 'very clearly despite the absurd relocation and in no small part due to an extraordinary performance by Grunpeter as Iago'. As a result, he noticed the audience were engaged and often rapt.

After *Othello*, Goold directed a production of *Twelfth Night* (ADC America Tour 1994). This was the first show he tried to approach 'theoretically'. He had been to see his youngest brother in a school play and become interested in 'the relationship between how parents watch school plays and how audiences watch professionals'. When a professional play is bad, the audience tend to have a bad experience, but with the school play, Goold noticed, 'the worse it got, the more beloved it was'. With his production of

Twelfth Night, Goold aimed to replicate the 'atmosphere' of the school play and elicit the same audience response. He describes the outcome of this experiment as 'embryonic of clowning' in the sense that it was 'sort of playful, quite alive, quite fresh'. While the show was on tour in the USA, he again had a chance to observe the reactions of different audiences. As with *Othello*, he could tell they were 'responding'. This gave him confidence: 'I thought I had a bit of an aptitude for this' (Goold 2018b).

Starting Out

The first play Goold directed after graduating from Cambridge was María Irene Fornés's *Mud* (Etcetera 1995). Fornés was a writer with no real reputation in the UK but whose spare dialogue and politics appealed to Goold: 'her writing felt raw and genuinely distinct, perfect for the fringe'. The production was self-produced on the London fringe, Goold having 'saved money from working overtime in a bar to pay for it' (Goold 2018b). Faber, who played the role of Mae, remembers it was done on a shoestring: 'None of us were paid a penny. Rupert was director, producer and on the lighting board every night. We rehearsed wherever we could find a room. The costumes were our own or from charity shops' (Faber 2019). The production was scathingly reviewed by Sara Abdulla in *Time Out*, who claimed the only good thing about it was that it 'closes on March 19' (Abdulla 1995). As a result, audiences stayed away. For Goold, this was a shock to the system: 'I'd just left university, I'd got a good degree, I'm being headhunted, I'd spent eight months trying to raise money and I'd lost it all overnight on a show that *Time Out* said reminds them why they get paid to do this job' (Goold 2018b).

A closer inspection of the *Time Out* review reveals Abdulla's main issue was with Fornés's play rather than Goold's production. She summarizes the action of *Mud* in the following terms:

> Mae and Lloyd are white trash (how very de rigueur) underneath the dirt. They spit a lot and clutch at their groins. Lloyd has prostatitis. Henry, on the other hand, doesn't, nor does he spit. At Mae's behest, Henry shacks up with the Family Flob, has an accident and is paralysed. Mae, having learnt to read, leaves. Lloyd shoots her.

While she dismisses the play as 'an utterly inglorious, dispiriting, dissipated hour of drivel', she identifies the company as 'talented' and laments that they are 'wasting time, energy and electricity' on Fornés's work (Abdulla 1995). Other critics praised the production. Laurence Kennedy in *What's On* proclaimed *Mud* 'one of the best shows on the fringe at present'. The production is 'vibrant', the cast 'impress' and Goold's direction is 'sharp and intelligent' (Kennedy 1995).

In April 1995, things started to come together again. On the same day, Goold was offered two opportunities: a Fulbright Scholarship to join the Performance Studies programme at New York University (NYU) led by Richard Schechner and the trainee director position at the Donmar Warehouse with Carlton Television. Goold turned down NYU to go to the Donmar, where he arrived at a mixed time for the company. Under Sam Mendes's artistic directorship, the theatre was enjoying critical success but the company's financial future was in doubt. In autumn 1995, the theatre's owners and their principal sponsor announced they would be withdrawing their funding from the following spring (Lister 1995). Threatened with imminent closure, the theatre was desperately seeking funding to stay afloat: 'everyone was very stressed'. During his time there, Goold assisted Mendes on productions of *The Glass Menagerie* (1995) and *Company* (1995). When *The Glass Menagerie* transferred to the West End, he also had the chance to work for Thelma Holt, 'a maverick West End producer' who had a 'great history and backed strange things'. Thelma became an influential figure for Goold. Whereas 'the Donmar felt like a taut, electric machine', with Thelma 'it was all weird anarchic folk band' (Goold 2018b).

Goold's time at the Donmar was not a great success. He felt he did not fit in. Referencing the theatre critic Kenneth Tynan, Goold identifies two different strains in British theatre: the Roundheads and the Cavaliers. Tynan associates the Cavaliers with the 1960s, with Oxford University, with 'flair, audacity, imagination, outrageous aplomb'. The Roundheads, by contrast, are indicative of the 1970s, associated with Cambridge University, with 'stubborn, obdurate, "hard hat" persistence' (Tynan 2002: 33). At the end of Goold's time at the Donmar, he had a 'pretty frank and brutal debrief'. He remembers an exec at Carlton suggesting, 'It would probably help if you cut your hair,' and thinking, 'My god, this is like the army'. For Goold, this offhand comment reflected the heart of what 'they thought about me'. Apprentices were expected to be Roundheads, to support and to subjugate their individuality. He was seen as too much of a Cavalier and his shyness meant that his ideas and demeanour were read as aloof and cerebral rather than charismatic. Goold felt caught in between 'wanting to wear a hair shirt on one level' but also 'as a director being drawn to flouncing around a lot!' Negotiating these impulses were, he says, 'part of growing up as a man and as an artist' (Goold 2018b).

Salisbury Playhouse

After the Donmar, Goold was awarded a place on the Regional Theatre Young Directors Scheme (RTYDS). It was his third application for the scheme. The first year, he had a 'really odd' interview where his hair again featured as a topic of conversation, one of the panel commenting: 'But doesn't he look like Byron, with his hair like that!' (Goold 2018b). The second year, he did not even make it to the interview stage. The third year, he was allocated one of the bursaries. That year, Salisbury Playhouse was one of the participating theatres. Jonathan Church was the artistic director at the time. He remembers some debate within the panel as to whether Goold needed the scheme. He had already 'done a year's training with a very successful director at a very brilliant organization'. Church, however, felt Goold would be a good fit for Salisbury. The theatre 'had been shut down' so 'the thrust of the policy was to re-open the building and to do a lot of work'. Church knew there would be 'an opportunity to direct' and so needed someone experienced. Ultimately, the panel decided Goold was the best candidate to deliver what Church required (Church 2018).

The posting was a 'blessing' for Goold (Goold 2018b). Instead of assistant directing, he spent time with the education department and the youth theatre. He showed an active interest in how Salisbury functioned: 'the daily life of the building and thinking about the programme and Salisbury audiences and what we did'. Church created opportunities for Goold to direct, initially in the smaller studio theatre. Having understood the ethos underlying Salisbury's programming, Goold was happy to support its remit, even though Church admits his assignments were 'counter-intuitive; in terms of everything he had talked about in his interview, and his background'. Church praises Goold's attitude, acknowledging that 'it's very easy for an assistant or associate to go, "I want to do the unknown Bulgakov play."' Goold, on the other hand, would say, "I'm happy to serve the cause of the-summer-show-needs-to-be-popular-and-light, so I'll do a P. G. Wodehouse."' Church found Goold had a talent for making 'whatever project he was given surprising': 'no matter how apparently cautious the bit of programming, his adventurousness as an artist transformed the work into something more than its component parts' (Church 2018).

The first show Church asked Goold to direct was the alternative Christmas show in the studio, John Godber's *Bouncers* (Salisbury Playhouse 1996). This was Goold's first professional production as a director. He took it very seriously: 'approached it as rigorously as Katie Mitchell[1] would'. Godber's play was originally set in a fictional Northern nightclub. Goold rethought the play as an 'Ibizan fantasy' (Goold 2018b). Church remembers that 'he made it an event'. After *Bouncers*, Goold had a lucky break when a more established director pulled out of a main house production, Giles Havergal's adaptation of Graham Greene's novel *Travels with My Aunt* (Salisbury Playhouse 1997). Goold was asked to take over. The adaptation was a four-hander with actors playing multiple roles. Goold cast four actors who could sing, turning them into a barbershop quartet and using this format to trace the geography of the journeys in the play through song. The show was a success and toured after its run at Salisbury. Pleased with Goold's work, Church 'made him an associate' (Church 2018).

During his time at the Donmar, Goold had started working on a Dennis Potter-inspired adaptation of Graham Greene's *The End of the Affair* (Salisbury Playhouse/Bridewell Theatre 1997) with Faber (writing under the name Caroline Butler). Initially, Goold and Faber each worked on adapting 'different sections of the book solo'. Goold 'worked on the first half, Maurice's story', while Faber 'worked on the section which is retold from Sarah's perspective'. They would then discuss the work together to 'make it cohere'. They wanted their adaptation 'to be a play with music and songs'. Greene's novel is set around the time of the Second World War, so they knew 'there was a wealth of material' they could draw on. They also wanted to use music to evoke the novel's 'sense of

---

[1] British theatre director known for an exacting approach to working on texts and with actors.

the sacred' (Faber 2019). This was the first show Goold worked on with Adam Cork as his composer. When the original composer Faber and Goold were working with became busy with other commitments, he asked Cork 'to share the job with him'. The original composer then dropped out completely, leaving Cork 'in the hotseat' (Cork 2019). For the show, Cork created a 'haunting soundscape' (Faber 2019) from which 'songs of the period emerged', sometimes 'pretty much as they were written', sometimes 'distorted' (Cork 2019). Cork, Faber and Goold presented an initial workshop of the piece at the Bridewell Theatre in London. On the basis of the workshop, Church programmed the piece in Salisbury's studio theatre. The Bridewell also programmed the finished show. Goold considers the show 'one of the best things I've done' (Goold 2018b). Church remembers its 'mixture of movement, visual style, semi-filmic and Adam's music' as having a 'theatrical richness to it': 'it was incredibly sophisticated, for a relatively young director' (Church 2018). The critics were generally complimentary. Brian Logan described the production as a 'compelling remembrance of fleeting happiness and lasting heartbreak' (Logan 1997).

Goold's next project was *Romeo and Juliet* (Greenwich Theatre 1998). Goold updated the play to a contemporary setting: 'a nineties world of cropped T-shirts, combat trousers and clumpy trainers' (Stratton 1998). He made several significant interventions. Goold argues that while 'there's enough fireworks and fun' in the first three acts of *Romeo and Juliet* to sustain the audience's engagement, the final two acts are hard going. In his production, Goold pushed the interval back to make the second half 'more manageable', moving it from after Mercutio's death (3.1), where it is traditionally placed, to after Capulet's sanction of Paris's speedy marriage to Juliet (3.4) (Goold in Neill 2011). In another intervention, Goold kept the chorus onstage throughout the play's action like an omnipresent 'malign Fate' (Bassett 1998); the chorus shadowed the lovers' moves, threw confetti at their wedding, and delivered the poison to Romeo. The two scenes in which the lovers lament Romeo's banishment (3.2 and 3.4) were intercut into a single simultaneous scene. Finally, Goold reversed the balcony scene. Romeo was positioned above and Juliet below as if 'he'd climbed into a walled garden rather than up to a balcony' (Goold in Neill 2011). The production received mixed reviews. David Benedict gave Goold 'full marks for bravery', predicting 'a bright future ahead of him' (Benedict 1998). Nicholas de Jongh noted 'a boldness to his approach which is heartening and attractive' (de Jongh 1998). For many, however, the production lacked consistency: 'Lots of nice and clever details' that 'don't quite cohere' (Macaulay 1998). Goold was accused of an over-reliance on 'deft directorial insights', which at times descended to 'tricksiness' (Benedict 1998): 'while he could be focusing on the text, he's too busy embellishing the action with stylistic gestures' (Stratton 1998).

Goold feels the production both undermined his 'confidence and certainty' and halted his progress. His output over the following five years is a 'ragbag' of 'odd regional theatre productions', 'a couple of underdeveloped plays at Hampstead' and 'a show at the Gate that was quite successful'. There is 'no governing ideology, or artistic sensibility' (Goold 2018b). The director Simon Godwin notes that emerging directors often have little real choice about the nature of their work: 'you're looking to make a living like all of us. If someone invites you to do a show anywhere, you're terrified if you say no they'll never ask you to do anything ever again' (Godwin 2019). During this period, Goold was 'just doing the work [he] could' and trying 'to make a living'. He felt pushed out into a theatrical wasteland. It seemed as if the industry didn't 'want me around', as if he was 'the wrong type'. His development as a director stalled: 'when I did *The End of the Affair* in 1997 I could have jumped to do *Paradise Lost* the next year but I was never asked to do that'. He 'couldn't get near the [Royal] Court or the National'. He felt like giving up: 'I wrote a load of letters to various publishers and literary agents advertising all sorts of jobs and didn't get any replies'. Goold reflects that making the jump from emerging to established director was and still is a challenge. An artist's late twenties and early thirties can be a difficult time: 'unless you're Sam Mendes or Robert Icke it's very rare you've got going but suddenly things get very real'. You are no longer doing it 'just because you like doing it. You want to have a career' (Goold 2018b).

CHAPTER 2
NORTHAMPTON: 2002–2005

In 2002, Goold was appointed as the artistic director of the Royal & Derngate in Northampton. Northampton provided Goold with 'a space where I could doodle artistically' (Goold 2018a), enabling him to develop a strong directorial voice and establish himself as a rising star within the industry. Simon Godwin, who worked alongside Goold at Northampton as an associate director, argues that watching Goold's work develop over his three-year tenure was like watching 'tectonic plates coming together, converging' (Godwin 2019). At Northampton, Goold challenged the received wisdom that regional programming means offering audiences a slate of safe but unchallenging work, such as pantomimes, comedies, thrillers and conventional adaptations of familiar stories from other mediums. Instead, Goold succeeded in re-energizing the organization and building an audience through a programme of work that included radical adaptations of classic texts, which at times verged on 'seriously weird conceptual art', alongside more conventional productions of P. G. Wodehouse, Alan Ayckbourn and Alan Bennett (Goold 2018b).

Northampton was low on culture when Goold arrived. It had a 'cool little indie music venue', 'a shoe museum' and 'some Victorian architecture'. Beyond this, local entertainment options were limited. Goold diagnosed the town as suffering from 'low self-esteem' and notes that 'even Milton Keynes was bigger and cooler' (Goold 2018b). The Royal & Derngate consisted of two theatres, which had been combined into one venue in 1999: the Royal, a 450-seat producing theatre dating from 1884; and the newer Derngate, completed in 1983, a 1,500-seat receiving house offering events ranging from classical concerts and opera to stand-up comedy and wrestling. Prior to Goold's arrival, the actor, playwright and director Michael Napier Brown had run the Royal for over twenty years. By producing a programme featuring regional staples alongside his own plays, he had managed to keep the theatre afloat through the funding crisis of the 1980s, a period during which many regional theatres had been forced to close. By the early 2000s, however, the theatre's artistic programme had 'fossilized' (Godwin 2019).

When Goold took over, Arts Council England (ACE) viewed the Royal & Derngate as struggling: 'it was seen as this limping, ridiculous failure'. Attendance was low, 'sort of on the floor' (Goold 2018b). Napier Brown was a popular figure within the community. After his departure, the theatre's audience had 'halved overnight' (Goold 2019b). As a result of the merger, the organization was in the middle of a £14 million capital project, which would physically integrate the two theatres into a single complex ('Boss Quits Royal & Derngate' 2005). At the same time, however, they were facing a significant decrease in local authority funding. Morale was low amongst the staff, partly because the theatre received little attention from the national press and partly because they were 'all disillusioned with the merger' (Goold 2019b). Finally, the addition of the Derngate meant it was now 'a real headache to try and make a narrative for the organization and still preserve an identity as a producing theatre within it'. To add to Goold's troubles, 'the chief executive left abruptly eight weeks after [he] arrived'. Until Donna Munday arrived eighteen months later, the theatre was run by a 'flat structure gang of four', consisting of Goold, the marketing director, the finance director and the general manager, who were divided as to how to programme the joint venues. The general manager was 'very much a believer that if it generates enough revenue, then that is how you can afford to subsidize the artistic work'. Others were adamant 'we weren't going to do work unless it conformed to our values'. Northampton did, however, have a range of things going for it. It was close enough to London for both national press and artists to come relatively easily. The Royal itself 'was a beautiful space' (Goold 2018b).

There was a sense that change was needed before Goold's arrival. Another director, Natasha Betteridge, had served as artistic producer at the Royal & Derngate between Napier-Brown and Goold's tenures. During her short tenure, she tried to move the theatre towards a more progressive programme, most notably by staging a production of Alan Ayckbourn's diptych *House* and *Garden* (Royal & Derngate 2001) across the two venues. Godwin, whom Betteridge appointed as her associate director, remembers she 'was absolutely about trying to bring change'. Together Betteridge and Godwin had programmed a season bringing 'a wider repertoire and a new breed of actors and designers to the theatre', which included a production of *The Seagull* starring Rory Kinnear (Godwin 2019). Betteridge left after less than a year. Godwin stayed on. Goold could see Godwin and Betteridge had begun a process, that there was already an 'interesting thing happening' upon which he could build (Goold 2018b). Godwin argues Goold was able to recognize, early in his career, 'that theatres that are not at their peak are really good theatres to inherit, because you've got all to find and all to discover' (Godwin 2019). There was 'no way but up' (Goold 2018b).

In order to establish himself within the community, Goold realized he would have to 'direct [his] way into an identity' (Goold 2019b). The budget for the year had been used up on the first two shows before Goold arrived, leaving him with limited finances. The first show Goold programmed was *The Importance of Being Earnest* (Royal & Derngate 2002), directed by Bill Alexander. The theatre subsequently received a financial uplift thanks to extra money the then minister for culture, media and sport, Chris Smith, provided for regional theatres. This enabled Goold 'to do one show to try and reassure the audience, get the reviews' (Goold 2018b). Goold chose Tom Stoppard's *Arcadia* (Royal & Derngate 2002). The character of Valentine was played by a young actor, Tobias Menzies, whom Goold had previously worked with on a production of Hristo Boytchev's *The Colonel Bird* (Gate Theatre Notting Hill 1999). *Arcadia*'s narrative is split into two different temporal strands. The first revolves around the events leading up to a hermit taking up residence in the grounds of an English country manor in the early nineteenth century. The second concerns a twentieth-century academic, Bernard, who is determined to prove Byron was the hermit. Stoppard weaves ideas relating 'fractal geometry, iterated algorithms, chaos theory and the second law of thermodynamics' into the telling of these two related stories

(Gardner 2002). Menzies remembers that Goold's production was 'on the face of it a relatively faithful rendering of Stoppard's play'. The play's 'DNA', however, was 'indicative' of where Goold's interests as a director lay. There were 'a lot of big ideas in there' (Menzies 2019).

The play provided an effective bridge between Goold's interests and the Northampton audience's needs. It was well received by local critics, such as Ruth Supple. Supple betrays the theatre's previously poor track record in her reluctance to venture out to review the show: 'Much of what I've seen at The Royal in the past decade has had a soporific effect, and I didn't relish braving the elements for another such evening'. *Arcadia* altered her expectations. She notes there are 'not enough superlatives to sum up how wonderfully brilliant' the production is: 'this complex script could be confusing to follow if not reined in with good direction and acting, which this production has in profusion'. At the end of the review, she articulates a complete change of heart: 'If they can continue to stage plays of this calibre, I would happily battle through any amount of bad weather to have my spirits lifted' (Supple 2002). Goold also invited national critics to review the show. Lyn Gardner came and gave *Arcadia* a five-star review, noting that it was 'a thing of wit, elegance and tantalizing wistfulness, and is acted with shimmering brilliance. Breathtaking, exhilarating and deeply satisfying' (Gardner 2002).

Godwin and Goold already knew each other from Cambridge. Once Goold arrived, they had to work out how they were going to balance their roles within the organization. Godwin ended up directing much of the Royal's 'conventional material', alongside tours of village halls and 'picnic champagne plays for the middle class'. Even with this more conventional work, however, Goold encouraged him to make it 'as diverse or surprising as possible'. When Godwin 'came up with the idea of doing *Everyman*' for a village hall tour, he remembers Goold was 'very excited' and 'very encouraging'. He was enthused by the idea: '*Everyman* was originally born as a regional tour, the first touring play, and going back to those village plays and posing big questions about life and death, which *Everyman* does' (Godwin 2019).

Goold followed *Arcadia* with a 'conceptually quite interesting' (Goold 2018b) production of Harold Pinter's *Betrayal* (Royal & Derngate 2002), which tells the story of a love triangle between Emma (Paula Stockbridge), her husband Robert (John McAndrew) and his best friend Jerry (John Lloyd Fillingham). The play starts at the end of Emma and Jerry's affair and winds its way backwards to the moment it started. Goold's production, designed by Ashley Martin-Davis, opened with 'furniture suspended from the ceiling', which then 'ends up on the stage as the plot unravels' ('A Fresh Twist on a Theatre Classic' 2002). One reviewer, Tim Ramsden, interpreted this central image as conveying the way in which 'people create the luggage of their lives': 'hanging over them is the weight these characters bear, the detritus of their lives suspended over the stage as furniture, lowered piece by piece, so less and less looms as time unwinds'. The walls of the set were covered with projected images of domesticity, which vanished during the course of each scene to leave bare walls 'fading their hopes and plans into blank existences' (Ramsden 2002).

At the beginning of 2003, money was still tight. Goold decided to deal with this by producing an 'Irish Season', a double bill of Conor McPherson's *The Weir* and Samuel

Beckett's *Waiting for Godot* (Royal & Derngate 2003) performed on a single set designed by Ray Lett. *The Weir* is set in a pub in rural Ireland and tells the story of a group of local men trying to impress a woman who has just moved to the area by telling ghost stories. Beckett's *Waiting for Godot* tells the story of two tramps, who are waiting for the mysterious Godot to arrive. The walls of the pub where *The Weir* was set became the ruins of a derelict building in *Waiting for Godot*. In addition to relocating *Waiting for Godot* to a rural Irish landscape 'of rocky outcrops and tumbledown stone walls', Goold added an opening sequence in which the boy who brings the news that Godot is not coming every evening is glimpsed 'sitting quite alone, watching and waiting' (Gardner 2003). In the programme, Goold justified the programming of the two plays together by arguing they were unified by their 'contemplation of inertia' and their attempt to examine 'how humanity clings to companionship and humour in the face of isolation and the seemingly arbitrary acts of God(ot)'. Rehearsing the plays in tandem, he argues, enables each play to be productively rethought through the lens of the other: 'the acute naturalism of *The Weir* has shed idiomatic light on the Beckett', while *Waiting for Godot* 'in turn heightened the deep sense of loneliness running through *The Weir*' (Goold 2003a). Not everyone was convinced, including the reviewer Jeremy Kingston: 'I don't entirely go along with the view expressed in his programme note that what occurs in one sheds light on the other' (Kingston 2003). Instead, Gardner argues, what fundamentally linked the two plays was Goold's use of a shared setting. The Irishness of the setting positions Beckett's tramps as 'a couple of chancers who lose their way home from the pub one night' (Gardner 2003). It was almost as if they had walked out of one play and into the next.

Othello[1]

Goold's next production was *Othello* (Royal & Derngate 2003), his third attempt at the play. Goold persuaded the American actor Ron Cephas Jones, who had recently appeared in *Jesus Hopped the 'A' Train* (Donmar 2002), to come to Northampton and play Othello. In order to make sense of his American Othello, Goold relocated the action of the play to the Second World War. Othello was reconfigured as a black GI, Desdemona (Kate Fleetwood) as the daughter of a high-ranking British official. In creating the world of 1940s Britain, Goold worked with the designer Laura Hopkins, whose work is heavily influenced by film. The production drew on the movies of Michael Powell and Emeric Pressburger. It opened in 'the interior of a taxi' speeding through city streets, the movement of the car created by 'film projected on the rear of the window', mimicking the techniques of 1940s cinema (Hopkins 2019). The 'muffled boom of distant bombing' conjured up London during the Blitz (Marlowe 2003). The action then moved to cabinet war rooms, 'a very dark world' full of 'secretive interiors' (Hopkins 2019). Cyprus was created using 'an enfolding set of De Chirico-like colonnades' (Billington 2003), which

---

[1] For production images, see http://laurahopkins.co.uk/shows/othello/ (accessed 28 February 2020).

could morph from an 'open square to a more narrow corridor of arches'. The set began as an 'open piazza' then developed into 'a more De Chirico dreamworld', ultimately becoming 'Escher-like'. Inspired by *Apocalypse Now*, Hopkins and Goold used the set as 'a metaphor for Othello's mind'. As he descended into jealous madness, the interiors became 'more and more twisted, distorted and interior' (Hopkins 2019). The period setting and intense atmosphere evoked through the set was supported by a score featuring 'noir-y', 'forties-style movie music' (Cork 2019).

Othello marked an increase in interest from national critics in Goold's work. While a few quibbled about the logic of 'an American general mysteriously attached to an otherwise very British army', most highlighted the effectiveness of Goold's Second World War setting. It captured the 'dynamism of the play' (Goss 2003). For Paul Taylor, the production had 'strength' in its 'depth', capturing the way in which, as the play 'gathers momentum, it becomes an appalling, unstoppable nightmare' (Taylor 2003a). Dominic Cavendish simply gushed: 'Goold's revival of *Othello* has so much to commend it, it's hard to know where to begin' (Cavendish 2003). The return of the national critics to Northampton improved staff morale; 'the oxygen of greater industry attention, both critically and in terms of excitement about the work' helped to put the venue back on track (Goold 2018b). Any doubters soon 'realized they were in a minority and it would be more fun to be on board this bus than to be standing outside it' (Godwin 2019). Once the critics and the staff were on board, it all became 'easier' (Goold 2019b).

Paradise Lost[2]

Goold 'had always wanted to do a version of *Paradise Lost* on stage' (Goold 2014a). While at Northampton, he had an idea for a manageable way of achieving this ambition, with 'a smaller cast' (Goold 2018b). By this point, however, he was busy with 'the basic grind of season programming and directing' (Goold 2014a). He needed some help. Godwin suggested Ben Power. Godwin had met Power when he returned to Cambridge to direct a production for the Marlowe Society in 2001 and had been working with him on 'a two-person adaptation of *Romeo and Juliet*' for a 'civic halls and school halls tour' for Northampton (Power 2019). Goold and Power met in the foyer of the National Theatre. At the time, Power was working in an administrative role at a health charity, while 'trying to work out what I was going to do in the theatre and how I was going to get a career making adaptations for the stage'. Power wrote a trial section of the *Paradise Lost* adaptation for Goold, 'Act One or maybe Act Four' (Power 2014). Goold remembers reading it and thinking: 'this is going to be brilliant' (Goold 2014a). Despite being excited, Goold was still concerned about how an adaptation of *Paradise Lost* would fare with Northampton audiences. Historically, the Royal 'would only play with more than 60 per cent with Ayckbourn' (Goold 2018b). Power

---

[2] For production images, see https://www.benstones.com/paradiselost and https://headlong.co.uk/productions/paradise-lost/explore/paradise-lost-production-photos/ (accessed 28 February 2020).

Figure 1 Left to right: Darrell D'Silva as Satan, Caroline Faber as Raphael and Jonjo O'Neill as the Son in *Paradise Lost* (Northampton Royal & Derngate 2002). Photo: Robert Day.

remembers the Royal as difficult even with such safe regional fare. Goold, he theorizes, came to the conclusion he had nothing to lose. If the audience 'won't come when we do P. G. Wodehouse and give them what we think they want' then 'we might as well stage *Paradise Lost* or an experimental reworking of Marlowe' (Power 2019).

In order to fund *Paradise Lost*, Goold needed to find a co-producer. Talking to other theatres, he discovered he had a competitor. He rang up Simon Reade at Bristol Old Vic and said, 'I know this is a crazy idea and it's never been done in 400 years but I've got this weird idea of doing *Paradise Lost* sometime in the late spring or summer. And there was a long pause and he said, "Oh, we're doing that as well"' – apparently, the writer and director David Farr had been working on an adaptation for Bristol while Goold was making plans in Northampton. The situation called for military manoeuvres: 'We both politely said, "Oh well, that's interesting. How funny!" Then both of us did what artistic directors do in those situations, which is to scramble all their fighter jets and drag the thing as early as possible to try and outflank the other one'. Both theatres, however, had advance programmed their Christmas shows. This meant the two versions of *Paradise Lost* ended up scheduled to open against each other in the first week of February. Bristol was one of the 'big ten [regional] theatres', so going up against them 'felt like David and Goliath' (Goold 2014a). In the end, having competing versions of *Paradise Lost* turned out to be 'the best thing' for both Bristol and Northampton as 'by doing two then of course all the national press reviewed both' (Goold 2018b).

By the time Goold was casting *Paradise Lost*, 'there was a bit of buzz developing around the work' in the industry: 'people were beginning to talk about us'. Goold offered Fiona Shaw the part of Satan. He remembers her being 'intrigued' but turning it down. She was intrigued enough, however, to come up to Northampton and see the show. Goold remembers spotting her in the bar with Deborah Warner and Saffron Burrows and thinking, 'Wow, we must be doing something right' (Goold 2018b). Jonjo O'Neill remembers a friend telling him: 'Look, if you have to kill someone to work with Rupert Goold, do it!' O'Neill auditioned for *Paradise Lost* and was offered the role of the Son, despite being a 'musical theatre boy' without any training in classical theatre. Goold, however, was convinced O'Neill had an aptitude for classical work: 'he said, "I think you'd take to it"'. O'Neill accepted the role.

Goold's *Paradise Lost* tells the story of the fall of Satan, his escape from Hell and his journey to Earth, where he successfully tempts Adam (Christian Bradley) and Eve (Leah Muller) into eating the forbidden fruit, unleashing Death (Antony Bunsee) and Sin (Caroline Faber) on mankind. The story is narrated by the Son (O'Neill), who is represented as a young man in a hooded tracksuit, whose bandaged hands hide the wounds of his future crucifixion. Satan (Darrell D'Silva) is a bloodied man in a slick white suit. The action of the story plays out in a dilapidated room designed by Ben Stones, which is empty except for a few wooden chairs. The use of a single location, within which the characters travel vast distances, evokes the idea that, wherever Satan is, he is always in Hell and brings it with him. When Satan holds his parliament of fallen angels, it is in front of a red curtain with a microphone as if in a seedy cabaret club. When he climbs up towards Heaven, it is via a ladder within the room, and as he climbs the room darkens and the cosmos appears projected behind him. Satan enters Eden through an emergency exit door at the back of the room, which opens to reveal green light. The same light then dapples the room in the third act, evoking Paradise. Instead of hanging from a tree, the fruit of knowledge, a red apple, sits on a wooden table in the middle of the room as Eve considers it. Sound was used to evoke the vast journeys the characters make. For the moment when Satan blasts off across the cosmos, Cork 'combined a whole load of different languages from different places' with sounds including 'jet planes', 'balloons popping and strange abstract bubbling organic life forms' to suggest the idea of 'swimming around in the cosmos' (Cork 2019). When Adam and Eve fall from grace, Cork created a long cue which 'started with a paradise of living unconsciously through sensuousness and ended up with the sound of pneumatic drills and traffic and all the ingredients of the modern world that completely mitigate against imagination and fantasy', so evoking a more everyday world (Cork 2019).

Overall, Goold feels Northampton's *Paradise Lost* 'came out a small points victory against Bristol' (Goold 2014a). Cavendish argues Goold's production was 'the grabbier of the two' (Cavendish 2004a). In reviewing the two productions, critics emphasized the different approaches they took to adapting their source material. Farr's version is identified as more dispassionate and high concept, Goold's as more voluptuous and with a greater emphasis on clear storytelling. Taylor reports being 'more emotionally engaged by the Northampton version' but felt 'a strong, if slightly distanced, admiration for the intellectual coherence and economy' of Bristol's (Taylor 2004). Ultimately, the real victory for Goold was that Northampton was being considered alongside Bristol: 'the fact that we were in the same discussion as one of the big ten'. It was 'the first time that Northampton felt serious' (Goold 2018b).

The show itself was not just a hit with the press, it was also a 'huge hit' with audiences, 'outselling the Ayckbourn'. Goold found this 'extraordinary' as 'the theatre really didn't have any kind of background in that kind of work at all'. For Goold, the audience's enthusiastic response 'legitimized real radicalism in Northampton' (Goold 2014a). Up to that point Goold's programming had been 'battling with how you managed that desire for the progressive stuff you wanted to do with the traditional audience' (Power 2014). The pairing of the naturalistic with the more conceptual in Goold's early programming – *Arcadia* with *Betrayal* or *The Weir* with *Waiting for Godot* – is indicative of this. Within this context, *Paradise Lost*, a difficult and unfamiliar classic text in a conceptual production, seems a risky prospect. Ironically, Power argues, it was when the programming 'started to be about what [Goold] wanted as an artist rather than trying to second-guess' his audience that they returned: 'everyone came to see that work because it felt different and really exciting' (Power 2019).

After *Paradise Lost*, Goold directed Terry Johnson's *Insignificance* (Royal & Derngate 2004), followed by Giles Havergal's adaptation of P. G. Wodehouse's *Summer Lightning*, a revival of a production he had originally created for Salisbury in 1998. *Insignificance* is about a set of imagined meetings between Marilyn Monroe (Gina Bellman), Joe DiMaggio (Steven Hartley), Albert Einstein (Paul McCleary) and Senator Joseph McCarthy (Alan Perrin). Like *Arcadia*, it is a play of complex ideas delivered in a relatively accessible form. For example, at one point Monroe explains the theory of relativity using a toy train. As Gardner noted, a pattern was beginning to become clear in Goold's programming choices: 'Shows that have an intellectual dazzle yet maintain an emotional strength in their secret hearts' (Gardner 2004). The national critics returned to Northampton again to review the show. The reviews are significant, not because of their assessment of the production itself, but in their reflection on Goold's tenure as a whole. Roderic Dunnett argues *Insignificance* 'confirms just how significant Rupert Goold's regime is proving' (Dunnett 2004). Cavendish agrees, noting that, with 'Goold striking home-run after home-run, the Theatre Royal, Northampton is fast becoming a regional player of national significance' (Cavendish 2004b).

Faustus[3]

The success of *Paradise Lost* raised the question of what Goold and Power would do next. Power was 'immersed in Marlowe' (Power 2014) at this point, having recently worked on

---

[3] For production images, see http://laurahopkins.co.uk/shows/faustus/ and https://headlong.co.uk/productions/faustus/explore/faustus-production-photos/ (accessed 28 February 2020).

Figure 2 Left to right: Jonjo O'Neill as Dinos, Scott Handy as Faustus and Stephen Noonan as Jake in *Faustus* (Hampstead Theatre 2006). Photo: Manuel Harlan.

an adaptation of *Tamburlaine the Great* (Rose Theatre Bankside 2003). They started talking about *Doctor Faustus* but were concerned about the weak quality of 'other hand' sections of the play (Goold 2014a). They 'wondered if there was a way to get rid of all the bad scenes and just do the good scenes', replacing the bad scenes with a contemporary narrative (Goold 2018b) that would work around the 'skeleton' of the 'extant Marlowe' (Goold 2014a). In considering adding material, Goold and Power were continuing a long tradition of augmenting Marlowe's text. The original frontispiece of the play states it already includes 'new additions' (Marlowe 1631).

Goold and Power did consider jettisoning the Marlowe and writing 'a new play about somebody selling their soul to the devil in some form or another' (Power 2014). Goold identifies two reasons for retaining the Marlowe, one commercial and one artistic. Despite the success of *Paradise Lost*, Goold was concerned 'a new play, anything that didn't say *Doctor Faustus* by Christopher Marlowe, would struggle' at the box office (Goold 2014a). The Marlowe was needed as a 'Trojan horse' (Power 2014) that could be used to 'smuggle' in a conceptual new play (Goold 2014a). The artistic reason was a question of structure. They felt the narrative of the extant Marlowe – 'Faustus gains the world, sells her soul, descends' – needed to be paired with an opposing journey: 'Would redeem her soul, lose everything, but transcend' (Goold 2018b). The original idea for the contemporary story was inspired by the work of Lars von Trier and based on the fundamental narrative underlying the journeys of his female protagonists in *Breaking the Waves*, *Dancer in the Dark* and *Dogville*, who all 'go through unbearable hellish circumstances and are redeemed through their essential purity'. Goold summarizes this as: 'The more she falls, the closer she comes to heaven' (Goold 2014a). Initially, the protagonist of the contemporary story was 'a Lithuanian immigrant called Helen' (Goold 2018b) but they struggled to find a 'sense of authenticity' in this narrative (Goold 2014a).

In 2003, the Chapman Brothers caused outrage in the art world when they exhibited a work titled *Insult to Injury*, which consisted of a set of original prints of the Spanish artist Goya's *Disasters of War* on which they had painted over all the visible faces with clown and puppy heads. Inspired by this intervention, Goold and Power talked about 'needing to do to the Marlowe what the Chapman Brothers had done to Goya's *Disasters of War*'. Eventually it became clear that the Chapmans themselves should form the content of the modern story. There was a clear link between them and Faustus: 'The Chapmans wanted to be iconoclastic; Faustus wants to be iconoclastic'. In May 2004, a real-life event created another parallel, when the Momart warehouse in East London, where a range of pivotal modern British artworks were stored, burnt down. Amongst the artworks destroyed was the Chapman Brothers' *Hell* (1999/2000), which featured 60,000 Nazi toy soldiers being chopped up and mutilated by skeletons, mutants and aliens. This 'felt Marlovian in all sorts of ways' and provided a climatic event for Goold and Power to juxtapose against Faustus's descent into Hell: 'just as Faustus goes on his big round-the-world journey and ends up in Hell, so would the Chapmans go on some post-success journey which would end in the Momart fire. These two fires would consume our central protagonists'. This storyline was problematic, however, because it paralleled the Faustus storyline rather than opposing it. Goold felt 'uncomfortable about being reactionary on both halves of the story': 'we were pro-Chapman and therefore by default pro-Faustus'. To make a complete equivalence between the Chapmans and Faustus's narratives was to say 'they should go to hell as well' (Goold 2014a). They realized 'the purchase of the Goyas could stand for the signature moment', which allowed them 'not to follow an identical arc in the Chapman story'. They still, however, did not know how to end the play (Power 2014).

Marlowe's play, Goold argues, articulates Chapman-like arguments about 'the author's intentions and their relevance'. Goold and Power realized they needed a moment that would challenge this position. They made an 'old-fashioned romantic decision' (Goold 2014a). Jake Chapman would meet his Helen of Troy 'at the same point Faustus meets his, and fall in love' (Power 2014). They took part of a speech on the power of beauty from the first part of *Tamburlaine* and divided it between Jake and Faustus, so creating an oppositional moment to the postmodern approach to art predominantly articulated in the play: 'the notion that art or culture aspires to transcendence or beauty was absolutely counter to the Chapmans' view' (Goold 2014a).

In creating the piece, Goold and Power worked collaboratively on generating ideas, then divided the initial writing between them: 'I'd take a stab at the Chapman stuff and Ben would rework the Marlowe and then we'd pass it between us'. The basic plotting of the sequence of scenes was modelled after *Arcadia*. The past and present began as separate alternating storylines isolated from each other but then, once established, merged: 'Marlowe, us, Marlowe, us, together'. The production opens with Faustus (Scott Handy) in his shadowy study, lit by a single candle. In the distance, monks take up a

Gregorian chant. As Faustus blows out the candle at the end of the first scene, the dark walls of his study suddenly wheel around to reveal the bright, white cube space of the Chapmans' studio. The chanting transforms into dance music. The Chapman Brothers, Jake (Martin Savage) and Dinos (Richard Katz), announce their intention to paint over the Goya etchings to a shocked art critic, Foster (Paul Chahidi). The action then returns to Faustus's study, where Faustus offers to give his soul up to Lucifer if Mephistopheles (Paul Barnhill) will agree to serve him. Back in the Chapmans' studio, the Chapmans are preparing to paint over the Goya etchings. Back in Faustus's study, Faustus is wavering over his decision to sign away his soul. The Chapmans appear above him. They are with an art dealer, sealing the purchase of the Goya etchings. Both the Chapmans and Faustus sign. This structure created two moments of shock for the audience. The first occurred when the first Marlovian scene ended and the space was transformed into a recognizably modern setting; the second, in Act One, Scene Five, when two worlds began to merge as the protagonists of both storylines sign (Goold 2014a).

Hopkins designed a set for the show, based on the kinetic work she had achieved with *Othello*, that could switch between the past and present 'very quickly and seamlessly' (Hopkins 2019). She modelled the world of Faustus and his study on the aesthetic of BBC Shakespeare, almost wilfully archaic. The main influence on the design, however, was the films of Stanley Kubrick, particularly *The Shining*. References to Kubrick in the design created a circular reference as, in interviews, the Chapmans frequently refer to Kubrick when discussing the act of painting over the Goya prints: 'We always had the intention of rectifying it, to take that nice word from *The Shining*, when the butler's trying to encourage Jack Nicholson to kill his family – to rectify the situation' (Jones 2003). The final image of the production was 'another filmic trope'. Hopkins created 'an overhead shot of [the Chapmans] starting to paint over the Goya prints', so enabling the audience to witness the act. In this scene, the rear wall 'was painted to look like the floor of the studio with floorboards'. There was an 'upturned table' in front of the rear wall. Two 'diving boards' were slid out with the actors playing the Chapmans 'lying flat on their stomachs' on them so the audience could see the tops of their heads and their hands working on the prints as if from above (Hopkins 2019).

Critics praised the show for its boldness of vision, 'its adventurous spirit' (Bassett 2004). Alfred Hickling awarded the show '[f]ive full stars', and admired the 'seamless manner in which the parallel stagings overlap', raising 'pertinent, keenly argued questions about artistic ownership and authenticity' (Hickling 2004). Other critics, however, were less convinced, observing that the two narratives felt forced together at times: 'its parallels don't always convince' (Marlowe 2004). Some were concerned that the piece was too wrapped up in its own cleverness to the detriment of its narrative: 'making a clever point isn't the same as delivering a satisfying drama' (Cavendish 2004c). Within the industry, Goold felt the response to his work at Northampton was shifting again. People were asking how he was managing to get away with it, 'to program this stuff' and still 'find an audience for it'. Goold was beginning to believe that his theory about the town's lack of self-esteem had been correct. The people who came to his shows wanted more than the town had been previously offering them in terms of culture and entertainment. They

Figure 3 Left to right: Tobias Menzies as Hamlet, Paul Shelley as Polonius, Tom Edden as the Player Queen, Dominic Colchester as the Player King, Michael Shaeffer as the Third Player, Aled Pugh as Guildenstern and Jamie de Courcey as Rosencrantz in *Hamlet*. Photo: Donald Cooper

loved the fact his productions offered them 'a totally imaginative world'. Though Goold remembers the local audience seeming 'utterly bewildered' during the first preview of *Faustus*, 'the weirder and more imaginative and bolder and stranger the worlds we created' the more Northampton appeared to lap it up (Goold 2018b).

Hamlet[4]

Goold's last production for Northampton was Shakespeare's *Hamlet*. It was also the final production before the theatre shut for the long-awaited refurbishment, so Goold's 'starting point was the space itself' (Goold 2005c). Goold and Hopkins wanted to create a production that would 'honour the theatre'. Hopkins's set for *Hamlet* 'reproduced the auditorium on the stage' (Hopkins 2019). Power remembers 'it was like there was a mirror on the proscenium and you were looking at an empty version of the theatre' (Power 2019). She gave both the real auditorium and the auditorium onstage a feeling of 'abandonment and neglect'. She 'scattered ash, dust around'. There were 'buckets collecting drips', 'piles of detritus and upturned chairs'. The abandoned theatrical environment

---

[4] For production images, see http://laurahopkins.co.uk/shows/hamlet-2005/ (accessed 28 February 2020).

Hopkins created for the play demanded a re-imagination of the court'. Goold came up with a poetic world for the play inspired by the work of dancer and choreographer Pina Bausch. The floor was covered in dirt and one party scene featured 'lots of people in shabby forties cocktail dresses dancing and stumbling around drunk'. It was as if a group of 'odd eccentrics had ended up occupying this abandoned theatre' (Hopkins 2019). The ethereal quality of Goold's poetic world was accentuated by the production's 'ghostly' soundscape which, inspired by the music of the Icelandic rock bank Sigur Rós, aimed to evoke a Scandinavian landscape, 'the frozen north' (Cork 2019).

The literal theatricalization of the space emphasized the ways in which *Hamlet* is a play about the 'nature of acting and theatre itself' (Goold 2005c). As Charles Spencer notes, 'much of *Hamlet* concerns acting, artifice and the vexed relationship between truth and illusion' (Spencer 2005). The players perform a play, an enactment of a fictional murder, to reveal Claudius's guilt. In Goold's version, Hamlet (Menzies) performs his own madness, for which he dons his mother's wedding dress and her red lipstick. Characters dissemble and spy on each other. Rosencrantz (Jamie de Courcey) and Guildenstern (Aled Pugh) pretend to be Hamlet's friends while reporting on his every move. Hamlet spies on Claudius's confession of his sins. Polonius (Paul Shelley) watches from behind a wall hanging as Hamlet berates his mother. The idea of performance was emphasized in Goold's staging of the first court scene, in which Gertrude (Jane Birkin) and Claudius (Hilton McRae) perform 'a sultry jazz number' while 'shadowy figures' lean over the balconies (Bassett 2005). John Peter argues Goold's staging blurs the line between the watcher and the watched, the performer and the audience: 'who will act, who will observe? I've never seen the near-identity of stage and audience more economically revealed' (Peter 2005).

The sense of the piece as a reflection on the theatre and its history was accentuated by the show's opening. An apologetic stage manager (David Ganly) comes onto the forestage to inform the audience that there has been 'an incident on the roads', delaying some of the cast. He leaves and then returns a few minutes later to reassure the audience: 'The actors have been sighted'. Having drawn the audience's attention to fundraising leaflets for the theatre's refurbishment, he proceeds to talk about the theatre's history, the famous people who have worked there and the theatre's ghost. He stops suddenly '*in absolute terror staring at the back of the theatre*' (Shakespeare 2005a: 1) and asks 'Who's there?' the opening line of the first scene of *Hamlet*, reconfiguring old Hamlet's ghost as a theatre ghost. With a '*spine chilling crash*' (Shakespeare 2005a: 1), the auditorium is plunged into darkness. In the darkness the audience hear Claudius's first speech – 'Though yet of Hamlet our dear brother's death / The memory be green' (*Hamlet*, 1.2.1–2) – as if playing on a crackly old radio. The safety curtain then rises to reveal the banquet scene, 'a twinkling ghost theatre' (Power 2019).

Though Goold had a poetic world for the play, he did not have a social world in which to set it: 'I began to worry the actors would need a more specific world ("where is Wittenberg?", "what kind of soldier am I?")' (Goold 2005c). He remembered a quote from Albert Camus's *The Myth of Sisyphus*: 'There is but one truly serious philosophical problem and that is suicide. Judging whether life is or is not worth living amounts to answering the fundamental question of philosophy' (Camus 2005: 1–2). The more Goold read about the birth of French existentialism 'coming out of the seedy postwar world of accusation, collaboration and cold war espionage, the more it seemed to fit the play'. So Goold excised the political aspects of Shakespeare's play, removing the Fortinbras narrative to foreground the existential nature of Hamlet's crisis (Goold 2005c).

Menzies, who played Hamlet, worked to bring a more physical edge to this existential struggle; not an 'elegiac beautiful existentialism' but a 'raging against the dying of the light', conveying how 'endlessly hard' it is in life 'to get it right or know what to do' (Menzies 2019). Though Goold and Menzies conceived the character more as a 'philosopher poet' than a 'revenging fury' (Goold 2005c), Menzies saw Hamlet's struggle as an embodied struggle of the heart as much as the mind: not 'cool and considered' but 'hot' and 'raw'. The production also focused on Hamlet's sexual obsession with his mother. Goold and Menzies represented this physically through having Hamlet dress in his mother's wedding dress during his supposed madness. It also visually conveyed a sense of Hamlet's increasingly becoming the wife his mother should be in his pursuit of justice for his father. It was an image they came to 'partly intuitively': Menzies notes that it is 'not entirely logical' but it was productive because it 'plugs into something on a non-intellectual level. It feels rich' (Menzies 2019).

In the reviews, Goold is positioned as an agent provocateur in both the positive and the negative connotations of the term. Michael Billington accuses Goold of being perverse in his directorial choices, specifically his excision of the play's political aspect: 'It must not be supposed that the director does this solely because it is wrong, though there is no other reason apparent'. While noting how Goold's radical productions have 'put Northampton on the map', he argues that the director's 'crusading adventure' now needs to be 'tempered by a strong dose of common sense' (Billington 2005). Spencer classifies the production as 'one of those flashy, look-at-me productions that initially seems more concerned with displaying the director's own brilliance than in getting to the mysterious heart of Shakespeare's inexhaustible play'. Despite finding it 'intelligent, eye-catching and involving', he advises Goold to concentrate 'more on the text and less on his own cleverness' (Spencer 2005). While Menzies feels the production had 'some amazing stuff in it', he wonders in retrospect if it was a little 'gauche': 'we were both young and maybe a bit punky about it and maybe showing off at times'. He argues, however, it was 'an emotional' interpretation. Its strength was that 'you saw a young man go through it' (Menzies 2019).

Despite the negative tone of some of the reviews, the local audience remained loyal. Goold remembers a 'sixteen-year-old girl coming up to [him]' one night after *Hamlet* and saying, 'I've seen all of these shows since *Othello* and they changed my life'. This encounter gave him faith that, despite the critical backlash, he had created something valuable during his time in Northampton; given a 'good energy to the place and really built an audience up' (Goold 2018b). Looking back, he classifies his project at the theatre as 'an existential enquiry' of which *Hamlet* is the culmination: '*Arcadia*, *Waiting for Godot*, *Paradise Lost* and *Faustus* have dwelt on recurrent themes of time, destiny and freedom and *Hamlet* is a distillation of many of these ideas'. One of the great privileges of working in regional theatre, he argues, is the close relationship you can build with the local community and the opportunity it offers 'an artist to enter into an ongoing dialogue with an audience and investigate these kinds of questions over a body of work' (Goold 2005c). As Goold notes of his time at Northampton:

> For some communities it is more appropriate to reach out to them and listen to what they want and the stories they are hungry to hear and tell about themselves but there is also a place for an artist to be resident and animate a community through the personality of their own work. In that sense I was inspired by the glory days of the Glasgow Citizens Theatre under my friend Giles Havergal or the mythical status of Pina Bausch in the smallish town of Wuppertal.
>
> (Goold 2018b)

Goold used his time at Northampton to develop a narrative around his work and build a following for it. *Paradise Lost* and *Faustus*, in particular, felt like 'part of a potential new enquiry' and would be revived during Goold's first season at Headlong (Goold 2014a). Goold feels his approach as a director was still developing at Northampton: '*Hamlet* was the first one I did with a bit more methodology'. Despite this, both *Paradise Lost* and *Faustus* contain elements that would become distinctive features of Goold's later work: 'intervention' in classical texts, which Goold compares to architect I. M. Pei putting a 'glass pyramid in the centre of the Louvre'; 'the Marlovian anti-hero' (Goold 2014a); and 'the appropriation of popular culture on stage' (Power 2014). Power sees *Faustus* as particularly formative in its clash of two unexpected elements. This would go on to be an important model for Goold. Power argues that 'suddenly having two things together in a way that wasn't really under control' became a defining feature 'both aesthetically and dramaturgically' of the work Goold would make in subsequent years (Power 2019).

CHAPTER 3
HEADLONG AND THE RSC – EARLY YEARS: 2005–2009

When Goold arrived at Headlong, the company was known as the Oxford Stage Company (OSC). Under Dominic Dromgoole, Goold's predecessor, the company had 'developed a distinct niche for rediscovering modern British plays or writers that have been neglected' ('Oxford Stage Company is One of the Leading National Touring Theatre Companies,' 2010). During Dromgoole's incumbency, the company produced alone: 'they would just finance it, they would lose their shirt, that was what the ACE [Arts Council England] money was for. It never had any commercial expectation at all'. By the time Dromgoole left, however, the company's business model was no longer working: 'It was starting to get into debt. Artistically it was mixed. I think audiences were expecting something different' (Finch 2018a).

Henny Finch joined OSC as executive producer a few months before Dromgoole resigned. 'Rupert applied and I saw his name on the list of people who asked for the papers'. She 'had heard amazing things about Northampton and what he was doing there'. She invited him for a coffee and they 'immediately hit it off'. It was clear to Finch that Goold would 'shake things up completely'. Although Finch was not part of the decision-making process, she 'was backing him from the start' (Finch 2018a). Power was 'initially sceptical about whether a touring company was the right context'. Goold, however, was 'really clear that it was a huge opportunity'. A touring company meant there would be 'none of the overheads or worry about the different stakeholders' involved with running a building (Power 2019). At Northampton, Goold had had to deal with a 'very long ten-year lottery-funded redevelopment that had been hanging over' the organization to make the merger of the two theatres physically coherent. There had been a 'great period of a couple of years after my first year and then increasingly it became all about the bricks and mortar'. As a senior management team, it became 'increasingly hard to feel you were part of an arts organization rather than a building project' (Goold 2019a). Goold also had practical reasons for wanting to move on. He was about to become a father for the first time. Working for OSC would enable him to be based in London with his new family. His son arrived after a forty-two-hour labour the day before his interview and in the same week his university friend and muse, Sacha Grunpeter, had died in a car crash while making his first film in Los Angeles. Despite suffering from a complete lack of sleep, the board told Finch Goold's performance was 'virtuoso': 'From the moment he walked in, it was always going to be him' (Finch in Trueman 2019).

Goold instantly faced a new set of challenges when he arrived at OSC. He 'was told the deficit was about £25,000' but soon discovered it was 'nearer £200,000' (Goold 2019a). Dromgoole and Goold had no real contact during the handover: 'He left me a bottle of crème de cassis on the desk and said, "I don't believe in handovers, good luck!"' Staffing needed to be rationalized 'in order to get back on an even keel financially'. It also needed refreshing, as the team 'had been used to delivering Dominic's kind of work, so had a different approach to artistic creation'. While Dromgoole was artistic director, there had 'been no other artistic voices' among the permanent staff based in the office: 'it didn't feel like there was a collective programming conversation going on'. Both Finch and Goold wanted to change that (Finch 2018a).

Goold was keen to bring Power to join him. Under Dromgoole, the 'company hadn't commissioned at all. It was only picking up revivals'. Finch agreed they needed to put a literary staff member in place 'in order to have a machine that could make new plays'. This move towards commissioning new plays was needed as Goold 'was hungry to be part of and influence the national cultural conversation that was leaping out of the early internet'. It would be hard to do through revivals. Initially, Finch hoped they would be able to book new plays into the touring venues but 'then it became apparent we couldn't' (Finch 2018b). The touring circuit traditionally favours classic titles, which are seen as safer draws for audiences. In response to this, the company developed a model over time where new work would be showcased first in order to raise its profile: 'opening at somewhere like Chichester and hopefully getting a lot of energy and touring in a second life off the first life' (Goold 2019a).

With the company in debt, they needed to find a reasonable justification for bringing in an additional member of staff. Power remembers the board being 'sceptical about whether you needed a non-directing full-time associate' (Power 2019). At the time, Power was working as a fundraiser for the London Library. In order to persuade the board, Goold suggested the company needed someone with fundraising experience as 'a way of smuggling in a literary manager' (Goold 2018a). The company advertised for a 'part dramaturg, part fundraiser' (Finch 2018b). Power applied for the job and was eventually appointed. Even though the job had been designed for him, there was a 'slightly nasty moment when I thought I wasn't going to get it' (Power 2019). In April 2006, just before Power arrived, the company also employed a new general manager, Jenni Grainger. In her interview Grainger remembers being asked by Goold: 'Would you like to work for a company that has great staff morale and shit artistic work, or would you like to work for a company that has low staff morale but great artistic work?' (Grainger 2018). Finch recalls that Grainger answered the question beautifully: 'She said. "My job would be to change the culture. I'd rather work for a company where the artistic output was good and I'd fix the rest"'. (Finch 2018b).

Finch, Goold, Grainger and Power went away for the weekend 'to try and do a business plan' (Goold 2018a). They put together a list of 'crazy goals' they wanted to achieve. These included: 'get an Arts Council funding uplift' (Finch 2018b); 'co-produce at the National'; 'a West End Transfer'; 'go to Broadway'; 'win Olivier Awards'; 'be not in the [Edinburgh] Fringe but part of the International Festival' (Goold 2018a); 'become a new writing powerhouse' (Finch 2018b); 'get a new play onto the A-level syllabus' (Trueman 2019) and 'to have the best and craziest parties in the industry'. In addition, they wanted to 'reflect the younger team at the company in the artists and audiences they worked with'. Despite the fact all these ambitions seemed 'incredibly' out of reach at the time, they 'managed them all in about two or three years' (Goold 2018a). Finch remembers 'the only one of those we didn't do was the Arts Council uplift' (Finch 2018b).

Soon after Goold's arrival, the board asked him to change the company's name. People often mistook the Oxford Stage Company for 'a student touring company' as it suggested an association with the University of Oxford (Goold 2018b). The company was also no longer based in Oxford, Dromgoole having moved its offices to London in 2001. Goold, Finch and Power considered several possibilities, including 'Blue', 'Infinite Space' (Grainger 2018), 'In a Nutshell' (Trueman 2019) and 'Isis' (Finch 2018b). The name 'Headlong' was suggested by Dee Miller (Power's girlfriend, now wife) and borrowed from *Paradise Lost*: 'Hurled headlong flaming from th' ethereal sky' (1.45). The 'rebranding was hugely freeing' (Grainger 2018) and was helped by the fact 'we were doing it at the same time as Rupert's career went from being artistic director of a not particularly high-profile regional theatre to being the most celebrated young director in the country' (Power 2018). There was, however, some anxiety that the name change 'could totally mess things up'. They all remembered that another company, Method and Madness, had 'changed their name and then completely disappeared' (Grainger 2018). The name change met with a mixed response. Some journalists questioned if it was just more 'Goold bar-rattling' (Halliburton 2006).

Initially, it was difficult for Headlong to establish their new brand. Being a touring company meant they tended to 'get subsumed by the venues [they] played in' (Roberts 2019). As Finch notes: 'People go to their local theatre, don't they? They don't go necessarily to see the company' (Finch 2018a). In addition, venues were often 'very protective' of their own brand (Finch 2018b). This manifested in concrete ways: 'We had a banner you could put up in a foyer and people would take it down and hide it'. The company 'spent a lot of time thinking about how you have any impact with audiences or press or industry when you are performing in someone else's house' (Power 2018). Clióna Roberts, the company's press and PR consultant, worked hard to ensure the company were recognized in the press: 'I had all critics and editors well versed on the company and the provenance of the show'. Occasionally, however, she would still have to 'get them to alter an online review' after publication. With time, the company did establish 'a recognizable template for producing vivid contemporary interpretations of classic texts and spectacular new work, which naturally evolved into a certain shorthand of "that's very Headlong"' (Roberts 2019). As producer Lindsey Alvis notes, 'Headlong became an adjective and it became easy to identify what the Headlong brand was' (Alvis 2019).

Finch and Goold drove around the country visiting various regional venues asking them 'what they wanted and how we could help' (Finch 2018a). They discovered that many of the venues 'weren't happy with what they had been getting'. They also 'knew what they wanted' (Goold 2018b) from touring companies: 'classic titles with a twist' (Finch 2018b). In addition, venues wanted to 'co-produce' (Goold 2018b) so they could be more 'involved creatively' (Finch 2018b). Co-producing had also become a financial 'necessity' for Headlong in terms of its development as a company. Coming from a commercial theatre background, Finch was keen for Headlong's work to reach a larger audience: 'I wanted to make shows that were going to be popular and widely viewed and so I was pushing to upscale'. This involved producing 'more plays than you could on a very steady weekly touring model'. Through co-producing, however, you can 'double your output' as 'you're sharing your risk with other theatres'. Finch argues that securing co-producers, however, depends on the quality of the company's work: 'to get theatres interested you have to have pieces that work, that are really desirable' (Finch 2018a).

'Reinventing the Epic', Goold's first season for Headlong, featured six productions, of which he directed five himself. Announcing a 'thematic' season of work, 'a bunch of shows that really spoke to each other', was 'a really radical thing' for a touring company to do, as it was a practice more associated with venues (Finch 2018a). Normally 'touring companies just announce one show at a time'. Grainger remembers it as feeling 'really impressive', like 'we were puffing our chests out' (Grainger 2019a). It was 'a declaration of "here we are and this is our style"' (Finch 2018a). Power argues, however, that while it is 'easy to look back and see certain policy strands' underlying each season's work, this is actually a bit of an illusion. The programming during his tenure was more 'about working with someone you are excited about'. There was not 'always a coherent vision thematically or formally about what those productions were doing': 'the best things that happened at Headlong had an air of improvisation about them' (Power 2019).

Goold wanted to include revivals of *Paradise Lost* and *Faustus* in the first season. He felt they were 'good calling cards for [his] work as a director to new venues' and wanted them 'to have a wider audience' (Goold 2018a). This presented him with a problem, however, as technically both shows were the intellectual property of Northampton. This led to 'a difficult negotiation with Northampton about whether they'd let me take them' (Goold 2019a). Power was keen to include Tony Kushner's *Angels in America* (Headlong/Glasgow Citizens/Lyric Hammersmith 2007) but getting the rights to revive the show was 'very tricky'. When the director Daniel Kramer came in to pitch some ideas to the company, it became evident he 'was obsessed with *Angels in America*'. Kramer managed to seal the deal: 'Daniel effectively doorstepped Kushner in America'. He was 'incredibly charismatic and passionate, and Kushner was charmed by it'. Goold also held the rights to Stephen Adly Guirgis's *The Last Days of Judas Iscariot*. He had been following the playwright since seeing *Jesus Hopped the 'A' Train*. Like *Paradise Lost*, *Faustus* and *Angels in America*, the play featured 'major spiritual themes, big abstract characters' so fitted well. All four productions were also linked by the presence of angels. Goold remembers thinking, perhaps 'naively': 'If we do these big mystic shows like *Paradise Lost*, can we take that round the country? Can we establish that as a brand?' (Goold 2018a).

The final two shows in the season were less obviously connected. The first was Edward Bond's *Restoration* (Headlong/Bristol Old Vic 2006) and the second an adaptation of Simon Schama's *Rough Crossings* (Headlong/Birmingham Rep/Liverpool Everyman and Playhouse/West Yorkshire Playhouse/Lyric Hammersmith 2007). Though they fitted less neatly with the spiritual concerns of the other four productions, both were epic in the Brechtian sense. Overall Goold summarizes the season as 'looking at the individual versus the establishment through divine metaphor' (Goold 2018a).

Speaking Like Magpies

As Goold was moving from Northampton to Headlong, he was also beginning to forge a place for himself as a director at the Royal Shakespeare Company (RSC). After seeing Goold's work at Northampton, Michael Boyd, the artistic director of the RSC, invited him to direct a new play, Frank McGuinness's *Speaking Like Magpies* (RSC 2005), for the company's 'Gunpowder Season', marking the 400th anniversary of the Gunpowder Plot. McGuinness's retelling of this historical event puts King James I (William Houston) at the centre, focusing on his fear of being killed in a Catholic plot and his troubled relationship with his wife, as a result of his attraction to young men. In parallel, it charts the story of a Jesuit priest, Henry Garnet (Fred Ridgeway), who reluctantly becomes embroiled with the plotters, Robert Catesby (Jonjo O'Neill) and Robin Wintour (Matt Ryan).

The production opened with what O'Neill terms 'the greatest opening sequence of all time' (O'Neill 2019). A line of gunpowder running across the centre of the stage spontaneously ignited as the audience waited for the play to begin. The flame moved towards the back curtain where it set off an explosion, sending sparks across the stage as the curtain fell, revealing a sparse, bomb-blasted landscape. Despite its explosive opening, however, McGuinness's play focuses on the events surrounding the Gunpowder Plot, rather than on the plot itself. The actual assassination attempt is only represented symbolically as part of one of James's nightmares. In McGuinness's text, this nightmare depicts a procession of conspirators '*robed in red, wearing black masks*' carrying '*banners of Catholic iconography*' and '*symbols of Catholic theology*' (McGuinness 2005: 85–6). Goold's staging, however, is more earthy than the letter of McGuinness's text suggests. The conspirators, in red robes and wearing crude wooden masks, advance threateningly on James in a tribal dance. They tie his limbs to ropes and raise him into the air. Guy Fawkes then enters with a flaming torch and relights the line of gunpowder. A flame starts to move towards the back of the stage as James frees himself from his ropes. James descends, stamping the fire out. The play's eschewal of any retelling of the events of the actual assassination makes the action of the play difficult for an audience not already versed in the details of the story to understand. As Jane Edwardes points out: 'If I hadn't recently read Antonia Fraser's book on the same subject, I would have been totally lost' (Edwardes 2006). While Goold's 'visually ravishing staging' was praised by the critics, it was seen as covering for the faults of McGuinness's play: 'a reminder of the lack of real drama elsewhere' (Gardner 2006).

The Tempest[1]

After *Speaking Like Magpies*, Goold returned to Headlong to direct their revival of *Paradise Lost* (Headlong/Royal & Derngate Northampton/Watford Palace 2006). He then went

---

[1] For production images, see https://www.rsc.org.uk/the-tempest/past-productions/rupert-goold-2006-production (accessed 28 February 2020).

straight back to Stratford to direct Shakespeare's *The Tempest* for the RSC's main stage, the Royal Shakespeare Theatre (RST). Before starting work on his version, Goold spoke to the director John Barton, who suggested the play could be done in 'only two ways': 'either in the manner of Peter Brook, spare and ritualised, or as a big show with lots of effects and magic'. Barton identified both approaches as problematic: 'the former never worked because it was just too portentous and dull and the plot was too silly to sustain such a reverent reading, and the latter was gaudy but at least had the virtue of the audiences enjoying it'. Goold controversially relocated the action of play to the Arctic. He sensed that its harsh mysterious landscape might provide an opportunity to bridge the gap between these two canonical approaches to staging the play: 'marry these "holy" and spectacular elements' by allowing for 'a staging that was theatrical and magical yet also hard-edged and cruel' (Goold in Bate and Wright 2008: 141). The 'shifting, evaporating, oft-claimed but never owned environment' also reflected the idea of the island being as much a state of mind as an actual place and the product of Prospero's need for revenge: 'just as Prospero's vengeance melts away, so maybe does his island' (Goold in Bate and Wright 2008: 133).

In his staging of the opening shipwreck, Goold aimed to 'convey the helpless fear one feels as a passenger when a storm hits'. Initially, Goold considered changing the shipwreck to a plane crash as 'most modern audiences will have more vivid and unsettling experiences of air travel than sea now'. Concerned a plane crash would invite comparisons with the television series *Lost*, Goold abandoned this idea and drew on his childhood memories of travelling in ships: 'being on cross-channel ferries and feeling very vulnerable and it struck me that the experience below deck is more frightening than above'. Goold's production begins with an image of an old-fashioned radio projected onto the curtain. As the shipping forecast announces bad weather, the radio's speaker becomes transparent, revealing 'a very claustrophobic navigation cell' below decks. Waves projected onto the curtain and a light swinging back and forth evoke a sense of queasiness. Inside the cell, guests in dinner suits and mariners 'pitch and panic' then abandon ship as Ariel (Julian Bleach) appears amongst them (1.1). As the scene ends the curtain darkens and the transparent circle rises to reveal the deck of the ship appearing to roll over as the storm strikes (Goold in Bate and Wright 2008: 127–8).

The curtain rises to reveal Prospero (Patrick Stewart) inside his wooden cabin, dressed in shamanic garb made of furs with a large fish bone as a hood, standing with his back to the audience, his hands raised. A blizzard can be seen raging outside the cabin. Miranda (Mariah Gale) enters and Prospero lowers his arms, quietening the storm. As Prospero takes Miranda to see Caliban (John Light), the hut walls disappear and a swirling blue snowstorm is projected onto a black curtain. This is then drawn back to reveal an icy landscape receding into the distance upstage. Caliban, dressed in furs like an Inuit, is asleep in a large wooden basket held above the snow on stilts (1.2). The majority of the action of the play plays out on this icy landscape, its location also evoked through Adam Cork's use of throat-singing in the production's score. When Trinculo (Craig Gazey) appears, Caliban hides under his basket, so the monster Stephano (Joseph Alessi) addresses later in the scene is a basket that rears up on four legs (2.2). Ariel blows snow over people to cast his spells. When a feast is brought on for the lords, it is a seal carcass, carried on a sledge pulled by Inuit. In the harpy scene, Ariel appears out of the carcass, his skin covered in blood, exposed white ribs visible on his chest. It is as if the seal has emerged from its own body (3.3).

For Ariel, Goold wanted 'to find something truly terrifying and threatening'. He was fascinated by resonances between *Dr Faustus* and *The Tempest*. Both feature 'god-defying magicians'. Whereas Prospero 'drowns his book', Faustus screams 'I'll burn my books', but 'at the moment of his damnation when it is too late'. In both, a spirit is 'the agent of the magic' and 'the source of the magician's power'. Goold's Ariel is 'Mephistophelean' (Goold in Bate and Wright 2008: 131). In rehearsals, Goold suggested Ariel might be 'fire-breathing' ('The Tempest: Rehearsal Note 1', 2006). In performance, his deathly white head first appears out of a flaming brazier, suggesting a hellish nature (1.2).

Images of fire and ice are woven throughout the production. The blessing of Miranda and Ferdinand (Nick Court) is performed by three goddesses (Allyson Brown, Golda Rosheuvel and Emma Jay Thomas) dressed in red. They blindfold the lovers, wash their hands and then aggressively dunk their heads into a bucket of icy water. They bring fire, waving it behind the lovers and smearing soot on their faces. They then push them to the ground, wave the flame over them and stand on their backs. They sit the lovers up, placing an untied cord over their hands. It snows on the lovers as the goddesses sing their blessing (4.1). The ceremony is broken as Prospero conjures a vision of the lords and their servants, split into small groups and lost out on the ice (5.1). The final scene takes place on the ice outside Prospero's cabin, which now looks ruined and leans at an angle. In the final moments of the play, as Prospero gives up his magical powers, he throws his staff into the cabin. Ariel is released and there is an explosion within the cabin. Flames can be seen flickering through the doorway (5.1).

A few critics balked at the inconsistencies between Goold's Arctic location and the text: 'It's made repeatedly clear in *The Tempest* that the King of Naples and his retinue were sailing across the Mediterranean from Tunis to Italy' (Spencer 2007a). For most, however, Goold's radical relocation reinvigorated a play that 'can easily languish as a beautiful poetic musing' (Benedict 2007). In contrast, Goold's production 'renews a feeling of the play's strangeness' (Taylor 2006) so that it seems 'refreshingly new-minted' (Benedict 2007). Accusations of showiness, however, still seeped through: '[the] staging is so exciting, his vision of the play so powerfully emotional, that he somehow gets away with his self-advertising desire for novelty at any price' (Spencer 2007a).

Restoration[2]

Back at Headlong, Goold decided he needed to start with a show that could act as 'a good bridge' between Dromgoole's tenure and his own. Dromgoole 'had made quite a name for

---

[2] For production images, see https://headlong.co.uk/productions/restoration/explore/ (accessed 28 February 2020).

the OSC for doing mid-twentieth-century proscenium repertoire'. Goold felt the need to reassure audiences, venues and critics 'we weren't jettisoning that'. Goold settled on Edward Bond's *Restoration* (Royal Court 1981) as the play both fitted within OSC's previous aim of reviving 'neglected, particularly British work' but pointed towards Goold's new remit of 'more political, Brecht-inspired, anti-Stanislavskian theatre-making'. Like Goold and Power's *Faustus*, *Restoration* repurposes a classical form for a modern audience, taking Restoration comedy and 'filtering it through [Bond's] Marxist lens'. The play tells the story of a penniless aristocrat, Lord Are (Mark Lockyer), who marries Ann (Dorothea Myer-Bennett), the daughter of an industrialist. When Ann dresses up as a ghost in order to scare Are into taking her to London, he runs her through with his sword and blames the murder on his servant, Bob (Mark Stobbart). Are manages to get Bob a pardon but Bob's illiterate mother (Beverley Klein) accidently burns the paper it is written on so Bob is hanged (Goold 2018a).

Restoration was the first show to go out under the Headlong banner. Power remembers it being 'a challenge for audiences': 'deconstructed Restoration comedy. It's tough. Tough with songs' (Power 2019). The critic Sam Marlowe remembers Goold's interpretation as grotesque and terrifying: 'absurd wigs and deathly makeup, and Oliver Fenwick's shadowy lighting give the performers a nightmarish, monstrous aspect'. At the same time, she praises Goold for effectively balancing the play's mixture of humour and brutality: 'Exquisitely funny yet brimming with contained fury and disgust, it's challenging, riveting and deeply disturbing – not least when it is making us laugh hardest'. The production was seen as 'a bold promising statement of intent' (Marlowe 2006) from the newly minted company, though a few critics still quibbled about the new name: 'Terrible name, good start' (Gore-Langton 2006).

The first year of Headlong was an exhausting time for Goold: 'taking over a new company', 'developing a relationship with the RSC' and, at the same time, 'having a little baby'. Being new to touring, he inadvertently created some unnecessary problems for himself. *Paradise Lost* was 'hell on the road, because it was very impractical to tour'. Touring shows have to get out of one venue on Saturday night and open again at another the following Tuesday. This means the get-in and technical rehearsal have to be completed in a very short time, so productions need to be designed to facilitate that. Goold had failed to factor this in when reviving the production. Goold also directed 'four shows back to back' (Goold 2018a). After *Paradise Lost*, he went straight into *The Tempest*. After *The Tempest* opened Goold immediately went into rehearsals for *Restoration*, and after *Restoration* opened Goold then went straight into rehearsals for *Faustus*. Goold's hectic workload continued into 2007, when he found himself directing two shows in the West End simultaneously. His well-received revival of *A Glass Menagerie* starring Jessica Lange opened at the Apollo in mid-February, while a revival of his RSC *The Tempest* opened at the Novello at the end of the same month.

Headlong's first few tours were not easy to book. *Restoration* only toured to four places as venues were put off by Bond's reputed 'cantankerousness'. *Angels in America* was also tricky 'because it was in two parts' (Goold 2018a). This was confusing for venues. Grainger remembers having discussions about how they would 'sell that to their audience'. The fact the company were 'doing something unique' at times made it 'harder to get the audiences in' (Grainger 2019a). The company was still struggling financially as a result of the debts it had inherited. Finch and Goold had to 'go to the Arts Council for some strategic support' (Finch 2018a). Arts Council England offered 'some funds to write off' the debt (Goold 2018a). In autumn 2006, Julie Renwick came on board as the company's new finance manager. The following year, the team was expanded to also include a part-time administrator. Lindsey Alvis applied for the job. Originally from Hull, she was completely new to London and the theatre scene: 'I didn't know what the National was, I didn't know what the Royal Court was, I didn't know what the Oliviers were'. She applied after seeing *Rough Crossings* at the Lyric, which she had seen 'because a friend of mine who I was talking to about what sort of theatre companies might be interesting to work with suggested Headlong'. She got the job and stayed with the company for eight years, developing into a producer. Despite the company's difficulties, it was an 'exciting time'. The team was 'really close knit, everybody had a clear sense of what their roles and responsibilities were, everybody felt a part of the work. It felt like we were all working together towards this shared aim and vision and it was really clear what that was' (Alvis 2019).

Macbeth[3]

Jonathan Church took over as artistic director of Chichester Festival Theatre (CFT) in 2006. He struck a deal with Goold, committing him to directing a show a year for three years in the theatre's studio space, the Minerva. Around the same time, Church was also talking to Patrick Stewart about coming to Chichester. They settled on a Shakespeare double bill, *Twelfth Night* and *Macbeth*. The initial idea was to transfer both to the West End if they were successful. Both Stewart and Church had the same idea about who should direct *Macbeth*: 'Patrick went, "There's a director I've worked with who I'd be very interested in," and I said, "Well of course I'd be very interested because I know Rupert very well"' (Church 2018).

For his version of *Macbeth*, Goold relocated the action to the social world of Soviet Russia. Despite the fact that the setting Goold chose was not specific to a particular Soviet era, it evoked Stalin's Russia. This was partly through Stewart's portrayal of Macbeth, which had strong echoes of Stalin. These are strongest in the banquet scene (3.4). Stalin is reputed to have enjoyed inviting members of the Politburo to drunken dinner parties at which he 'forced brandies and vodka on his guests – and stood back and waited for them to blurt out some secret' (Service 2005: 437). In Goold's *Macbeth*, the banquet scene is characterized by the same terror-ridden revelry. Goold evokes this mood of enforced drunkenness, frivolity and terror by inserting a movement sequence featuring a game of 'musical mop' between the two appearances of Banquo's ghost. Having toasted the absent

---

[3] For production images, search for 'Macbeth' in the Chichester Festival Theatre Online Archive http://passiton.cft.org.uk/archive/ (accessed 28 February 2020).

Figure 4 Martin Turner (centre) as Banquo with the company of *Macbeth* (CFT 2007). Photo: Manuel Harlan.

Banquo (Martin Turner), Macbeth puts on a polka. Chanting the refrain of 'Our duties and the pledge', everyone grabs a partner and polkas around the room, except for Ross (Tim Treloar), who is handed a mop to dance with instead (3.4.91). Whenever the music stops, there is a desperate scramble for new partners, as no one wishes to be singled out as a weak link; the losing guest finding themselves condemned to dance with the mop. Goold's use of this Stalin parallel clearly establishes the power relations within Macbeth's regime by referring the audience to a recognizable historical model.

Goold's poetic world for the production is the horror film. His stated aim for *Macbeth* was to make it 'scary' (Goold 2019b). The presence of an old lift as the only visible entrance onto and exit from the stage suggested the action was taking place in a subterranean world, a hell into which the characters descend. The play's soundscape was full of ominous rumblings, the grating of metal on metal, the clanking of the lift. Scenes were reconfigured within the style of the genre. Macbeth's visit to the witches (4.1) was relocated to a morgue, complete with bodies in body bags, which convulse and are reanimated as the spirits speak through them. In the sleepwalking scene (5.1), when Lady Macbeth (Kate Fleetwood) washes her hands in a sink, the taps run with blood.

Critics found the production 'terrifying' (Clapp 2007a), 'heart-stopping' (Marlowe 2007), and 'pulse-quickening' (Taylor 2007). 'Two days on', Spencer claimed, 'this production still haunts my memory like a vivid nightmare that taints the waking day' (Spencer 2007b).

As well as keeping 'the spectators on the edges of their seats' (Billington 2007), viewing the play through this lens serves to support its more difficult moments to stage, such as the murder of the Macduff family (4.2). Part of the problem with this scene in the original play is the fact the audience are meeting the family for the first time and so have no relationship with them. Goold both expanded the Macduff family by adding two sisters and made them more present in the play by having them accompany Macduff (Michael Feast) to Macbeth's castle (2.3), in order to build the audience's investment in them. The murders themselves are evoked by a series of tableaux. At the end of Act Four, Scene Two, the murderers enter in silence. One of them ominously rips a piece of gaffer tape off a roll, before the audience is plunged into darkness. The lights flash up. A child screams. We see a tableau of Lady Macduff (Suzanne Burden) being forced to watch as her children are 'Savagely slaughter'd' before being plunged into darkness again (4.3.205).

The witches (Polly Frame, Niamh McGrady and Laura Rees) are reconfigured as nurses. At the beginning of the production they wheel in a wounded man on a gurney and attend to him (1.2). Once alone with him, however, 'they pulled his life-support machine out and you realised they were not what they seemed'. The witches are positioned as an ever-present force. Their nondescript grey uniforms double as maids' uniforms. They haunt the edges of the action as nurses, kitchen staff and servants, conveying the idea 'Macbeth wasn't in control' (Seymour 2019). In Macbeth's final scene (5.8), Goold splits Macbeth's last line to indicate the witches' power. Macbeth delivers the line 'And damn'd be him that first cries, "Hold"' to Macduff as a challenge. As Macbeth holds Macduff at his mercy, the witches appear. Seeing the witches Macbeth surrenders to Macduff, directing his final word 'enough' to them (5.8.34).

The production is set in a kitchen, whose bare tiled walls are also used to evoke a hospital and war rooms. Within this space, food preparation takes on a symbolic significance. The sound of chopping and of knives being sharpened evokes the butchery of the murders that will be served up (1.6). Food is used to symbolize communion. Macbeth shares his sandwich with Banquo's murderers, who look at it considering if they want to partake (3.1). After resolving to commit the murders, the Macbeths return to the dinner party hand in hand holding cake and wine, evoking the body and blood of communion as they bring Duncan (Paul Shelley) his last supper (1.7).

Goold's production offers the audience several glimpses of the characters' subjective view of what is happening. The most effective use of this is in the banquet scene, which Goold stages twice, once before the interval and once after. In the first version of the banquet scene, the audience see and hear what Macbeth sees and hears. We are party to his conversation with the murderer. When Banquo's ghost enters, he strides out of the lift, onto the table and stands menacingly over Macbeth. At the beginning of Act Two, the scene repeats but now the view is that of Lady Macbeth and her guests. The conversation between Macbeth and the murderer is mimed as it goes unheard. Macbeth cowers suddenly and inexplicably at vacant air. This second version of the scene is imbued by the remembrance of the first version. The audience can both see and not see Banquo's ghost. Both Macbeth's response to the ghost and the guests' response to his seeming madness become equally understandable.

The critics were gushing in their praise for the production: 'five stars across the board' (Goold 2018a). Goold's 'astonishing' production made Billington 'experience the play anew' (Billington 2007). Georgina Brown pronounced it to be 'the most powerful and blood-curdling production of Macbeth I've seen' (Brown 2007). This was the first time Goold had received such universally rapturous reviews. They felt like a 'benediction' (Goold 2018a). Church attributes the production's success to two elements. Firstly, Goold's conception and direction: 'the combination of the craftmanship of the work of the director with the company, combined with this staggering visual world'. Secondly to the fact the show opened in a relatively small studio theatre: 'it was a big production done in an incredibly intimate space, and the power of it' (Church 2018). The production transferred straight from Chichester to the West End earning Goold Olivier, Evening Standard and Critics' Circle Awards for best director. It transferred to the Brooklyn Academy of Music (BAM) in New York in February 2008 and then moved directly to Broadway. The success of the production was productive for Headlong, despite the fact they were not directly involved: 'it helped with our brand and our commercial heft, because people really wanted to work with him' (Finch 2018a). Personally, thinking 'in terms of directing as a craft that you can study and learn' (Goold 2018a) and therefore as something 'you can get better at' (John, 2005), Goold considers *Macbeth* an exemplar of his best work: 'the most consistent and the most rigorous thing I've made' (Goold 2018a).

After the success of his Chichester *Macbeth*, Goold was approached to do a film version. The first offer 'smelt wrong'. This was partly because the company was reluctant to allow him to direct: 'They said, we're bringing in another guy to direct it. You can co-direct it with him. We'll handle the camera stuff. You just put your play on and we'll film it. I felt patronized by that' (Goold 2019c). Stewart had recently worked on a BBC television film of the David Tennant *Hamlet* directed by Gregory Doran (RSC 2008) with the independent production company Illuminations, who had developed a model for filming stage productions in which they would 'translate it to ideally a single location away from stage and outside of a film studio and shoot a low-budget film version quickly with the original cast and with the original stage director'. This was cost-effective as 'a single location could give you lots of possibilities in your set designs' while at same time enabling you to 'establish a production village there so you weren't continually moving on to another location in a way that conventional TV drama does' (Wyver 2019). Stewart recommended Illuminations to Goold. The company's co-founder, John Wyver, had 'more of an arts background' than the previous producers did and was willing to let Goold direct, so Goold decided to jump ship: 'I could sense this was a chance to really try and learn about camera as well as capture the film' (Goold 2019c).

The budget for the film was modest. Wyver remembers it as being just over £1 millon. Despite this, Goold was keen to 'be as cinematic as possible' (Goold 2019c). Finding a single location that could facilitate this by offering a range of different environments was 'absolutely crucial' (Wyver 2019). Wyver's producing partner Sebastian Grant found a location for the film at Welbeck Abbey in Nottinghamshire, famed for its network of 'underground tunnels'. The abbey had been leased to the Ministry of Defence in the 1940s and was used as an army training college until 2005. The 'weird mixture' of spaces at the abbey appealed to Goold: 'sort of eighteenth-century land, nineteenth-century underground tunnel system and ballrooms, and then this sort of Lindsay Anderson-esque sort of 1960s/70s MoD décor that had all been stripped away and left derelict' (Goold 2019c). Illuminations had to build a couple of sets within the abbey. They brought in 'half of a train carriage', and the kitchen was replicated as it 'had been done on stage with the white tiles and the fridge' because 'there wasn't a room there that had that particular kind of sterile domesticity'. They also licensed footage from the Soviet documentary film, *Turksib* (Turin 1929) and employed a digital house to make a computer-generated image of the top of the lift. All the other locations, however, were 'relatively lightly dressed' pre-existing spaces within the abbey itself (Wyver 2019).

Goold feels he was 'lucky' in his producers (Goold 2019c). Grant and Wyver had worked out that 'you could do these adaptations with the stage director if you got three things more or less right'. Firstly, partnering the stage director with 'a sympathetic director of photography (DoP) who would help them realize their vision' (Wyver 2019). Goold requested Sam McCurdy as his DoP, who had been the cinematographer on the horror film *The Descent* (Marshall 2005). Secondly, the stage director needed a good first assistant director to 'build your schedule, keep you as far as possible to schedule and also make sure that you didn't make stupid mistakes like crossing the line and not getting the continuity you needed'. Goold was supported by Richard Styles. Finally the stage director required 'a really good editor' (Wyver 2019). Goold's editor was Trevor Waite, 'who worked a lot with [the film director Michael] Winterbottom' (Goold 2019c). One thing Goold felt he could bring to the table was his experience of working collaboratively: 'recognizing it's not all on you, that the DoP is there to bring ideas, and production design. You curate all that'. The original cast were able to return for the film and were headed by Stewart, 'who really knew screen acting'. Goold was able to work efficiently because the actors 'knew the piece inside out'. This meant he 'could really concentrate on how to shoot it' (Goold 2019c). The tight budget meant the film had to be shot quickly in around three weeks. Wyver estimates they were achieving 'eight to eight and a half minutes of finished screen time a day'. In comparison, in 'standard TV drama you probably aim to get five minutes, and feature film you've probably got the luxury of getting two and a half to three minutes' (Wyver 2019). Goold had 'never worked so hard in [his] life'. Wyver describes the pace as 'efficient, not rushed' (Wyver 2019). The restricted budget meant they had to 'put every single penny on the screen' (Goold 2019c).

The finished film builds closely on the theatre production, embracing its style and structure, retaining a claustrophobic quality in its use of underground locations but opening the action out to roam across multiple spaces. Despite the logistical constraints of the shoot and Goold's inexperience as a film director, it was a success, winning a Peabody Award. Wyver puts this partly down to the fact that Goold's theatre work is 'highly filmic'. The original production was 'steeped in cinema references', so it translated well to screen

(Wyver 2019). Deputy stage manager Lorna Seymour remembers Goold's filmic vision for the production revealed itself in rehearsals for the theatre version: 'he's got these filmic ideas that we do our best with, but we can't always quite achieve them on the stage'. For example, Goold requested 'real carcasses' in the kitchen and 'German Shepherd dogs' (Seymour 2019). Within the context of theatre, the first request was a health and safety issue, while the second was too expensive. In the film, he was able to have both.

Rough Crossings[4]

Around the time he started at Headlong, Goold was 'actively looking for intellectual voices' who were 'theatrical in sensibility'. He gravitated towards this after seeing Simon McBurney's *Mnemonic* (Complicité 1999), which reminded him of the new historicist training he had had at Cambridge: 'You take this tiny thing, like the finding of a man in the ice in the alps, and then extrapolate huge arguments about memory and identity and history and the self, all through this gorgeous physical theatre'. Goold became interested in Simon Schama's work after reading *Landscape and Memory*, 'a book about the relationship of landscapes to social psychology and history'. With Power, he explored the idea of making the book into a show but struggled as it 'didn't really feel like it had a structure'. Goold got wind, however, that Schama was about to publish a book to coincide with the 200th anniversary of the outlawing of the slave trade in Britain, *Rough Crossings*. The book tells the true story of a failed British attempt to repatriate a group of freed American slaves who had fought for the British during the American Revolution by creating a state in West Africa for them (Goold 2018a).

Goold was aware, however, that the story was really neither Schama's nor his to tell, and started to investigate if there was a black writer who would be interested in adapting it. The British-Caribbean writer Caryl Phillips 'was suggested by a literary manager at the National' (Goold 2018a). Phillips's adaptation of *Rough Crossings* is, as the critic Nicholas de Jongh notes, very much his own: 'He has taken a few threads from Schama's 500 pages and woven them into a narrative, both political and personal' (de Jongh 2007). The play's central conflict is between two black men, David George (Peter de Jersey) and Thomas Peters (Patrick Robinson), who represent different approaches to the black struggle. Phillips positions George as a man of God who advocates non-violent means and integration. In contrast, Peters advocates any means necessary and believes that separation is the only path to freedom. Phillips's adaptation favours Peters's views, as by the time George takes charge of the colony at the end of the play, it is clear he has absorbed some of Peters's philosophy: 'some intemperate part of you is Thomas Peters' (Schama 2007: 125). In the staging of Peters's final scene before his death, Goold positions him as a Christ-like figure, lighting him in a beam of white light.

---

[4] For production images, see https://headlong.co.uk/productions/rough-crossings/explore/ (accessed 28 February 2020).

Phillips's adaptation is epic in the Brechtian sense, travelling in space and time from the American South to Nova Scotia to London and then to Sierra Leone over a period of around twenty years. Goold found it 'deeply cinematic' (Goold 2018a). Laura Hopkins's original design for the production reflected this: '[an] incredibly complicated double decker set with a roaming frame that could expand and contract and shift [...] to frame any action on this structure'. Practically, the design was problematic. The images within each frame would 'require the most exquisite composition'. The show itself required 'quite a big cast'. This would have meant actors 'going up and down ladders and getting out of the way and coming into frame' in a relatively limited space. When they showed the model box to the company on the first day of rehearsals, both Goold and Hopkins realized it needed to be redesigned. Hopkins's reworked design featured 'a big square floating platform that was raised and could pivot, could tilt' and so could suggest a range of locations from ship decks to below decks, from battlefields to town halls. Above the platform was a white sail on which flags and clouds, maps and pamphlets could be projected. Once the characters reached Africa, the sail rose up into the flies and was replaced by a projection of a red African sun (Hopkins 2019).

The first section of Phillips's adaptation juxtaposes the cruelty of the slave trade with the luxury of London life. In the opening scene, slaves on a ship are forced to dance. One is shot when he tries to save another slave who is sick from being tossed overboard. The slave ship then transforms into a barge on the River Thames, on which a soirée is taking place. A white woman, Eliza (Miranda Colchester) sings Handel as the bodies of drowned slaves roll in the water. A group of slaves, chained together, sit and rock as the white guests discuss slavery, unaware of the enslaved women beside them. The guests' comfort is portrayed as built on the slaves' suffering: 'the most profitable business ever known to man' (Schama 2007: 36). The idea the white characters are slaves to commerce is threaded through Phillips's adaptation. At the end of the play George reminds a white abolitionist, John Clarkson (Ed Hughes): 'No man owns allegiance to commerce, but a slave. And slaves come in all shades' (Schama 2007: 126). Phillips sets Clarkson up as a white saviour figure, but then complicates this narrative by positioning him as the one who needs to be saved. Clarkson's scheme to set up a colony in Sierra Leone only comes to fruition because Peters is willing to provide him with colonists. After Peters's death, Goold literally plunges Clarkson into darkness and the audience watch him fumbling around in the blackness, unable to find his way. The different worlds of the play are defined through music. Cork contrasts the 'Handelian British baroque sounds of empire' with spirituals from the American South. Sierra Leone is conjured through the rhythms of traditional West African music, created by the percussionist, Ben Okafor, who 'created his own beats around [Cork's] choral arrangements' (Cork 2019). Goold's production ends on a hopeful note with Clarkson ceding his governorship of the colony to George. In the final moments, all three musical styles come together in a single melody suggesting hope for harmony.

Despite the presence of a black writer in the creative team, Goold is aware that today the production would be seen as problematic in terms of both ownership and voice: 'Now I'm not sure I would have felt I had the right to direct it' (Goold 2018a). As Phillips points out in the adaptation, only those who know what it is to 'lose their freedom' can 'truly understand' (Schama 2007: 126). The critics were divided about the production. There was praise for the company for tackling a 'compelling and important story' (Spencer 2007c). Others felt that in attempting to take on such a complex story, the company had bitten off more than they could chew. For Susannah Clapp, the production was 'bogged down by the weight of information and good intentions' (Clapp 2007b). Ultimately it was seen as 'bravely ambitious' but 'a problematically rough ride' (Bassett 2007).

The Last Days of Judas Iscariot[5]

The final play in the season, *The Last Days of Judas Iscariot*, stages a court case over the fate of Jesus's infamous disciple Judas. The trial takes place in some 'downtown Purgatory' (Guirgis 2006: 10) that, Spencer observes, 'bears a strong resemblance to the meanest neighbourhoods of New York' (Spencer 2008a). The play opens with Judas's mother (Amanda Boxer) bewailing the death of her son, arguing that if God were cruel enough to commit her son to Hell after all his suffering, the very act would prove that there was no God: 'If my son is in Hell, then there is no Heaven – because if my son sits in Hell, *there is no God*' (Guirgis 2006: 10). The action then moves to a courtroom as the trial of '*God and the Kingdom of Heaven and Earth versus Judas Iscariot*' commences (Guirgis 2006: 11). During the trial the defence and the prosecution call a range of witnesses to testify for and against Judas, ranging from biblical figures such as Mary Magdalen (Poppy Miller) and Pontius Pilate (Ron Cephas Jones) to more contemporary figures like Mother Teresa (Doña Croll) and Sigmund Freud (Josh Cohen). In the final moments of the trial, as Judas (Joseph Mawle) is losing ground, he accuses Jesus (Edward Hogg) of betraying him. Despite this, the jury find Judas guilty on all counts. Jesus comes to Judas and washes his feet with his tears.

For Power, the play's reworking of myth and religious text felt 'really dynamic and contemporary and sexy'. The play, however, was not without its problems: 'it was, in places, dramaturgically incoherent'. Goold and Power worked to fix it: 'we created new bits of action to try and join the story up'. For example, in the original script the movement from Judas's mother's opening speech to the court scene was abrupt. The monologue was 'standalone, never referred to, and then in the next scene, another woman, for reasons that aren't revealed, is defending Judas in a sort of heavenly court'. Goold and Power connected the two scenes: 'as the monologue was finishing and Judas's mother was saying "my son killed himself and it's not fair that he gets fucked" the lights reveal that Susan Lynch, playing the defence attorney, had been listening, that the whole thing was for her, and she said "Mrs Iscariot, you need a lawyer". Smash cut into court scene'. This also grounded the action of the play in a clear genre: 'a classic Erin Brockovich-style, one woman against the system courtroom drama' (Power 2019).

---

[5] For production images see https://headlong.co.uk/productions/last-days-judas-isacriot/explore/ (accessed 28 February 2020).

The reviews for *The Last Days of Judas Iscariot* were polarized. The critics who disliked it, despised it: 'over-long, over-written, it basks too much in its own cleverness' (Letts 2008); 'A fleetingly interesting notion, for sure, but it wore a bit thin as the hours dragged by' (Walker 2008). The critics who loved it gushed about it. Spencer argued the play made 'most contemporary plays seem safe, timid and dull' (Spencer 2008a), while Billington found it 'a gloriously intoxicating brew' (Billington 2008a).

By now, the idea that both Goold and Headlong had a particular style and approach was becoming more prevalent in the industry: 'there was this perception of my work as sort of almost wilfully, self-consciously taking perverse choices' and 'having a lot of loud bangs intellectually and visually'. An assistant director shared with Goold an account of how Ian Rickson had described the director's style:

She'd been around to see Ian, who'd been making something with some peppers, and she said, 'Oh I'm about to go and see this Rupert Goold'. And he said, 'Oh yeah, that's interesting'. And she said, 'Well what's his work like?' [...] And he sort of paused for a long time and he said: 'Well. Look at this pepper. You see, I'm trying to get the maximum peppery-ness out of this pepper. I'm considering how much oil to cook it in. I'm trying to think whether it needs its skin on or off to make it more pepper-ish. You know, where is it best placed to get the hit of the pepper-ness. And Rupert Goold would go, "Oh look, a hat"'.

(Goold 2018a)

Goold also suffered from the impression he had skyrocketed to fame: 'a young, talented director in a hurry to make his name' (Spencer 2007b). This was despite the fact he been working as a director for over ten years. Headlong was seen by some as arrogant and pushy. Finch argues this aggression came out of a desire to protect 'the quality of the work' (Finch 2018b). Power sees it as an attitude born of the realities of touring: 'How does any touring company make an impact? The only way to do it is to be aggressive. You've got to be piratical by nature. Because you turn up for whatever, twenty-four hours or seven days, in someone else's theatre' (Power 2018).

Headlong's second season was announced in January 2008. It included three productions directed by Goold: *Six Characters in Search of an Author*; *King Lear* (Headlong/Liverpool Everyman and Playhouse/Young Vic 2008) and *ENRON*. These were joined by three shows directed by other directors: Richard Bean's *The English Game* directed by Sean Holmes (Headlong/Yvonne Arnaud Theatre Guilford 2008); . . . *SISTERS* created by Chris Goode (Headlong/Gate 2008); and Anthony Neilson's *Edward Gant's Amazing Feats of Loneliness* directed by Steve Marmion (Headlong/Nuffield Southampton 2009). Goold was still 'incredibly busy' (Goold 2018a). Alongside his Headlong commitments, he was committed to a revival of *No Man's Land* (2008) for the Gate in Dublin; a West End revival of Sam Mendes' 1994 production of Lionel Bart's musical *Oliver!* (Drury Lane 2009); a revival of *Time and the Conways* (2009) for the NT; and a new production of *Turandot* (2009) for English National Opera (ENO); alongside both the New York transfer and the film of *Macbeth*. By his own admission, he was 'slightly over-working'. The problem was he was being made offers he could not refuse. This was particularly true of *No Man's Land*: 'I didn't really have space for it at the time but it was clear Pinter didn't have long to live and I thought, god, what if I turned down the chance of working with him?' (Goold 2018a).

Six Characters in Search of an Author[6]

Six Characters in Search of an Author is the show Goold considers to be 'the apex' of his collaboration with Power. Goold and Power found the play when they did a check on what had recently fallen out of copyright and Pirandello came up. *Six Characters in Search of an Author* had both 'a good title to take out on the road' (Goold 2018a) and fitted with ideas they were exploring around the same time in relation to 'authorial intention and how in making an adaptation of something you want to try and go back to the moment of creation and the feeling for an audience at a first night of a performance' (Power 2014). During the first performance of *Six Characters in Search of an Author* in 1921 in Rome, audiences had rioted 'chanting "madhouse" and "buffoon" – because of its shocking structure and subject' (Sheaffer 2009). Goold and Power were interested in reversing the play's slide into 'a staple of commercial, jolly commercial theatre' and recapturing its provocativeness (Power 2014).

Pirandello's original play is set on a stage and begins with a theatre company rehearsing his 1918 play *The Rules of the Game*. Suddenly six characters (Father (Ian McDiarmid), Mother (Eleanor David), Son (Dyfan Dwyfor), Stepdaughter (Denise Gough), Boy (Jude Loseby or Edward Searle) and Girl (Freya Parker)) burst in and demand the company tell their story instead. The company attempt to perform the characters' story but the characters cannot agree on the correct set of events. Preoccupied with their squabbles, they fail to notice that the Girl has fallen into a fountain and drowned. They also fail to notice when the Boy leaves and commits suicide by shooting himself offstage. At the sound of the gunshot, the family stop quarrelling. When the Boy is brought on, he seems to be actually dead. The Producer, fed up with all the arguing over what is reality and what is make-believe, calls for the house lights to be put back on. The rehearsal is over and the company leave. The Producer, left alone, encounters the six characters again but now there are only four.

In Goold and Power's version, the action of the play is relocated from a theatre to a studio in which a drama-documentary about assisted suicide is being edited. One of the most important influences for this relocation was Andrew Jarecki's documentary *Capturing the Friedmans*, which tells the story of an American family, the Friedmans, whose world is turned upside-down when the father and the youngest son are accused of molesting schoolchildren. The family were addicted to recording their lives in home movies, which Jarecki dissects for clues as to the guilt or innocence of the father and son.

---

[6] For production images, see https://headlong.co.uk/productions/six-characters-search-author/explore/ (accessed 28 February 2020).

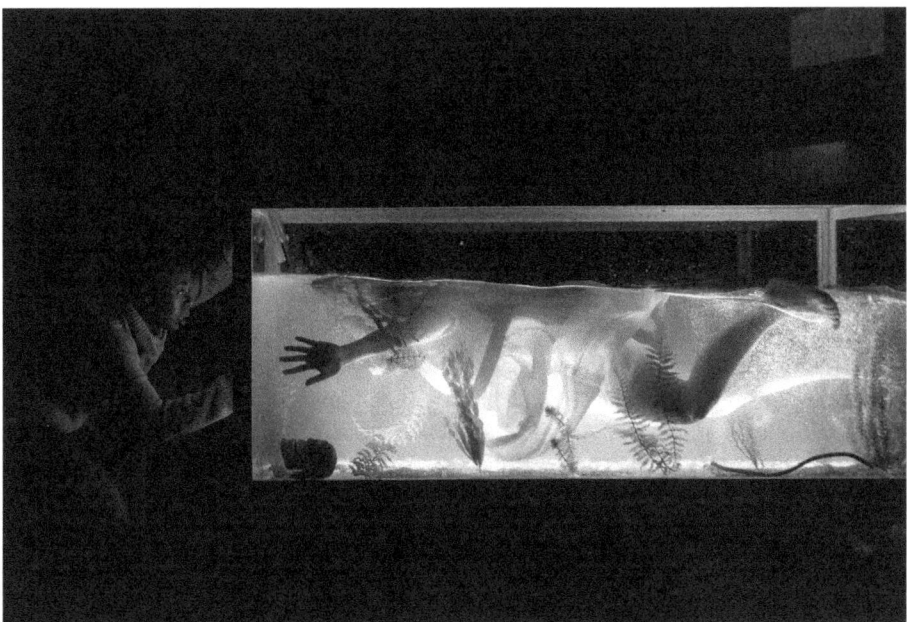

Figure 5 Left to right: Noma Dumezweni as the Producer and Freya Parker as the Girl in *Six Characters in Search of an Author* (CFT 2008). Photo: Manuel Harlan.

The documentary 'made an impact' on Goold on two counts. Firstly, it is inconclusive: 'you get to the end of the film and you think, I'm not sure anyone's done anything, but one of the children has gone to prison for twenty years, and so has the father [...] you can't work out what's true and what's not'. The Friedmans felt like the six characters in that they had a story that needed to be told but the truth of their story seemed inaccessible amidst the multiple perspectives. Goold had also seen a Richard Jones production of *Six Characters in Search of an Author* in 2001, in which 'the characters were real and the director and performers were very sort of fake'. Goold and Power decided to flip that idea on its head: 'we make the people making the work ultra-verité and the characters extremely heightened but arguing that their form of heightened is more real'. The idea for the subject matter of the docudrama in the play came from an interest in Barthes' 'Death of the Author'. Goold and Power felt the 'thesis of the Pirandello' was also about 'killing the author' or, in terms of the world of the play, the Producer. Linking this idea to the idea of fiction and reality as indistinguishable, Goold latched on to the provocation of 'If you knew the truth about the inadequacy of reality versus the power of fiction, you'd kill yourself'. Dignitas was 'just coming into the news then, this idea of voluntary euthanasia' and it seemed to fit (Goold 2018a).

They started work by dividing the adaptation between them: 'I wrote Act One. Ben wrote Act Two. I think we wrote Act Three together'. Then they would 'swap them'. Goold and Power added a fourth act to Pirandello's three acts, which 'came out of brainstorming'. They hit upon the idea of what Goold describes as 'a series of thought experiments about how you could kill an author, which had Ben and me in it at one point and then we get killed' (Goold 2018a). At the end of the third act, as the Boy lies dying, Goold and Power's version breaks from Pirandello's. Instead of dismissing the Boy as pretending, the Producer (Noma Dumezweni) picks him up and goes to get help, blundering into the middle of a musical running in the theatre next door; *The Music Man* in Chichester and *Les Misérables* in the West End. Failing to find help, she attempts and fails to commit suicide. Act Four, which Power identifies as inspired by the way the narrative 'fractures' in the Charlie Kaufman film *Adaptation*, starts with a re-run of the first scene of the play with a director's commentary, as if the audience were watching the DVD extras (Power 2014). It then cuts to an office in which two theatre-makers resembling Goold (Jeremy Joyce) and Power (Jake Harders) are trying to persuade an Executive (John Mackay) to fund their radical reworking of Pirandello. It then switches to a garret where Pirandello is struggling to write *Six Characters in Search of an Author*. Then to Hamlet reciting 'O what a rogue and peasant slave am I!' (*Hamlet*, 2.2.544), a speech which is then taken over by the Producer, who commits suicide assisted by the six characters. Though they came up with the idea for the final act in a single afternoon, they 'spent months and months and months, both on the first outing and the second outing, trying to refine' it (Goold 2014a).

Act Four generally met with reprimands from the critics: 'wildly self-indulgent and obscure' (de Jongh 2008); 'in-jokes about re-working Pirandello for Chichester become tortuous and tiresome' (Taylor 2008); 'What has been deliciously clever becomes torrentially clever-clever' (Shuttleworth 2008a). At the same time, however, a number of the critics recognized Goold and Power were attempting something in the spirit of Pirandello: 'the excessive twists are Pirandellian' (Bassett 2008b). Audiences struggled with the show in Chichester. Power remembers 'terrible walkouts during previews' (Power 2019). Grainger remembers 'you could see them at the Minerva just walking to the car park' (Grainger 2019a). There was also 'anxiety about the child actors in *Six Characters* and the adult themes they were potentially being exposed to' (Power 2019). The moment in the production where the Girl drowned caused particular concern, despite the fact the Girl was actually played by an adult actress, Parker. Seymour remembers the audience finding it 'very unsettling. There were people really looking to see if she was all right' (Seymour 2019). Grainger remembers it was even 'nerve-racking as a producer to sit and watch'. The moment was staged in a large fish tank. Hidden in amongst the pond weed in the bottom was a breathing pipe. In the event the actress couldn't find the tube, she was supposed to turn over and float face upwards. The actress would flap around in the tank as if she was drowning to cover the action of finding the breathing tube: 'because I knew what the trickery was, I could see her trying to get the pipe to breathe. And there were times where I'd sit there going "just turn over, just turn over," because she took a long time to find the pipe and I could see that she wasn't breathing yet, that she was still struggling' (Grainger 2019a).

Despite the critics' reservations and the challenging nature of the show for audiences, it transferred to the West End. Goold and Power, 'taking all the critical notes on board, completely rewrote' the fourth act. They removed some of the in-jokes: 'We got rid of some of the slightly knowing references to Patrick Stewart' from the Chichester version. They also cut a section at the end of Act Three, where the Producer met sixteen versions of herself: 'all the other actors dressed like Noma [Dumezweni] wearing masks, which was just weird and like slightly creepy in the wrong way' (Goold 2018a). The critics who reviewed the show both in Chichester and the West End noted that while the performance was much improved, both in terms of the script and the production values, the fourth act still seemed 'superfluous' (Billington 2008b) and 'self-indulgent' (Hart 2008). Power, however, argues that the brilliance of Act Four lay precisely in its audacity and pretentiousness. Of the scene featuring Goold and himself, he notes that 'it existed on a knife-edge because, of course, it was indulgent and ludicrous and self-involved, but the source play contains those elements as well. They're bound up in what the play is about' (Power 2014). It nearly led to him having to go on and play himself during the production's tour of Australia. The actor playing Power, Harders, dislocated his shoulder and was then given too much pain medication so 'he was completely out of it' (Grainger 2019a). In the end Harders managed to go on, but Power remembers standing in the wings 'inches away from playing myself, which was probably a Pirandellian twist too far' (Power 2014).

Goold positions *Six Characters in Search of an Author* as the first production in which 'we formalized what I now think of as the Headlong process'. The process was dialectical, taking the form of an 'A/B dialogue'. It started with a dialectical proposition: 'we'd take a statement like "fiction is more truthful than fact"'. Then by arguing it out, pitting A against B, they would try to develop, nuance and complicate the argument through provocations – for example, 'Who's more real, your great-great grandfather, or Hamlet?' – in order to 'try and get to something that was interesting'. Act Four of *Six Characters in Search of an Author* embodies this process, with each scene countering and complicating the gesture of the one before, like a series of ever-expanding footnotes (Goold 2018a).

King Lear[7]

After the success of *Macbeth* for Chichester, Finch was keen for Goold to do something similar for Headlong. Goold felt that it needed to be a Shakespeare: 'And I'd done *Othello*, I'd done *Hamlet*, I'd done *Macbeth*. *Lear* was the last big tragedy' (Goold 2018a). Liverpool was the Capital of Culture in 2008 and Headlong were eager to be part of it. Goold had previously worked with Pete Postlethwaite on *Scaramouche Jones* in 2001 and was keen for him to play Lear. Postlethwaite was deeply associated with the Liverpool Everyman and Playhouse as it was where he had started his career. The theatre's history acted as the stylistic inspiration for the show: a 'sense of what the Everyman had been in the 1970s, the Alan Dossor Everyman, the politics of that and the specificity and regionality of that'

---

[7] For production images, see https://headlong.co.uk/productions/king-lear/explore/ (accessed 28 February 2020).

(Power 2019). Goold and Power wanted to create a production in that spirit: 'really punky', 'non-reverent and non-RSC-like' (Goold 2018a).

Spatially, Goold was thinking about the relationship some Northern cities have with the moors, where the heath 'sits so near to the streets' (Goold 2018a). Power, who is from the North-West, remembers 'spending hours just talking about the landscapes that I'd grown up in and the community that I remembered from my childhood'. For him, the production was reflecting on a specific form of patriarchy that had been woven into industrial Northern communities. The Northern elements of the production, Power argues, took the play 'away from the regal and put it into a different kind of status, a different sort of political landscape' (Power 2019). Ultimately, the production's Northernness linked back to Postlethwaite 'because that was what Pete was, it was all Pete' (Power 2019). Socially, Goold was interested in the idea of the 1970s as marking the death of the nuclear family in Britain, as evidenced by a huge rise in the divorce rate. He felt there might be a connection between the idea of the heath and the death of the family: 'the Moors murderers maybe precipitated that' (Goold 2018a). He was also interested in Margaret Thatcher's statement, 'There is no such thing as society' (Thatcher 1987), and what that meant for the North-West as an area. He felt it had a possible parallel with 'what happens to the nation in Lear' (Goold 2018a).

In developing the production, Power and Goold took the question of 'Why do you always forget one strand of Lear?' as their starting point. In order to address this, they cast fourteen actors, each of whom had 'different flavours' and were powerhouses in their own right (Goold 2018a). O'Neill argues that every actor in the production 'thought they were the lead, or thought it was about them' (O'Neill 2019). Menzies remembers Goold allowed space for each of the actors' 'personalities to express themselves' (Menzies 2019) in the rehearsal room, so producing a group of performances that were 'gladiatorial' in character (O'Neill 2019). Grainger argues that you 'could feel that on stage' (Grainger 2019a).

The production was set in a Northern town in the late 1970s. Giles Cadle's set featured weed-ridden grey stone steps leading up to a corrugated metal fence covering the derelict facade of a building behind. There was 'a sense of riots going on offstage' (Seymour 2019). It opened with a recording of Thatcher reciting St Francis of Assisi's prayer, 'Where there is discord, may we bring harmony' (Thatcher 1979). Stylistically, its atmosphere was a touch '*Hobson's Choice*, crossed with *The Sopranos*' (Bassett 2008c). Lear (Postlethwaite), reconfigured as a Northern patriarch, divides his kingdom up at a 'family tea party' (Billington 2008c), whipping off a tablecloth to reveal a scale model of his dominion in three vitrines underneath. His daughters, Goneril (Caroline Faber) and Reagan (Charlotte Randle) are positioned as 'Thatcher's children, believing that greed is good and that society is dead' (Brown 2008). Goneril is heavily pregnant in the first scene and later her baby is pushed around the stage by her emasculated husband, the Duke of Albany (Michael Colgan), the unlucky heir to all his family's strife. Lear's followers are reconfigured as football hooligans and the Fool (Forbes Masson) as a 'Working Men's Club-style comedian' (Bassett 2008c). The Fool's demise was delayed and his part extended: 'A clutch of brief additional scenes and/or reassignments of lines gives the Fool

[...] the progression he so keenly needs through the second half of the play' (Shuttleworth 2008b). The Fool is eventually shot by Edmund, his demise the punchline of a joke: 'Edmund: "Knock, knock". Fool: "Who's there?" Bang!' (Riches 2008). Goold also adds a new character to the play, the Boy (Jacob Anderson) who, his face painted with a St George's cross, is 'a reluctant witness to events' (Shuttleworth 2008b).

Goold worked beat by beat on the production, trying to subvert some of the play's established staging clichés. Goold realized the climatic fight between Edgar and Edmund (5.3) was always done 'with big broadswords'. Goold stripped the scene back to its essence: 'two brothers fighting'. He remembered how his brother and he 'would fight with toys' and 'hurt each other'. It would get 'really nasty'. This led him to wonder whether you could 'kill someone with a toy sword'. Goold staged the Edmund/Edgar fight with plastic toy swords, symbolizing the idea of them putting 'an end to [their] childhood bond'. The fight culminated with 'Edgar literally choking Edmund with his plastic sword'. Goold's staging of the blinding of Gloucester (3.7) was inspired by an account of a football hooligan sucking out the eyeball of an enemy and biting it off in Bill Buford's book *Among the Thugs*. He staged it with 'Reagan sucking Gloucester's eye out and spitting it into a cow trough'. This staging, even close up, looked incredibly real: 'every night we had people faint or throw up' (Goold 2018a).

On its opening in Liverpool, the production received disappointing reviews. Many of the critics felt Goold had gone too far: 'self-indulgent and reductive, drawing flashy attention to the director's role of theatrical razzle-dazzler without serving the text' (Spencer 2008b); 'a near-parody of his best work. In the theatrical equivalent of necrotizing fasciitis, his hallmark techniques have begun to eat up the play' (Clapp 2008). While there were many interesting ideas in the production, it was felt that it lacked a unifying concept: 'full of short-term effects rather than long-range vision' (Billington 2008c); 'the series of arresting moments never coheres into a satisfying, plausible whole' (Brown 2008). Postlethwaite appeared to lose faith in the production during the run at the Everyman 'and said we're going have to remake it, we're going to transform it'. Power ascribes this loss of faith to Postlethwaite's theatrical taste being 'maybe more conservative than Rupert's'. Postlethwaite had previously worked on Shakespeare plays with the Royal Exchange and the RSC 'that had been more conventional in setting and performance style'. Power remembers Postlethwaite as being 'anxious that we were somehow patronizing Liverpool, that we weren't giving them Rolls-Royce Shakespeare, we were giving them *Coronation Street*'. Despite Postlethwaite's fear, Power observed that Liverpool audiences loved the show: 'they couldn't believe that he was there in front of them doing it, and it was electric' (Power 2019).

Goold and Power reworked the show prior to its London run at the Young Vic, dropping the opening Thatcher speech and the model of Lear's dominions. Power argues the London version of the production was not really a radically different show. The changes they had made, however, meant Postlethwaite and the company 'believed in it by the time it opened at the Young Vic' (Power 2019). In London, the reviews were more polarized. Some reviewers, while acknowledging the changes as improvements, concluded that 'some of the touches still smack too much of gimmickry' (Cavendish

2009) and there still was 'no coherent overview' (Gardner 2009b). In contrast, Andrew Haydon hailed the show as 'extraordinary theatre' (Haydon 2009) and gave it a six-star review. The audience in London were more enthusiastic than many of the critics: 'it sold really well and again there was a standing ovation every night' (Seymour 2019).

Goold remembers the critical response as 'the first real drubbing I'd had'. He notes that *King Lear* 'didn't have an easy legibility in the way [his] *Tempest* or *Macbeth* or *Merchant of Venice* did'. It lacked a two-word concept. Reading the reviews, he also realized he needed to 'calm down'. *King Lear* can be seen as the end of an escalating pattern of risk-taking for Goold which had its seeds in Northampton: 'if you take a big risk and it works, take an exponentially bigger one each time and see where it ends up'. This 'sort of perverse iconoclasm and undermining everything that feels easy' reached its peak in *King Lear*, bringing both Goold and Headlong 'crashing' down. When considering the question of 'what was the most Headlong show?' however, Goold names *King Lear*. It was 'the famous failure', but 'in many ways, even though it wasn't a new play and nor was it addressing a specific political argument, in its uncompromising energy, European aesthetic and performance style and sheer desire to jolt an audience into a reaction, however unsettling or vulgar that might be, it was maybe the most Headlong show' (Goold 2018a).

CHAPTER 4
HEADLONG AND THE RSC – LATER YEARS: 2009–2013

King Lear marks both a high and a low point in not only Goold's trajectory but Headlong's as well. It is in many ways, the most extreme of Goold's interventionist re-imaginings of classic texts. After *King Lear*, trajectories changed: Goold's focus shifted from classic texts to new work as the commissions Power had secured for Headlong began to bear fruit. After seeing Goold's *Macbeth*, Nicholas Hytner, the artistic director of the National, invited him in for a chat. Both Finch and Goold felt 'a co-production at the National would give the company much more status'. Goold pitched some of the plays Headlong were developing, including *ENRON* and *Earthquakes in London* (NT 2010). Hytner, however, was not interested in a co-production at this point. Instead, he was looking for a director to revive a play from the 'twentieth-century British repertoire': 'an Osborne or something'. Goold said, 'The only play I like from that period is *Time and the Conways* [...] he said that would be great' (Goold 2018a).

Time and the Conways[1]

J. B. Priestley's *Time and the Conways* tells the story of the wealthy Conway family. The first act is set during the birthday party of one of the daughters, Kay, in 1919. The war has ended and the family are full of hopeful ambitions for the future. Kay (Hattie Morahan) experiences a moment in which she accesses events in her family's life twenty years in the future. She sees how none of the family's ambitions will be fulfilled (Act Two). She then returns to 1919, retaining her memory of the future events she accessed (Act Three). Priestley's play is an exploration of J. W. Dunne's theories about time. Dunne believed all moments in time co-exist at the same time and so might be accessible under the right circumstances. The play's unusual temporal structure is difficult to convey effectively in performance, particularly in the third act. Goold was attracted to the challenge the play presented: 'the idea of exploring time sort of theatrically was interesting' (Goold 2018a). In order to do that, however, he felt it would be necessary to 'make some intervention into the third act' (Goold 2009d).

Goold recruited Laura Hopkins to work on the design. She interpreted Dunne's theories as referring to the idea that 'time is a series of moments that accumulate' and sought to represent this through her design for the production (Hopkins 2019). Hopkins

---

[1] For production images, see http://laurahopkins.co.uk/shows/time-and-the-conways/ (accessed 2 March 2020).

Figure 6 Left to right: Hattie Morahan as Kay and Paul Ready as Alan in *Time and the Conways*. Photo: Manuel Harlan.

used the set from the original 1937 production of the play as her starting point. She replicated this set and then sought to 'subvert' it and see it from a 'modern viewpoint' by applying a series of different 'temporal effects' to it, effects which would serve to illustrate her reading of Dunne's theories of time (Goold 2018a). Goold and Hopkins came up with three ideas for effects that could represent the play's non-linear temporal frame through evoking 'non-linear space' (Goold 2018a). These were based on the ways in which 'film approaches time', particularly in the work of early filmmakers such as Eadweard Muybridge (Goold 2009d). These temporal effects were supported in turn by Adam Cork's score for the production, which played with 'time and tempo, suggesting different rates of experience and hopping back and forwards from decade to decade' (Cork 2019).

The first effect, at the end of the first act, aimed to give the impression of suspended time by creating the theatrical equivalent of a 'bullet-time shot', as first used in the film *The Matrix*: 'to have a frozen moment in time and us able to travel around it'. At the end of Act One, Kay is writing, leaning on an open portfolio of papers. She freezes as her papers fall and freeze in mid-air before they touch the ground. The circular love seat she is sitting on would begin to turn in one direction while 'the entire room would then start to travel in the opposite direction' in order to create the bullet-time shot. For the effect to work, however, 'you have to absolutely fool the eye': 'the entire room needed to move [...] and wipe from one side to the other, and more stuff come on that hadn't been in your vision before that'. The effect was not fully achieved at the National: 'we weren't able to accommodate enough set on the side to come on around and into shot'. The solution was to hinge part of the set back rather than 'tracking' it out of view. The compromise was 'a big mistake'. The illusion was 'broken immediately by this one bit of set. Most of the set moved round, but this one bit moving in the opposite direction destroyed it'. In the final production, an incomplete version of the effect was presented. Kay froze, her papers froze in mid-air, the love seat turned but the walls of the room stood still (Hopkins 2019).

The concept behind the second temporal effect, at the end of Act Two, was 'to have a sequence of moments in a gesture broken up into those moments'. At the end of Act Two, Kay turns to look at herself in a mirror over a fireplace. The lights darken around her and six identical fireplaces are revealed behind her, 'diminishing in size and basically stretching to infinity'. At each fireplace is another Kay, 'dressed identically'. As Kay moved they repeated her moves, a slight time lapse between each one creating a 'canon of gestures'. The effect was 'like a photograph where you get the trace of the movement' (Hopkins 2019). The effect was supported by music suggesting a slipping 'in and out of the temporal flux' (Cork 2019).

The final temporal effect at the end of Act Three used 'a moving Pepper's ghost', which Hopkins and Goold planned to employ to have 'the old and young selves occupying the same space' on stage during the third act. Hopkins had seen this effect perfected by a Canadian company called Lemieux Pilon 4D Art in a show called *Norman* (2007): 'They had a man interacting with a projection [...] He could move around it and it could move around him, and the work is extraordinary because you cannot see how they do it'. The trick is created by an image being projected onto an inclined mirrored film membrane, but because the membrane affects the quality of the sound it needs to be taken in and out during the course of the performance without the audience noticing. Initially Hopkins and Goold 'couldn't find a way to introduce the membrane into the space in a way that wasn't clunky'. Even when they did manage to introduce a large area of the film, it proved difficult to keep the film taut. The membrane 'would bag, and then you got a very distorted image on it' (Hopkins 2019). The solution they came up with was to employ 'a huge truck' which 'trundled downstage with this membrane already in place' (Hopkins 2019). At the end of Act Three, after Carol's last line, a red curtain descended in front of the stage. Carol (Faye Castelow) stepped forward to dance in front of it, while behind the curtain the truck with the film moved into place. The curtain opened to reveal Alan (Paul Ready) talking to a projection of Kay, aged twenty-one, as they deliver the final lines of the play. A clock starts to tick and Kay enters in 1930s clothing to deliver a line from Act Two: 'Remember what we once were and what we thought we'd be' (Priestley 2000: 59). A projection of 1930s Alan then appears. The characters dance and their projections repeat their motions after them. Voices echo from both time periods. The sequence ends with a line from Mrs Conway (Francesca Annis): 'I'm not one of those people who remember graves, it's human beings I remember' (Priestley 2000: 49). Alan and Kay's future and past selves appear beside them. Past Kay reaches out and touches future Kay, then vanishes as the lights fade to black.

Rehearsals were challenging for Goold as he prefers to leave actors to work out the biographical hinterland of their characters on their own: 'You know the actors' role is to dream. And you can shape those dreams and you can stimulate the dreams absolutely, but so much of the inner imaginative life has to come from the performer'. This is one of the reasons he is drawn to new writing and 'auteur classical texts', such as Shakespeare, Pirandello and Pinter, where any notion of the characters' prior lives is less relevant. With *Time and the Conways*, however, the characters' backstories and inner lives were 'important' because the play depicts a family with complex interpersonal dynamics at two different moments in their lives. Goold solved this problem by giving the actors an exercise through which they could share their inner lives with each other without his direct involvement. Goold asked each actor to 'handwrite a letter as their character to one of the other characters for each year been 1919 and 1938'. He made time at the end of the rehearsal day for them to do this and then stage management would post the letters to the actors playing the characters they were addressed to: 'some of them found it a chore, but a lot of them really loved doing it, and I think they all loved getting letters. And you know they'd come into rehearsals each day and raise an eyebrow at each other as if some secret had been exchanged in 1931 between two characters' (Goold 2018a).

For *Time and the Conways*, Goold was keen to find a movement director whose style was less rooted in Lecoq or Frantic Assembly: 'something a little bit more lyrical'. Trevor Jackson, the casting director for the revival of *Oliver!* Goold had directed, recommended Scott Ambler, who was a founding artistic associate of New Adventures. Over the next few years, Ambler would become 'a key part of [Goold's] and Headlong's work'. Working with Ambler was instructive for Goold. From Ambler, he learnt that 'if you love your work and you show people that love, there's nothing, nothing people cherish more' (Goold 2018a).

ENRON[2]

ENRON was the first fruit of Headlong's move into new writing. Power had seen Lucy Prebble's first play, *The Sugar Syndrome* (Royal Court 2003), and invited her for a meeting soon after he arrived at Headlong. 'We talked about a series of ideas that she had and we were saying we were going to commission a tiny slate of things, but that they had to be formally ambitious and with dialectic and for Rupert to direct'. Prebble pitched a musical of the rise and fall of the American energy company, Enron. Power commissioned it: 'It felt really obvious. I didn't know the story, and as soon as she started telling me I knew this was going to be great for us' (Power 2019). Prebble took the commission. Headlong's offer to writers was particularly attractive, as unlike other new writing-focused companies, Headlong had 'a commitment to producing the plays' it commissioned (Grainger 2018).

The 2008 financial crash happened during the rehearsals for *King Lear*. 'I remember the actors coming in and going, "Fucking hell, what's going on?"' *ENRON* had already been announced as part of the second season, but Goold decided to push it forward: 'I remember saying to Ben, I know Lucy's got hardly anywhere with this first draft, but this idea of doing *ENRON* feels like we should do it soon'. At the time, *Gulliver's Travels* was slated to be the final show in Goold's trio of shows for Chichester and had also been

---

[2] For production images see https://headlong.co.uk/productions/enron/explore/ (accessed 2 March 2020).

Figure 7 The company of *ENRON* (Royal Court 2009). Photo: Manuel Harlan.

booked for the Edinburgh International Festival. Goold talked to Jonathan Church and he agreed to take 'a punt' on *ENRON* instead, so Headlong pulled out of the Edinburgh International Festival, 'much to the director's annoyance' (Goold 2018a).

ENRON's protagonist is Jeffrey Skilling, the company's chairman and later president. The plot follows his implementation of dubious practices at the company that initially cause it to flourish, but eventually lead to its crash. The story of the play was initially structured around the story of the company: 'She literally went, okay, I'll begin the story at the beginning of the company and end it at the end' (Goold 2018a). Power remembers 'trying to work out how you could put a sort of Shakespearean shape onto the story, make Jeffrey Skilling a classic tragic protagonist' but at the same time leave space for the 'playfulness' she wanted to create with 'her incredible ideas for the Lehman Brothers as Siamese twins, the raptors, all that stuff' (Power 2019). As the play progressed, 'it moved more and more onto the character of Skilling as protagonist, away from just the kind of sheer rapacious anarchy of the corporate thing'. Goold remembers sitting reading the rehearsal script and thinking, 'Wow, this is a brilliant, brilliant play'. What particularly caught his eye were the 'extraordinary' monologues, for instance the 'bubble speech the analyst gives about the financial system being a plane kept in the air and what if the plane only stayed in the air because everyone believed it would, and if they stopped believing it would fall' (Goold 2018a). Church remembers reading the script for the first time and thinking it was 'complex': 'it wasn't a play where you went, "this is instantly going to work," you went, "there's some dazzling and brilliant ideas but it's bonkers"' (Church 2018). Lindsey Alvis remembers that 'even on the page, there was a sense that it was going to be something unique' (Alvis 2019).

As a director, Goold sees himself as associated with new plays that are 'impossible challenges' to stage: 'the number of times I've had actors come in and go, "Good luck with directing this!"' (Goold 2018a). Lorna Seymour remembers the production as complex to manage: 'it was a big spectacle and an ensemble cast with loads of people playing lots of different smaller roles'. Anthony Ward's set featured a 'mesh tower at the back which had a platform in it halfway up so you could have a room in there'. Across the middle of the tower was a ticker 'that showed the stock price'. They used the tower to project onto. The different technical aspects of the show were 'so closely integrated' that teching the show 'took ages'. There was a scene 'where Skilling, the main character, would say whether he was happy or sad and the stock price would go up or down responding to him'. Seymour remembers how 'they had to programme it so that it was in time to how he said it' and it 'took quite a while to sort out'. There was 'furniture on wheels that could whizz on and off really quickly' and 'grey boxes that could be used in all different configurations, stacked up or whatever. Some of them had a drawer or cupboard door in them so you could hide props inside'. There was 'a grid of lighting tubes that could change colour [. . .] so they could be used to change the setting quite easily'. When Skilling's protégé Andy Fastow was 'in his lair with his dinosaurs, they all went red [. . .] At the end four of them flew in to make a [prison] cell around Skilling'. Even with all this, there was 'still a big open space for all the choreography'. For stage management, 'it was a bit mental' (Seymour 2019).

Goold argues that while some of the moments in *ENRON* demanded the discovery of an inventive way to stage them, 'a lot of things that were acclaimed about the production were ideas from the play. The theatricality was in the writing' (Goold 2019b). Goold staged one scene about the collapse of the Californian energy system (Act Two, Scene Six), by creating a movement sequence in which the traders used light sabres to represent the circulation of energy-as-a-commodity. The inspiration for the sequence is rooted in Prebble's text. The stage directions at the top of the scene call for the traders to be '*manipulating California's electricity market by moving energy around*' (Prebble 2009: 79). In reality, the Enron traders were 'geeks who were always using *Star Wars* terminology' (Goold 2018a), particularly in the naming of their shell companies (Barboza 2002). Goold 'thought light sabres would be cool' (Goold 2018a). Ambler developed a physical language for the show based on the movements traders use: 'We went down to the trading floor to look at how they were moving and a lot of the physicality in the show came out of watching those trading floor exercises' (Goold 2019c).

The play also features a 'career-defining role' for an actor in the character of Skilling. The actor that Goold cast in the role was Sam West, who 'was a union man, a socialist, believed in the ensemble, anti-capitalist, and yet also understood Skilling's basic "I think I can do this and I think maybe I can do it better than everyone else; I think I might be the smartest guy in the room"'. West's relationship with Skilling was a prime example of 'the role and the actor coming together'. To some degree, Goold thinks that finding this synergy is a matter of luck. It's difficult to predict: 'We had a wonderful actor [Norbert Leo Butz] do it on Broadway, but the show wasn't the same [...] somehow the essence of the actor was different' (Goold 2018a).

The show was a huge hit with critics. The play was immediately recognized as an outstanding piece of political drama: 'one of the most incisive, most grown-up political dramas of the past ten years' (Clapp 2009); 'one of those rare works that crystallizes the mood of its age' (Spencer 2009). Goold's direction, though still full of razzle-dazzle – 'an eye-socking, mad cabaret of flickering stock prices, neon cityscapes, ticker-tape blizzards and floor traders gyrating with adrenaline' (Gore-Langton 2009) – was identified as appropriate, coherent and grounded: 'a production that shows Goold's bold showmanship at its very finest, allied to a sense of empathy that makes this an emotional experience too' (Maxwell 2009). Frustratingly, Clióna Roberts struggled to get Headlong's role in creating the production recognized in the press at times: '*ENRON* particularly fell victim to some lazy thought; occasionally in print, journalists, not necessarily theatre critics would always assign credit to the Royal Court'. Michael Billington stepped in to redress the balance: 'he rather brilliantly wrote a piece giving Headlong the full credit, which helped stem this ongoing misunderstanding' (Roberts 2019).

Goold remembers the reviews coming in. He rang Prebble because 'it is so rare when you have those moments' and said, 'This is really special, you must hold on to this'. They had not been expecting such a rapturous response: 'We were sort of hoping we might get away with it'. Within two weeks they had 'every New York producer wanting to take it to America. It was going to be the Great Play about the post-crash'. The production secured both a West End and a Broadway run. The West End run of *ENRON* was a success, however, the Broadway production bombed (Goold 2018a).

Goold was still managing a heavy workload. Between opening *ENRON* at the Royal Court and opening the play on Broadway, he also directed the West End transfer, a production of *Turandot* (ENO 2009), a low-budget film of *Macbeth* and a production of *Romeo and Juliet* for the RSC. The American producers needed *ENRON* to open before the Tony Award deadline, so rehearsals started without Goold. Prebble and Sophie Hunter, the associate director, took the lead in his absence. Goold arrived two weeks in. *Romeo and Juliet* had just opened. The night before his first day of rehearsals in New York, he had been at the Oliviers in London picking up the award for Best Director for *ENRON*. He arrived in rehearsals the next day straight off the plane and feeling 'crappy'. The company decided to play a practical joke on him: 'The musical director said, "Do you want to hear some of 'Commodities Chorus'?" and they sang it and it was unbearable. And of course, it was a joke, but I was too tired and hungover to really appreciate it'. All in all, 'it was a very disorientating twenty-four hours' (Goold 2018a).

Amidst the whirlwind of events, Goold also had an 'odd' feeling 'something was going to change'. Then Power announced he was leaving Headlong to take up the role of dramaturg at the National. Goold was 'unquenchably and regrettably really angry about it': 'I really thought Headlong was going to go on for ever and we were going to make films and books and installations and it would be great and we were at our absolute height' (Goold 2018a). Part of the pain, for Goold, was the sense he was constantly being 'asset stripped' as artists he had put energy into developing were poached by better-resourced organizations. Both Northampton and Headlong were like 'feeder football teams' in that they were 'mid-scale organizations for early-career practitioners to come to and develop and move on' (Goold 2018c).

Goold knew the Broadway production of *ENRON* was in trouble before it opened. The political atmosphere in New York was different to that of London: 'New York is a democratic town with Wall Street. And that's a real contradiction for them'. Headlong were coming over with a show saying 'the financial system was the problem, not the Texans': 'New Yorkers didn't want to hear that'. The form of the play was also an issue:

> In London the first three scenes, which were quite naturalistic, were fine, good, really worked, and then the play sort of worked into these madcap Brechtian song-and-dance numbers, as the Enron company emerges. And I always feel like the audience always went 'Woah!' at that point. In New York it was almost exactly the opposite. They really enjoyed the familial nature of the first three scenes and then when we threw the tap-dancing at them and it confused them, they didn't like it.

In Goold's experience, New Yorkers 'tend to like really high and really low culture': 'they love serious art and talking seriously about serious art. And they also love ribald musical comedy'. *ENRON* was rooted in a more British tradition of combining both, which Goold traces back to Shakespeare: 'America doesn't really have that tradition massively. And even more it doesn't have a tradition of satire. And all these things conflated'. The show's mode of production was also different in New York. In Chichester, they had been a mid-scale subsided show taking a swing at capitalism, but in New York they were 'a multi-million-dollar commercial show'. They had become the thing they were satirizing and 'so there was a righteous swing back' (Goold 2018a). The production was killed off by Ben Brantley's review in the *New York Times*. The play, he decreed, 'made the same points so arduously and repeatedly that there isn't much room left for discussion'. It also suffered from metaphorical overkill: 'When, toward the end, a character steps to the edge of the stage to announce that she has "the best metaphor" for "the values that define price," your instinct is to cry out, "Please, not another metaphor!"' (Brantley 2010). The show closed two weeks after opening. Despite this, Goold remembers the experience as 'extraordinary': 'we were there, as Headlong, in Times Square with our gang with one of our shows. Even though it bombed you can't take that away, that thrill, the ecstasy in that bubble' (Goold 2018a).

As a result of *ENRON* 'things changed for Headlong as a company and for me as an artist'. The show defined a winning formula for Headlong: 'get the intellectual enquiry right, make it a new play, try and build it around an emerging artist, don't build it on an actor because you can't tour that, get the theatricality of the production high enough'. The show itself needed to be the star: 'if you get a show that can exist for an audience outside of the flavour of the original cast, you know if you can create a *History Boys* or a *War Horse* or an *ENRON*, then that's gold for a touring company, that's absolute gold'. Today Goold still believes in the same basic model:

The absolute centre of the bullseye as a producer is a major new play that speaks to the times with real scale, defines the times even, from an artist who has been awaiting their defining work and delivers the defining work with that play. Ideally they are a less-known voice. And better still if that work anchors on a protagonist that in turn creates a career-defining role for an actor whose own circumstances align with the role.

For Goold it was the first time he had worked with a living writer whose talent and sheer creativity 'was so much more obviously greater than mine'. This placed him into a new position within the creative process: 'I'm not the author of these ideas' (Goold 2018a).

Romeo and Juliet[3]

Goold's next production was *Romeo and Juliet* for the RSC, which opened just before *ENRON* opened on Broadway. This was his second attempt at the play and his first production as an associate director with the company. In conceiving his approach, he drew on his experiences of working on the earlier Greenwich production. He kept the intercutting of the banishment scenes (3.2 and 3.3) and again chose to place the

Figure 8 Left to right: Sam Troughton as Romeo and Mariah Gale as Juliet with the company of *Romeo and Juliet* (RST 2010). Photo: Ellie Kurttz.

---

[3] For production images see https://www.rsc.org.uk/romeo-and-juliet/past-productions/in-focus-rupert-goold-2010 (accessed 2 March 2020).

interval later in the play's action than is customary, between Capulet's (Richard Katz) agreement to wed Juliet (Mariah Gale) to Paris (James Howard) and the lovers saying their goodbyes before Romeo (Sam Troughton) is banished (3.4 and 3.5). Goold concluded that the central problem with many productions of *Romeo and Juliet* is that 'Romeo and Juliet aren't as interesting as the characters around them'. He decided to try to find a way 'make them special'. Goold was initially inspired by one of his cousins, who was affected by schizophrenia and had found love despite difficult circumstances: 'In care he met a girl who had real problems with depression and schizophrenia and they fell in love'. He remembered being at their wedding and feeling that their love was more special and fragile than most: 'The whole room was willing them on to be together' because 'there was so much at stake'. Goold thought if you could make the audience feel like that about Romeo and Juliet then 'that would be kind of special'. Goold considered setting the production in a secure unit but struggled to work out where the familial conflict, 'the Montague and Capulet thing', would fit within that social world. He then came across the story of Sophie Lancaster and Robert Maltby, who had been viciously attacked for being Goths. Lancaster had been killed in the attack: 'two again rather fragile people that a lot of society might look at and go, "losers"'. The story deeply affected Goold and formed the basis of his poetic idiom for the show (Goold in Neill 2011).

Goold's production linked the idea of love to an exploration of the nature of faith in the modern world. In our current 'less ecclesiastical age', Goold argues, 'our new god' is 'romantic or sexual love' and he positions Romeo and Juliet as its patron saints. In his production, Romeo and Juliet, like Christ, 'go through a passion together'. While Christ is literally resurrected, Romeo and Juliet are metaphorically resurrected: 'through the enacting of the tragedy they become immortalised' (Goold in Neill 2011). This idea is emphasized in Goold's production in an additional scene in which Romeo comes to meet Juliet for their wedding night (between 3.4 and 3.5). As they kiss on her balcony, light illuminates a golden frame behind them, 'burning through the oily surface' and visually transforming them into a religious icon (Scutt 2019). They are positioned as 'secular saints' (Goold in Neill 2011).[4]

Goold was also interested in the idea of pilgrimage, particularly as the play was being staged in Stratford-upon-Avon, a place to which people come to 'pay homage' to Shakespeare: in the same way that some people would 'go on a pilgrimage like going to Lourdes, they go to the RSC to see the greatest love story ever told'. Goold envisioned his lovers as such visitors, who find themselves magically inside Shakespeare's play: 'like us, they just turned up on some pilgrimage or strange exploration and go through this sort of like Alice in Wonderland experience, dropped down the rabbit hole' (Goold in Neill 2011). Goold and designer Tom Scutt emphasized this idea by setting the action of the play in a cathedral 'dedicated to the figures that are Romeo and Juliet' (Scutt 2019). The production opens with Romeo entering the cathedral, listening to an audio guide playing the prologue. A time shift is indicated by a blend of ancient and modern sounds

---

[4] See cover illustration.

in the soundscape, the sound of cars, a siren, a Gregorian chant. A hooded monk enters the space and then exits through a metal grate. Romeo follows as if accepting an invitation to enter the past. Goold relocated the action of *Romeo and Juliet* to 1548 Castile, a period close to Shakespeare's but more pervaded by religious and ethnic tension, providing 'a world that is Catholic dark, full of the sepulchre', and with 'a bit of sex and heat' helping Goold to create a space in which the play's contradictory elements, 'death and yet also explosive and riotous and sexual', could be reconciled. Within this world, Romeo and Juliet wear modern clothes, singling them out from the other characters in period dress. Elements of the contemporary seep into the period world: 'as Romeo and Juliet become tainted by the High Renaissance world that they're in, equally they pollute the period world'. For example, in the scene where Juliet refuses to marry Paris (3.5), Lady Capulet (Christine Entwisle) smokes a cigarette. In the final moments, the image is reversed. Romeo lies dead in Juliet's lap, his head resting on her figure in her High Renaissance wedding dress. The parents gathered around the tomb are now dressed in contemporary clothes: 'By the end [Romeo and Juliet] are the pilgrims in high Elizabethan costumes and through their dramatic action they have become transcendent and their families are exposed as quotidian and banal'. Through enacting the tragedy, these contemporary lovers become 'immortalised' like their Shakespearean counterparts (Goold in Neill 2011).

Tom Scutt's set for the show was black, reflecting the deathly darkness of the play's High Renaissance Spanish world. This initially worried Goold: 'we can't do Romeo and Juliet on a black set' because 'the midday sun rips through the whole play'. In order to solve this problem, Goold used another dominant image pattern in the play, 'images of fire and gunpowder' to 'mitigate against the aridity and weight of the mausoleum' (Goold in Neill 2011). The finished production is full of fire: flaming torches, flame bowls, a tall burst of flame that erupts from a metal grating during fight scenes. The presence of fire supported Scutt's desire for his black environment to be 'oily and flammable' in quality (Scutt 2019). The use of fire also visually emphasized a key metaphor in the play linking both violence and passion – 'These violent delights have violent ends / And in their triumph die, like fire and powder, / Which as they kiss consume' (2.6.9–11) – which captures the idea that when 'you put things together they explode in a moment', which in turn reflects what happens to Romeo and Juliet (Goold in Neill 2011).

The production was a triumph. Billington praised it to the heights: 'I can't recall as exciting a revival since Zeffirelli stunned us with his verismo in 1960' (Billington 2010). Goold was praised by many of the critics for delivering 'a surprisingly straight version of the play [...] there is none of the extreme Gooldification we have come to expect' (Shuttleworth 2010); 'chimes exactly with the spirit of the play' (Billington 2010); '[a]live to the shades and textures of the play' (Hitchings 2010a). Spencer felt Goold's time-blending device captured 'the heart of our modern experience of the play': 'When we read *Romeo and Juliet*, we are simultaneously in the past and in the present, caught up in the drama itself and our own vivid memories of teenage love. Goold's staging allows us to experience this jolting double-take in the theatre' (Spencer 2010a).

Earthquakes in London[5]

Goold unveiled Headlong's third season in the autumn of 2009. It included five productions, two of which were slated to be directed by Goold: Mike Bartlett's *Earthquakes in London* and Goold and Power's 'nascent middle-eastern reading' of *Gulliver's Travels* (Goold 2018a). The latter promised to 'filter "the spirit and the ambition of the novel through the lens of contemporary culture" in a "visceral satiric exploration of identity, sanity and international relations"' ('Goold Unveils Headlong's 2010, Reworks *Gulliver*' 2009). Tom Scutt worked on the design for *Gulliver's Travels* as one of the winners of the 2007 Linbury Prize. His brief was to design a 'tourable' set that 'managed to harness the expanse of the novel'. Goold suggested Scutt consider what would happen 'if there was one space for this piece'. Scutt found this note productive, as it suggested a tension between a 'minimal design space' and 'huge and expansive' ideas. This tension became a key element of Goold and Scutt's work together: 'a principle almost of starvation and reward that you hold back for an audience. You limit the visual vocabulary in order to earn these moments of growth and expanse'. For example, in *Romeo and Juliet*, Goold wanted to use the golden frame that lights up when Romeo and Juliet kiss on the balcony several times.[6] Scutt argued against this: 'You've got to hold this back. This is one moment'. Scutt's idea for the design for *Gulliver's Travels* positioned Gulliver as 'an architect who was in charge of the redevelopment of an old asylum': 'it was all about scale, about the architect looking down on the scale model of the institution, the Lilliputians, and then he disappeared into his model and was scrutinised by the Brobdingnagians' (Scutt 2019). The other three productions in the season were: *Orson Welles in the Land of the Peas*, a new play created by Anthony Neilson '[e]xamining the clash between art and commerce'; a David Eldridge adaptation of *The Threepenny Opera*; and a Jamie Lloyd-directed revival of Oscar Wilde's *Salome* ('Goold Unveils Headlong's 2010, Reworks *Gulliver*' 2009). The unexpected success of *ENRON* and Power's departure from the company, however, meant only two of the shows announced were actually produced: *Salome* (Headlong/Leicester Curve 2010) and *Earthquakes in London* (NT 2010). *Gulliver's Travels*, *Orson Welles and the Land of the Peas* and Eldridge's version of *The Threepenny Opera* remain unproduced, the latter due to the strictures of the Brecht estate, who would not countenance Eldridge's setting of the play during the period after the death of Princess Diana.

Power had seen some of Bartlett's early plays at the Royal Court and commissioned him 'to make a piece of work that does all the things you're not really allowed to do. Big cast, massive idea, write it for a big space'. Originally *Earthquakes in London* was 'a three-play saga'. The first part, the basis for *Earthquakes in London*, was set in the present day. Another, called *No Snow in Moscow*, was set in the near future: 'a Chekhovian play about a family in an old house and sitting outside London going, "one day we'll go to London [. . .] but London has become a catastrophe due to climate change"' (M. Bartlett 2019). The

---

[5] For production images, see https://headlong.co.uk/productions/earthquakes-london/explore/ (accessed 2 March 2020).
[6] See cover illustration.

remnants of *No Snow in Moscow* survive in *Earthquakes in London*'s final scene, which is set in the '*kitchen of a large country house*' (M. Bartlett 2010: 166). Other elements – the country house, the Chekhovian form – can also be discerned in Bartlett's later play *Albion*: 'even though it wasn't, it was a sort of companion piece of *Earthquakes*' (Goold 2018d). Bartlett notes that the two plays were 'born of the same impulse' (M. Bartlett 2019).

Goold remembers the first draft of *Earthquakes in London* as 'pretty disorganized' (Goold 2018a). He was concerned it was not 'going to fly'. Then Bartlett had a brainwave about 'trying to write formally what climate change might look like. Could a play be too much of everything? [...] The ocean's full of plastic, what is the dramatic form of that?' (Goold 2018d). The play was rewritten around this idea of excess: '*The stage should overflow with scenery, sound, backdrops, lighting, projection, etc. Everything is represented. It is too much. The play is about excess and we should feel that*' (M. Bartlett 2010: xi). The finished version of *Earthquakes in London* tells the story of three sisters. The eldest, Sarah (Lia Williams), is the minister for the environment. The middle sister, Freya (Anna Madeley), is pregnant and suicidal, struggling with the idea of what having a child might do to the planet. The youngest, Jasmine (Jessica Raine), is a hedonistic student. The play draws on Chekhov in its presentation of three sisters who are all adrift in their lives, but is also mythic, in terms of its representation of Freya, whose wanderings across London have echoes of Odysseus, Orpheus and Dante. In its climatic moment, in which Freya falls off Waterloo Bridge to her death, only to be resurrected in 2525, it draws on the messianic. After working on *ENRON*, Goold had become confident that, even with a new play, a director still had a contribution to make: 'you could be a secondary artist and still a very involved artist'. When directing a classic play, Goold argues 'the director's job is to take care of the bad bits'. With a new play, 'if something wasn't working you could just get rid of it if the writer was in agreement'. This meant 'the starting point changed', allowing Goold to investigate new ways of approaching a text, trying to find 'a poetic, formal or tonal quality, as opposed to a concept' (Goold 2018d).

The show was conceived as site-specific, in the loosest sense of the term. It was a show about London in London. The theatre sat right by Waterloo Bridge, the setting for Freya's climactic fall into the Thames. Miriam Buether's design consisted of two letterbox stages at either end of a bright orange catwalk that snaked through the space between them like a river, embodying 'the play's serpentine approach to storytelling' (Hitchings 2010b). The audience stood or sat on bright orange bar stools around the catwalk. Goold felt the show captured a sense of Bartlett's generation's experience of London: 'modern urban life under thirty-five, what that meant'. He remembers looking down at 'the audience around the catwalk and it felt, I mean people talk about gig theatre now, but it felt like club theatre': 'it just felt generationally kind of alive, and not didactic, even though it had a strong message' (Goold 2018d). With its pumping music and concert-like staging, Grainger argues the production was indeed an early precursor of 'gig theatre' (Grainger 2018).

While audiences responded enthusiastically, the critics were not so sure. The general consensus was that the production was highly likeable but '[u]ndeniably flawed' (Hitchings 2010b): 'the theatrical equivalent of a thrilling roller coaster ride. It swoops and twists, rushes and soars, and provides a great shot of adrenalin-fuelled excitement

[. . .] and at the end exhilaration gives way to a slight feeling of anti-climax' (Spencer 2010b). Though Bartlett succeeded in his aim of creating a play of excess, the structural relationship between the idea of excess and climate change seemed to pass the critics by. As with *ENRON*, Goold felt 'there was this perception that I'd sort of dressed up the play. When that really wasn't the case at all' (Goold 2018d). Many moments that were praised as Goold additions, such as a singing and dancing chorus of '*mothers in black with black prams*' (M. Bartlett 2010: 65), actually originated in Bartlett's play: 'the text of *Earthquakes* is actually far more visually exciting than the production I actually made' (Goold 2018d).

The Merchant of Venice[7]

After *Earthquakes in London*, Goold returned to the RSC to direct *The Merchant of Venice*. He relocated the action of the play from Renaissance Venice to contemporary Las Vegas. Looking back, he sees *The Merchant of Venice*, together with *Turandot*, as the 'most extreme version' of his interest in challenging 'pomposity' in high art, such as 'the reverence around verse speaking or the operatic canon as sort of an exclusive club', by 'very actively putting accessible playing styles, performance idioms, into contact with core repertoire' (Goold 2018d).

Identifying *The Merchant of Venice*'s strong and weak points, Goold concluded the Portia scenes were always 'a secondary element in a production of this play'. In the play, Portia's father has died, leaving both her and the fortune she has inherited as a prize to be won by whichever man can solve the lottery he set before he died. The scene in which the idea of the lottery is introduced (1.2) is 'one of the hardest scenes in Shakespeare'. At the same time, it is absolutely vital because it explains the lottery's rules: 'it has to print because you've got to engage with that storyline'. This led Goold to think of 'a game show of three caskets'. This in turn became linked in his mind to an idea of an 'inane, performative vapidity, Disney Club vapidity', which then led to 'the Britney Spears thing'. This became his poetic idiom for the production. The idea for Las Vegas as the social world of the production came from Patrick Stewart, who played Shylock and was interested in the fact the city had originally been established as the legal gambling centre of America by the Jewish Mafia. Goold thought it was 'a world, but not a meaningful world'. The combination of this social world with Goold's poetic idiom, however, sparked the question: 'what is a Las Vegas Portia?' Then 'everything mapped on from there' (Goold 2018d).

Goold's production relocates the action of Shakespeare's play to a casino in Las Vegas whose logo, 'a micro-skirted hostess with her arms outstretched like a come-hither venal parody of the crucifixion' hints at the religious conflict underlying this city in which money appears to be the only god. Capitalism is productively equated with gambling through the figure of the merchant Antonio (Scott Handy), who is reconfigured as a heavily indebted gambler (Taylor 2011). To achieve the design, Scutt had to go against his

---

[7] For production images, see https://www.rsc.org.uk/the-merchant-of-venice/past-productions/rupert-goold-2011-production (accessed 2 March 2020).

usual minimalist instincts: 'the right thing for this production was to throw absolutely everything at it and assault Stratford with garish visual spectacle'. Goold and Scutt looked at 'Venetian architecture and styles and the Rialto and we sort of ingested that and spewed it out over the stage' (Scutt 2019).

For all their glitz and glamour, both Belmont and Venice are presented as hotbeds of racism and anti-Semitism. In the gaudy 'Destiny' gameshow, a cross between 'The Bachelorette' and '*Deal or No Deal*', each contestant is ridiculed by the use of exaggerated racial stereotypes. The Prince of Morocco (David Ononokpono) is a heavyweight boxer, while the Prince of Aragon (Jason Morell) looks like a member of a mariachi band. Portia's distaste for anything but a WASP-ish lover is emphasised, so linking her racism directly to the anti-Semitism Shylock suffers. As the gameshow prize, however, the vapid blonde Portia (Susannah Fielding) is also positioned as the victim of oppression at the hands of a patriarchy whose reach extends beyond death. Fielding argues that as the 'presenter and the prize of her own game show', Portia is merely a piece of property to be passed from one man to the next (Fielding 2019).

Shylock is presented as a wealthy property developer despised by his Christian patrons. In a city where everything can be bought and sold, the inability of Portia and Bassanio (Richard Riddell) to buy Antonio's life pits new forms of compensatory justice against older forms of revenge justice, positioning Shylock as standing outside of capitalism's systems in his refusal of the money. As such, he represents a threat to them. When Antonio cannot repay the money himself, he is subjected to a Mafia-style trial in a meat factory, where he is saved by Portia (4.1), who in a *Legally Blonde*-esque transformation, has been revealed to be a highly intelligent brunette: 'actually there was an amazing brain under it all and she'd just been subject to this horrific game that her father had left her with' (Fielding 2019). The production ends with Portia's realization that Bassanio's affections lie with his friend Antonio and not with her. In the final image, Portia is left alone, twirling on the spot, 'doing this extraordinary almost music-box-type spinning to Elvis's "Are You Lonesome Tonight?" on one stack-perspex-platform heel, carrying her blond wig in her hand' under a 'canopy of lurid stars that were also Vegas casino bulbs' (Scutt 2019), so conveying a sense of someone 'who'd been trying to be these two different people for so long falling apart' (Fielding 2019).

The Merchant of Venice is the most full-throttle example of Goold's relocations and reconfigurations of Shakespeare. For some critics, the 'outrageously inventive production' (Edwardes 2011) effectively excavated the themes underlying Shakespeare's play, the Las Vegas setting 'a perfect metaphor for a world of financial and romantic fantasy' (Billington 2011a). Others argued it was revelatory in terms of its representation of Portia, making her 'interesting rather than simply disjointed' (Clapp 2011a). For many critics, however, it was emblematic of Goold at his worst: 'too many moments that show the director's cleverness but don't necessarily reflect the text' (Lee 2011). Charles Spencer saw it as 'director's theatre run riot', arguing it made Goold's '*The Tempest*, set on an Arctic island, and *Macbeth* located in a Stalinist dictatorship, seem almost staid' (Spencer 2011). Patrick Carnegy, tired of Goold's dramatic relocations, dubbed the director a 'theatrical travel agent' (Carnegy 2011).

But the show thrilled audiences. Before the play started there was a thirty-minute 'pre-show, which was like a Las Vegas nightclub and so the audiences would come into that and you'd see the shock horror on people's faces. They'd expected to see ruffs and doublets'. Fielding remembers hearing people saying, 'This can't be it! This can't be it!' (Fielding 2019). Handy remembers the audience excitement as palpable, particularly in the first few moments of the actual show. When 'Elvis came up through the crap table and started singing', he could hear the 'whole audience literally breathe in together in shock' (Handy 2019). The production transferred to the Almeida in 2014. For Goold, however, the revival never quite recaptured the energy of the Stratford production. Despite the fact that only three years had passed between the two versions of the show, Goold remembers thinking, 'This feels dated to me, but also dated to theatre'. The production seemed very much of its moment. In the 2000s, 'You had Žižek writing about Darth Vader and it just felt like a very playful, early social media-influenced anarchy and a way of breaking down reverence to art' that felt useful in terms of making classical work accessible to a wide range of people. Goold, however, was reaching the end of an era in terms of his approach to Shakespeare. *The Merchant of Venice* can be seen as both the height and the end of 'these huge, these big-scale shows, totally as imaginative playthings' (Goold 2018d).

A distinct shift in Goold's approach to Shakespeare can be discerned in his next Shakespearean project, a screen version of *Richard II* for the first season of the BBC's *The Hollow Crown* (2012). Goold had thought about directing *Richard II* for stage, when he was planning to do a production for the RSC: 'I set it in late Michael Jackson Neverland. That was my social world. I hadn't quite got a poetic world'. For the film, however, he 'completely set it in period'. From working on *Macbeth*, he had identified that Shakespeare on film works better when shot in real environments: 'the moment you film Shakespeare in a studio it's utterly dead. It feels completely fake' (Goold 2019a). The 'Soviet elements that I felt were really strong' on stage 'just didn't quite work on screen' (Goold 2018d). Shooting *Richard II*, Goold insisted 'everything was in real spaces' so 'it lives' (Goold 2019a). Inspired by the film director Terrence Malick's work, he approached the film as 'a meditation on the land and leadership against the backdrop of kingship and the speech of kingship'. The film's cinematography is infused with a Malick-esque transcendent representation of nature: 'I remember constantly saying to the producer, "I want to go and shoot some more grasses, and we need some clouds", you know, and trying to get that Malick-y feel'. It was only afterwards, in the editing, Goold began to realize 'how much of that came just in the rhythm of your frame selection' (Goold 2018d). *Richard II* marks the beginning of a movement towards a quieter, less interventionist approach to directing Shakespeare and won Ben Whishaw a BAFTA for Best Actor in the title role.

Decade[8]

Now that Power had left for the National, Headlong needed to find a new associate to replace him. The director Robert Icke first met Goold at an Almeida fundraising gala in which Kate

---

[8] For production images, see https://headlong.co.uk/productions/decade/explore/ (accessed 2 March 2020).

Figure 9 Left to right: Tobias Menzies, Amy Lennox and Cat Simmons in *Decade*. Photo: Tristram Kenton.

Fleetwood was performing. Icke, who had been rehearsing the actors involved in the gala and was feeling out of place 'surrounded by all these very rich people in the Almeida lobby', had taken refuge in the theatre's green room: 'Rupert came down and I'd seen a bit of his work and we just got chatting to each other'. Initially, Icke did not consider applying for Power's role. A chance encounter with Goold changed his mind: 'I bumped into Rupert in the street and he said, "Are you going to apply for Ben's job?" And I said, "No. I'm not a dramaturg". And he said, "You don't need to be a dramaturg, we're going to make the job around the person"'. Icke applied to be Power's replacement and came in for an interview. He remembers thinking, 'My odds of getting this are zero. So I'm going to be really honest and say what I actually think' (Icke 2019a). In the interview, Goold recalls that Icke was 'really impressive'. The panel 'couldn't quite believe his chutzpah, but also his insight' (Goold 2018b). The applicants for the role were all asked to critique a play from Headlong's back catalogue. Icke picked *ENRON* and argued the problem with the play is 'it doesn't know whether it's the story of [Skilling] or the story of the company [...] and it can't be both of those things' (Icke 2019a). Goold remembers Icke 'showed me stuff about the play that I thought I knew backwards'. He thought, 'Wow, let's take a punt on this person' (Goold 2018b).

The first show that Goold and Icke worked together on was *Decade*. While he was in New York working on *ENRON*, Goold remembers 'walking near Ground Zero and thinking, "I'd really love to make a show about 9/11"'. Alongside this, Goold also had an instinct that 'doing something site-specific was the next step for the company' as working in established theatre venues meant audiences were still not always aware they were seeing Headlong's work: 'The host venue would always be the foregrounded visual partner'. Working in a non-theatre venue would foreground the company as the undisputed authors of the work (Goold 2018d).

Initially, Goold was interested in exploring 'something more choreographic' (Goold 2018b). Over time, Tobias Menzies observes, influences from 'dance theatre' can be perceived as increasingly 'bleeding' into Goold's work. He hypothesizes this is because 'modern dance has a purity of communicating something that is non-linguistic, pure emotion. You can get something just because of the way someone moves and how that is with the music. That bypasses argument and plot'. It's an extension of Goold's impulse to physicalize both ideas and emotions (Menzies 2019). Goold had seen a French film, *Le Bal*, which was set in a dance hall and explored its history through the history of dance. Inspired by it, Goold became interested in making a dance piece set in Windows on the World, the restaurant at the top of the North Tower of the World Trade Center:

> You'd see all the customers at the restaurant that you would eventually realize were there on the day of 9/11. Silent. Because they were voiceless. Because we don't know what happened to them or who they were in some cases. And then you'd hear lots of voices from the ten years following, and somehow the silent section, which was half of the show, would be choreographic, and be about panic and also community.

Goold and Icke started to 'gestate' these ideas. The idea developed from a pure 'dance show' to a dance show 'with devised elements in it'. With Scott Ambler, they developed a 'choreographic language' for the piece. They ran a workshop with actors, in which they improvised a range of different scenarios: 'different architects pitching what the tower to replace Ground Zero would be' and 'sort of comic ones round Blair and Bush'. Eventually, they decided they needed a writer but 'no one writer wanted to take the whole thing on'. So instead they decided to use the piece as 'an opportunity to have lots of different voices' (Goold 2018d).

The project gave Headlong the opportunity to 'meet a whole load of writers, internationally as well as at home' (Icke 2019a). They took a group of British writers away on a retreat and held a workshop in New York with American writers in conjunction with the Public Theater. In the end, there were twenty-seven writers 'writing pieces for the show, knowing that only ten would get selected' (Grainger 2019a). Talking to the writers, Goold realized 'everybody felt, "Oh I can't write a play about it"' but 'everyone wanted to tell you what they did on the day'. So they asked the writers to write about that. For Goold, this reflected 'the Aristotelian element of 9/11'. There was a 'place, time and action singularity' as 'the whole world watched in real time'. The event also had a compelling dramaturgy: 'the horizontal, the planes going into the two verticals and the descent as being a sort of primal geometry' (Goold 2018b).

During the process of making *Decade* (Headlong/CFT 2011) Goold led on the direction of the show with Icke and Nadia Latif, the other associate director, also staging some sections. The acting company was put together before Goold and Icke had determined exactly what the text would be. In the end, there was 'way too much material' and more material kept appearing: 'some writers were delivering during rehearsals' (Goold 2018a). The final text of the production was put together in the rehearsal room and in previews. Icke did most of the dramaturgical work: 'what order did the scenes go in, how did they split up, how did they structure?' (Icke 2019a). Menzies remembers that 'the writing was coming in as we were working and it was changing'. While 'the fluidity' of the process was 'exciting', at times, it could be 'pretty bewildering to be in rehearsal' (Menzies 2019). Lorna Seymour found it difficult to keep track of all the scripts: 'every day there'd just be so many scripts being emailed through'. In the rehearsal room, they attempted to manage the situation with a big chart on the wall: 'Moving things up and down this chart, what order things might be in, or whether they're in it at all'. She remembers it was 'really hard to keep on top of what the script was going to be, let alone write any blocking down'. During previews, it got worse: 'All of the lights and sound were programmed sequentially for the order they were in when we teched them'. When the structure of the performance changed, they 'didn't renumber anything. We just had to reprogramme it. So cue 300 might then link to cue 25'. With the cue numbers all out of sequence, 'you have to just trust that you've written it down right and that you've programmed it right'. Constantly changing the running order also affected the actors. Sometimes, they 'just couldn't remember what was next' (Seymour 2019).

Many of the pieces were dropped before press night. Writers whose work made it into the final version included Lynn Nottage, Alecky Blythe, Rory Mullarkey and Ella Hickson. The spine of the final version was provided by Matthew Lopez's piece 'The Sentinels', which tells the story of three 9/11 widows who meet each other every anniversary in the same coffee shop. Its eleven scenes were interspersed across the evening, with scenes from the other plays woven in between. Scott Ambler choreographed dance sequences, which were integrated into the piece between scenes. Mike Bartlett's contribution, 'The Enemy', features a journalist interviewing the man who shot bin Laden. It takes the form of a duologue written almost entirely in 'single-syllabic words'. Through writing it in this form, Bartlett unwittingly created something that could not be cut: 'the actors told me a lot of the other pieces were coming in and out; they weren't sure which ones were going to be in it. But mine required such learning and rehearsal they'd all agreed if they were going to do it, it had to stay in' (M. Bartlett 2019). For *ENRON*, Adam Cork had created an elegiac chorale which used text messages sent on 9/11 as its source material. For *Decade*, he created a very different piece, this time using a larger selection of text messages as a starting point: 'There was more of a journey. It lasted longer. The texts started out positive, they were kind of everyday, and then developed into the nightmare that was 9/11'. The text fragments were woven into 'a mosaic structure which built and built and built to a climactic toppling' (Cork 2019).

Finding a venue for the show was not easy. They looked at a warehouse, out at the end of the Docklands Light Railway line. They viewed a huge empty space under the Trocadero. With the help of an event production company, Finch and Grainger eventually found a venue for the show in an old trading hall in St. Katharine Docks. Finding the venue was only half the work: 'As a company we'd never had to deal with anything like that: needing to create dressing rooms; adding additional electrical power to the building because, for a show with lots of lights, sound etc., it didn't have enough; security; running our own bar' (Grainger 2019a). Alvis remembers it was 'a massive undertaking for the small team' (Alvis 2019). The National supported the production by selling the show's tickets through their box office. The show was not a sell-out but ticket sales were good (around 60 to 65 per cent). Kym Bartlett argues, that, given it was new writing and in a 'hard-to-reach venue and fairly unknown, non-theatre-y area', the production 'did extremely well sales-wise' (K. Bartlett 2019).

The set, designed by Buether, was a recreation of the Windows on the World restaurant. At either end of the hall, the huge windows of the restaurant were reproduced; one with a view of Manhattan looking downtown, the other looking uptown. The audience sat in booths and at the tables in the restaurant with the action being played amongst them and around them. In addition, there was a round stage in the middle of the space and a gallery running along one of the long sides, its windows looking out over the playing space, echoing the windows of a floor of the World Trade Center. On entering the building, audience members had to pass through security checks: 'We had all these tables lined up, we had American TSA border police uniforms and as they came in they would be called up to a table and we would question them, as if they were entering the country' (Menzies 2019). After this the audience walked onto a balcony overlooking the playing space and then down a red-carpeted flight of stairs to their seats in the restaurant.

The critics' assessments of *Decade*'s faults and strengths were often in opposition to each other. The only matter on which they agreed was the show's length: 'half an hour too long'. On everything else there was disagreement. Some critics felt the show, because of its many authors, was only 'intermittently successful' (Billington 2011b): 'less than the sum of its parts' (Bassett 2011). Others, however, argued that a 'kaleidoscopic approach seems the only possible way of responding' (Spencer 2011) to 9/11 and that it was remarkably coherent: 'it's in danger of giving multi-authored multi-media theatre a good name' (McGinn 2011). Some thought the play added little to the conversation around 9/11: 'doesn't stump up anything hugely startling to say about it' (Szalwinska 2011). For others, the play's decision to circle the event rather than directly comment on it was highly effective: 'the most probing scenes are the most oblique' (Clapp 2011b). Neil Norman felt he had spotted a common theme in Headlong's choice of new plays: 'Headlong have nonetheless cornered the market in Disaster Theatre, with *Decade* now joining *Enron* and *Earthquakes in London* in their portfolio' (Norman 2011). For the company, *Decade* 'felt like a really rich creative time', 'a great engine room for meeting new creative voices' and, for Goold personally, 'the mature high point of Headlong, or my time at Headlong' (Goold 2018d).

When it came time to launch Headlong's next season, Goold struck upon the idea of making a video trailer. Grainger remembered it made complete sense at the time, as theatre marketing was beginning to move increasingly online: 'paper landing on someone's desk felt a bit redundant' (Grainger 2018). It took Headlong 'a while to find a building that would let us film' (Grainger 2019b) but they eventually secured a location in a derelict building on Southampton Row that had once been part of Central Saint Martins. The whole trailer was shot in a single day on a tiny budget. This involved a 'major pulling in of favours' (K. Bartlett 2019). Goold used a DoP recommended to him by Danny Cohen, the DoP he had worked with on *The Hollow Crown*. They used stage management they knew and could trust and called in actors who had worked with them on previous projects. They found someone happy to edit the video at cost.

The resulting video, entitled *Falling Headlong* (Goold 2012d), cryptically introduced the company's fourth season by following a group of figures, each of whom represented a different show, through an abandoned building. A man (Orion Lee) in a white shirt carrying two plastic bags represented Lucy Kirkwood's *Chimerica* directed by Lyndsey Turner (Headlong/Almeida 2013) about a photographer's search for the man who stood in front of a tank in the aftermath of the 1989 Tiananmen Square protests. A woman (Charlotte Randle) sitting amongst a room of balloons with soft toys tied underneath them watching a young boy playing with them stood for Mike Bartlett's adaptation of *Medea* (Headlong/Glasgow Citizens/Watford Palace Theatre 2012). Ella Hickson's *Boys*, directed by Robert Icke (Headlong/Hightide/Nuffield Southampton 2012), a play about a group of co-habiting university students, was represented by a binman carrying bin bags. A woman (Mariah Gale) holding a bottle of pills as the walls closed in around her stood for Lucy Prebble's *The Effect* (Headlong/NT 2012). Roberto Aguirre-Sacasa and Duncan Sheik's musical adaptation of Bret Easton Ellis's *American Psycho* (Headlong/Almeida 2013) was a suited man (Hywel John) cutting the word 'exit' into his arm with a knife. At the end of the trailer the name of each show was revealed above the figure associated with it. The video trailer sparked online debate within the UK theatre community about the future of season announcements. While Chris Unitt criticized the effectiveness of the trailer as a marketing tool (Unitt 2012), Jake Orr praised it as not just as 'a piece of marketing material' but as 'a piece of art in itself' (Orr 2012). The trailer received more than 2,260 views on YouTube in the first two days after its release (Alberge 2012).

Around this time, there was a sense of 'Headlong aspiring to be a state of mind rather than a company': 'in five years' time we'd want people like *The Economist* or the Tate to come to Headlong and go, I wonder what Headlong's take on this would be'. Within the company, there was an idea of Headlong as a verb as well as an adverb or adjective. There was a sense things could be 'headlonged': 'unashamedly provocative, enquiring, political in places, theatrical, noisy in all forms, a bit irreverent'. There were even vague discussions about monetizing by selling a Headlong state of mind to the business world: 'About corporates coming and going, "What is this for your business?"' Some aborted attempts were made at trying to find a radical Headlong voice for social media: 'Headlong energy on social media would have been great'. Being creative with social media was problematic, however, for as much as you 'curate and try and do interesting things with it, you have to keep churning out a degree of "this show's on" or "here's some offers"'. The company wanted something more 'pure', where 'you didn't have to do anything other than sell ideas'. At this point, I entered the frame, coming on board as an associate artist with an initial remit to develop a content-driven website that offered 'a curated, magazine-like way of thinking' and positioned the company as an idea factory, in which theatre was just one of many ways of generating ideas (Goold 2018c).

During late spring 2012, Goold co-directed a production of *The Lion, The Witch and The Wardrobe* (ThreeSixty) in a tent in Kensington Gardens, for which he had also provided the adaptation. He had done it for his children but partly for the 'wrong reasons': 'I thought it was going to be a big hit to be honest'. The practical set-up for the production was awful: 'the venue didn't work at all, it wasn't supported properly'. For Goold, 'despite beautiful designs and score, it was really not a great piece of work'. He was beginning to realize that he needed to be more discerning in his approach to taking on work: 'I'd done these bunch of shows I'd done for the wrong reasons. I think maybe I had been a bit over-anxious about trying to make a living and nine times out of ten that doesn't work, if you go in that way. So it was all a bit of a quagmire' (Goold 2018d).

The Effect[9]

Prebble's second commission for Headlong had originally been 'a play about the golden age of magic'. She had then changed direction and said she wanted to explore the idea of clinical drug trials, but 'she didn't really tell me what it was about at all. And just gave me a script' (Goold 2018d). The play tells the story of Connie (Billie Piper) and Tristan (Jonjo O'Neill), who meet as participants on a drug trial for a new anti-depressant. They fall in love but cannot be sure if they are really in love or if their feelings are just a chemical side effect of the drug being tested. At the same time, the play follows the story of the two doctors involved in administering the drug trial, Lorna (Anastasia Hille) and Toby (Tom Goodman-Hill). Toby thinks that depression is a chemical imbalance that can be cured with the right balance of chemicals. In contrast, Lorna, who suffers from depression and refuses to medicate, believes that depressed people 'actually have a more accurate view of the world, a more realistic view of ourselves and others' (Prebble 2012: 85). Although the play tackles issues related to big pharma, Goold found it a 'struggle to resolve' the 'pure romantic story and the more political big pharma story'. He 'gravitated more intuitively to the love story', which lies at the heart of the play and asks the question of whether love is something transcendent or simply the effect of a chemical reaction.

The Effect was programmed into the Cottesloe at the National. Buether's design for the show transformed the theatre into the residential research unit of a pharmaceutical company, with the audience sitting around the edges of the stage on clinical beige banquettes. Each audience member was issued with a medical-style wristband on entering the theatre, as if they were also being admitted to take part in the trial. There was a nod to Headlong with a fish tank, 'a reference to *Six Characters*', placed at one end of the stage (Goold 2018d). Prebble had written the play with specific actors in mind for some of the parts. Tristan and Connie were written with O'Neill and Piper in mind respectively. Prebble and Goold wove elements of O'Neill's skillset into the character to spectacular effect. O'Neill 'could tap dance' but had 'never used it in a show' (O'Neill 2019). Prebble inserted a moment into the script where Tristan does a trick to impress Connie, '*a tap dance*' (Prebble 2012: 52). In the production O'Neill performed 'an old

---
[9] For production images, see https://headlong.co.uk/productions/the-effect/explore/ (accessed 2 March 2020).

Hollywood tap dance': 'the lights came on in the whole room, and the tables I was tap-dancing on were mic'd underneath, and what became lo-fi little taps on the shoes became this whole musical number' (O'Neill 2019).

Goold approached the show with the aim of doing 'as pure and simple a directing job on it as possible'. His focus was on foregrounding the play and the acting. Goold tried to direct the show around 'physical rhythm'. Whenever they were stuck, he would try to find a physical rather than an intellectual solution to the problem: 'a specific bit of staging would solve something; sometimes quite kinetic, sometimes quite formal' (Goold 2018d). Goold's direction took a back seat, evidencing a move towards a quieter style. O'Neill noticed the change: 'It was very restrained theatrically, quite simple, more mature maybe' (O'Neill 2019). Reviewers also noticed it was an 'unusually subdued' production (Allfree 2012): 'Goold can be a bit of a flash harry as a director, but there is a beautiful tenderness and grace about this production' (Spencer 2012). The reviews were generally enthusiastic and focused mainly on the high quality of the cast's performances. Goold identifies Hille's performance as the research doctor Lorna as 'one of the best performances I'd ever had in a show'. As with West, he puts this partly down to the alchemy between the actor and the character: 'She's a brilliant, brilliant actor but I think the role kind of met her' (Goold 2018d).

The Effect was an important show for Goold. It 'wasn't as exuberantly fun as doing *Earthquakes* or even *ENRON* as a rehearsal process. And it wasn't as sort of intellectually complex and challenging or problem solving as *Decade*. But it was the purest, most tender thing I'd been part of'. Goold sensed he was coming to 'the end of something'. He remembers one specific revelatory moment during rehearsals:

> I remember doing one of the runs and, because we were in traverse staging, I remember looking across at Tom Goodman-Hill, who had been in *ENRON* and *Earthquakes*, doing his brain speech and looking at Jonjo [O'Neill] and Billie [Piper] and Lucy [Prebble] and Ben [Power] and Audrey [Sheffield, the assistant director] all watching. I had this very vivid sense that my life had become my work. That the rehearsal room had just melded with life [...] Billie was very famous at that point and had become a good friend. Jonjo, who I'd done all that work with back in Northampton. Ben, who I'd known for ten years but who was now working at the National. Lucy, who I'd had this very close relationship with over *ENRON*. And Audrey, who I'd known back since we were nineteen when she had been going out with my friend Sacha, and I remember thinking, 'Can you live in the theatre? Can the work become your life and your life become the work? Where are the boundaries?'

After *The Effect*, Goold started to think about leaving Headlong: 'It was partly that sort of thing you feel as an artistic director going, "Could this get stale?" And it was partly pragmatic. Touring was becoming harder and harder'. It was also partly a sense of having achieved what he could with the company (Goold 2018d).

By the time Goold departed from Headlong, the company had established a strong and clear identity: 'Everyone knows what a Headlong show looks like and feels like'

(Grainger 2018). Ironically, Finch argues, the 'most Headlong-y season' was the season that coincided with Goold leaving, which included *The Seagull*, directed by Blanche McIntyre (Headlong/Nuffield Southampton/Derby Theatre 2013), *Chimerica*, Icke and Duncan Macmillan's adaptation of *1984* (Headlong/Nottingham Playhouse 2013) and *American Psycho*: 'It was the finest expression of something we'd been trying to do' (Finch 2018). Summing up the work he did with Headlong, Goold notes the productions were 'wildly ambitious about the possibilities of what theatre could be'. This he puts down partly to the freedom of being a touring company. With no regular audience to satisfy, 'there was only a discussion with the artist and us'. They were able to place work with the venues they thought would provide the best audience for it: 'We'll find the right home for it. Just write the story and we'll either put it in a studio theatre or tour or whatever, maybe a different art form altogether' (Goold 2018a). For example, with *The English Game* 'you tour that to cricketing towns all over the country. With *ENRON* you go to the Royal Court' (Power 2018). Not being tied to a building meant being 'very lean on the overheads', so more of the company's subsidy could be spent on making work. The company also benefited from the more generous funding environment that existed before the Conservative government's austerity policies, which forced Arts Council England to make significant cuts and prompted the introduction of standstill funding in 2011. Before this era of austerity, they could subsidize their projects 'to an enormous extent which very few companies can do now' (Finch 2018). While his time at Headlong – characterized by artistic freedom and creative innovation – had been productive, Goold was ready for a new type of challenge.

CHAPTER 5
ALMEIDA: 2013–2017

In the autumn of 2011, Michael Boyd announced he would be stepping down as artistic director of the RSC. Goold was tipped by Michael Billington as one of the two most likely candidates to replace Boyd (Billington 2011c). Being artistic director of the RSC was Goold's 'wildest possible dream'. Even three years earlier, the idea he would actually be considered for the position would have seemed 'ludicrous'. Goold was given 'a lot of favourable steer on it'. He put in an application. The following day he withdrew it: 'I couldn't face doing that much classical work. I wanted to be doing new work'. Goold had directed five stage and two film Shakespeares over the previous five years. If he 'hadn't done all those Shakespeares', he thinks he would 'have leapt at it': 'It was always the pinnacle for me'. Then, in spring 2013, Nicholas Hytner announced he would be stepping down as artistic director of the National. Goold was approached but felt it 'wasn't my time' (Goold 2018d).

Late 2012 and early 2013 became one of those 'funny merry-go-round periods in [British] theatre', with many of the major artistic directors stepping down and being replaced. Goold was concerned that if he 'didn't go for one of them and stayed at Headlong for another round' he 'would never leave' and instead become permanently associated with one company, like Simon McBurney at Complicité or Declan Donnellan at Cheek by Jowl. This was partly a question of how much further he could push his work within the context of a mid-scale touring company: 'If I just stayed at Headlong, going up and down the touring circuit, could I re-invent it enough?' It was also partly a feeling that he 'was going to be left by everybody'. The director's path always seemed 'a longer and a slower one'. Many of the artists he had both worked with and developed had leapt ahead of him. Power had gone to the National. Prebble now had substantial interest from film and television (Goold 2018d).

Michael Attenborough then announced he was stepping down from the Almeida. Goold had enjoyed working at the theatre when he directed *The Last Days of Judas Iscariot*, and Headlong had two co-productions programmed there for 2013, *Chimerica* and *American Psycho*. In addition, it left his career prospects more open-ended. He was still only in his early forties: 'I remember thinking if I go to the RSC and do that for ten years, then I'm fifty and then what? Who does anything after those big jobs? They're just dead! I don't want my career to end that early' (Goold 2018d). When the job was offered to him, he took it. For Henny Finch, while Goold's decision to move on from Headlong was a shock, it was understandable: 'He wanted to stop touring and have his own space, and actually continue the Headlong project at the Almeida really, but with more resource and more decision-making power and not having to work in partnership on every project, which just takes so much time' (Finch 2018).

Goold spent most of 2013 directing the film *True Story* (Plan B/Regency Enterprises 2015). He was relieved to have the Almeida to come back to. He was at a difficult turning point in his career: 'I was really struggling in moving from being perceived as boyish or, God forbid, wunderkindy into a middle-aged maturing artist, but my art had never been very middle-aged or mature so what would that mean for me?' His experience on *The Effect* had changed how he felt about directing. Previously, Goold had always felt he was working on an equal footing with other artists when creating a production: 'The actors bring it and the writer brings it and the director brings it and we all make it collaboratively'. During *The Effect*, however, he had felt 'secondary': 'I remember feeling what I offer is so much less than what Lucy [Prebble] is bringing to this evening in terms of the writing. My job was to bear witness as sensitively and compassionately as possible and therein lay a new kind of satisfaction' (Goold 2018d).

When Goold arrived at the Almeida, he faced a completely different set of challenges to those he had faced at Headlong. By the time he started, he was feeling 'under-energized'. He was leaving Finch and Alvis behind at Headlong, Grainger having left in 2012 to take up a role at Told by an Idiot. There was a level on which Goold wanted to take Headlong to the Almeida with him, but he thought that would cause a 'revolt' (Goold 2018d). With Headlong co-producing two shows there in 2013, there was already some speculation within the industry the two organizations might merge. The current Almeida staff 'assumed I was just going to parachute Headlong into the Almeida and do a takeover, and they wouldn't have any ownership over it' (Goold 2019b). This was exacerbated by the success of the shows in Goold's final season for Headlong. They 'all ended up having commercial lives', which meant he was still at the company in spirit 'for a good length of time after he left' (Finch 2018). In the end, the only staff member Goold brought with him was Icke.

Goold's arrival at the Almeida was smoothed by the success of the season of shows Attenborough had programmed during the transition: 'We got off to an absolute flying start' (Goold 2019b). *Chimerica* and *American Psycho*, the two Headlong shows, were both big hits. The show in between them, *Ghosts*, directed by Richard Eyre (Almeida 2013) was also a resounding success. *Chimerica* and *Ghosts* both secured West End transfers and scooped eight Olivier awards between them. Goold brought in Denise Wood as an executive producer to help him. He had worked with Wood at the RSC: 'She was a huge supporter of the artist first and foremost and I felt like I was really needing that as well as her having great organizational experience' (Goold 2018d). The Almeida took time to get used to Goold's way of working, especially his tendency to programme late in the day. Under Attenborough, Icke thinks 'everything had been programmed well in advance': 'it was a steady operation that looked well ahead'. It took staff 'a couple of months to realize that Rupert wasn't going to do that' (Icke 2019b).

Icke argues Goold and he were clear as to where the organization was headed artistically when they arrived: 'We sort of lifted the Headlong philosophy and dropped it into Upper Street [the location of the Almeida], including some of the commissioned plays' (Icke 2019a). There was a gulf, however, between Headlong's philosophy and the character of the Almeida. Attenborough had 'done the most important thing any theatre needs which had been he'd kept an audience, and a big healthy audience' but that audience had got 'a little bit tweedy' (Goold 2019b). Like both its audience and its location in Islington, the theatre itself was perceived to be 'emblematically middle-class' (Lawson 2014). This raised questions about how to shift the public's perception of the theatre: 'Is that just the work you put on? Do you have to keep feeding them a bit of what they're used to so you don't have empty houses while you find your new audience? How do you bridge that gap?' (Icke 2019b). There was a question of whether gradual or immediate change was best. Do you 'go in soft or go in brave?' Do you 'try and keep some Attenborough or do you go, "This is the new sheriff in town"?' (Icke 2019a).

The biggest challenge Goold has faced as artistic director of the Almeida is financial. In 2011, the Arts Council cut the theatre's National Portfolio Organisation (NPO) funding by 39 per cent (Sharp 2011). Since then the organization has faced standstill funding. Austerity has also affected the wider economic climate, creating additional financial pressures: 'Costs of making shows are going up because inflation is going up'. Living costs are rising for both staff and artists. One of the impacts of this is a decrease in the diversity of artists, as those from economically deprived backgrounds find it 'harder and harder to get by'. Financial pressures put pressure on ticket prices and consequently also on the accessibility of theatre to a more diverse audience, who become increasingly excluded as ticket prices increase. This raises several challenges. Firstly, 'how do you make ticket prices stop creeping up and up?' Secondly, with regard to artists from economically deprived backgrounds, 'how do you make entry points into the industry?' Thirdly, with regard to accessibility, 'how do you make the work genuinely affordable?' In order to keep ticket prices down, the Almeida has become 'more and more reliant on what we raise privately, either from individuals or corporations'. Goold identifies the current economic situation as 'more problematic and damaging' than any he has faced to date (Goold 2019b).

American Psycho[1]

While in New York in 2008, Goold had met the singer-songwriter Duncan Sheik and the writer Steven Sater, whose musical version of Frank Wedekind's *Spring Awakening* was running on Broadway at the same time as *Macbeth*. Sheik loved *Macbeth* and approached Goold about the idea of a musical version of Bret Easton Ellis's novel *American Psycho*. They workshopped the idea together and Goold 'just loved' it (Goold 2018d). *American Psycho* tells the story of a young investment banker, Patrick Bateman (Matt Smith), living in Manhattan in the 1980s. Bateman is a controlling perfectionist, obsessed with his appearance and his designer lifestyle. After murdering a rival, he descends into a killing spree. Ellis links Bateman's violence to the inherent violence of capitalism, as Bateman's initial monologues about his morning routine, fashion and pop music give way to monologues describing his sexual encounters and then his murders in graphic detail.

---

[1] For production images, see https://almeida.co.uk/whats-on/american-pyscho/3-dec-2013-1-feb-2014 and https://headlong.co.uk/productions/american-psycho/explore/ (accessed 2 March 2020).

Figure 10 Left to right: Cassandra Compton as Jean, Ben Aldridge as Paul, Katie Brayben as Courtney, Matt Smith as Patrick, Susannah Fielding as Evelyn, Jonathan Bailey as Tim, Gillian Kirkpatrick as Patrick's Mother and Tom Kay as Sean in *American Psycho* (Almeida 2013). Photo: Manuel Harlan.

Bateman confesses his serial killings to colleagues, who fail to take him seriously, hearing his confessions to 'murders and executions' as 'mergers and acquisitions' (Ellis 2014: 197). By the end of the novel, it becomes unclear if Bateman's murders are real or just a figment of his troubled mind. Sheik's musical, a collaboration with Roberto Aguirre-Sacasa, who wrote the book for the musical, follows the narrative of Ellis's novel, interspersing it with original songs about consumerism, perfectionism and murder alongside rearrangements of classic Eighties pop songs including Phil Collins's 'In the Air Tonight' and Duran Duran's 'Hungry Like the Wolf'. A nightmarish ending is added for Bateman, in which he finds himself married to the long-time girlfriend he cares little for, Evelyn (Susannah Fielding). Goold argues *American Psycho* is 'strangely my most personal show in all its iterations'. Alongside his interest in the Marlovian anti-hero, Goold has also always had an interest in 'transgressive but depressive or marginalized figures'. While Goold did not identify with Bateman's 'violence and womanizing', he found himself 'emotionally' drawn to the character's 'deep loneliness' and his position as an 'isolated outsider' (Goold 2018d).

Es Devlin's design for the production was 'based on the top view of a Walkman' with two small revolves, one at either end of the stage, to facilitate the quick shifts in staging the show demands. The design was a reflection on capitalism, a 'consumerist sort of cathedral of things'. This element was inspired by both a visit to a Volkswagen factory, watching 'car parts coming through on conveyor belts' (Devlin 2019), and Michael Landy's performance installation *Break Down*, for which he constructed a 'production line' and then 'directed the cataloguing and destruction of all his possessions, right down to the last sock' (Cumming 2002). The revolves functioned as a production line endlessly delivering new things, ranging from furniture to 'beautifully wrapped Christmas gifts' to 'chopped-up lumps of body parts'. This reflected the structure of Ellis's writing, which will be 'chumbling along in the porn mode' when it switches to 'horror mode'. It catches you in 'this aroused state and then slams a chopped-up bit of meat in your face and says "wake up to that"' (Devlin 2019).

Part of the magic of the design was the fact that the Almeida has no backstage space directly around the stage itself. Watching the show, there is a sense of an impossible plethora of objects and people appearing from nowhere. In order to facilitate this, Devlin created a proscenium arch around the stage, allowing for a small amount of wing space on either side. To block the view of the wings from the auditorium, 'flapping slatted curtains' like those 'you would have on a conveyor belt at an airport' were added to the entrance and exit of the revolves (Devlin 2019). Fielding remembers it was 'frantic backstage': 'sometimes people didn't make it to the stage because they simply couldn't get to the entrance because there was so much set, so many people, so many costume changes'. At other times 'people would be knocked off the revolve by bits of furniture or the wrong costume would come around' (Fielding 2019).

The production had 'incredible energy' (Goold 2018d). Fielding remembers Goold was 'brilliant at evoking atmosphere': 'at the top of the show we were all standing in the audience in these macs looking all film noir and the lights would come up very slightly so the audience could see us, very slightly, and the cast sang an amazing a cappella harmony that kind of vibrated through the whole auditorium' (Fielding 2019). The audience loved the show: 'people turned up in costume all the time'. One man turned up with 'a fake machete and things hanging off his belt, and a trench coat' while 'his girlfriend had this dress covered in blood' (Seymour 2019). It also felt special in that it was a transitional production, being both Goold's last show for Headlong and his first show as artistic director of the Almeida. For Headlong, the show felt 'right on brand' (Alvis 2019). For the Almeida, the production was 'cool' at a point when Goold felt the theatre 'needed a bit of that' (Goold 2018d).

Critics recognized the production as a statement of new intent at the Almeida: 'a decisive move' (Clapp 2013). While critics noted the production was polished, 'wickedly slick' (Murphy 2013), some found its slickness difficult to fathom: 'is it "purposely mock superficial", as Bateman says of a painting he owns, or superficial superficial?' (Maxwell 2013). For some critics, the production's hollow sheen was just hollow: 'But as for the "why", I still don't know' (Murphy 2013). Others read it as a critique of the vacancy of the capitalist system: 'Some might find it vacuous and empty, but that is the point' (Cook 2013). Andrzej Lukowski concluded it was a critique both of capitalism and of the musical form itself: 'characters with no soul singing trashy, narcissistic pop songs about their empty inner lives – a mischievous contrast to the faux profundity most musicals peddle' (Lukowski 2013).

While there was confusion over what was at the heart of the production, critics were in little doubt a West End transfer was 'inevitable' (Spencer 2013), but the West End transfer never came to pass. When the show finally transferred to Broadway in 2016, it was a flop. Ben Brantley killed it off by deeming it 'neither scary nor sexy' (Brantley

2016). Devlin argues the show would have fared better in New York if it had started off-Broadway, 'somewhere gritty and dirty, and allowed people to enter its world and fall in love with it and beg it to come to Broadway'. For her, the straight-to-Broadway version lost something in its 'gleaming-ness' (Devlin 2019). For Goold, the Broadway show 'died far too young, because I could feel the audience loved it' (Goold 2018a).

After Goold's arrival, the Almeida was rebranded, with the word 'theatre' turned upside down in its new logo suggesting things were about to be turned on their head. Alongside *American Psycho*, Goold's first season at the Almeida featured a transfer of Robert Icke and Duncan Macmillan's *1984*, which had been 'critically successful in a way that nobody, including us, ever really saw coming'. Goold 'was very speedy about saying he wanted it for the Almeida once he set eyes on it in previews' (Icke 2019a). Next came Goold's production of Mike Bartlett's *King Charles III* (Almeida 2014). Then finally a second production directed by Icke, Anne Washburn's *Mr Burns* (Almeida 2014), which tells the story of how the narrative of the *Simpsons* 'Cape Feare' episode is slowly transformed into a religious text by survivors of an apocalyptic event living in a post-electric society. This show was hated by critics but a success with audiences: 'It emptied the theatre until it filled the theatre because it felt like something different and new' (Goold 2018d). In retrospect, Icke observes that Goold's first season looks like a clear statement of intent: 'Big crazy new plays: one brand new, English, a little bit counterculture; one American, very counterculture; two huge adaptations of major novels in formally unusual ways' (Icke 2019a). All four productions were formally inventive, cementing the idea things were changing and bringing a new, younger, edgier audience to the Almeida.

King Charles III[2]

Bartlett's *King Charles III* had originally been commissioned by Headlong but moved to the Almeida with Goold, along with a number of other projects, including Ella Hickson's *Oil* (Almeida 2016). The play is set in a near-future Britain, in which the Queen is dead and Prince Charles is finally able to ascend to the throne. Building on Charles's real-world reputation for meddling in politics, Bartlett imagines him abusing the royal prerogative and dissolving parliament when asked to sign a bill he disagrees with. The play is a modern Shakespearean history play written in iambic pentameter: 'like a Shakespeare play that wasn't off-putting for people' (M. Bartlett 2019). The modern language and familiar characters make the play accessible to a modern audience, while the Shakespearean form infuses it with a sense of grandeur. The actions of the royals echo those of some of Shakespeare's most well-known characters. Prince Harry, like a modern-day Prince Hal, mixes with commoners and considers revoking his royal privileges (as the real-life Harry would later choose to do six years after the show's premiere). Kate urges William to seize the crown like Lady Macbeth. Charles is haunted

---

[2] For production images, see https://almeida.co.uk/whats-on/king-charles-iii (accessed 2 March 2020).

Figure 11 Left to right: Richard Goulding, Tafline Steen, Nyasha Hatendi, Tom Robertson, Katie Brayben, Lydia Wilson, Miles Richardson, Nicholas Rowe, Margot Leicester, Tim Pigott-Smith and Adam James in *King Charles III* (Almeida 2014). Photo: Johan Persson.

like Hamlet by Diana's ghost, who like the witches in *Macbeth* issues direful prophecies. Eventually, like Richard II, Charles relinquishes the crown. When the play had its first reading, Goold remembers 'feeling the same thrill as when I read Ben's script of *Paradise Lost*, and going, "Wow, this is so alive, the verse is just singing"' (Goold 2018a).

Goold's approach to directing the play was a further development of the quieter approach he had taken with *The Effect*. Whereas *The Effect* retained a little of the Goold glitter in the form of projected brain scans and a scrolling ticker tape displaying dosage levels, *King Charles III* had nothing beyond masks and candles. Goold 'knew [he] wanted to do it with nothing and make it purely about the language and the words and that staging' (Goold 2019b). Seymour identities it as 'the quietest show we've done' (Seymour 2019). Goold initially considered three different versions: a 'Ruritanian' version set in an imaginary country; a 'Peter Brook' version; and a 'Shakespearean' version (Goold 2019b). Tom Scutt remembers the latter as 'doublet and hose', 'swords and floorboards', 'the Royal Shakespeare Company basically'. Scutt argued the design needed to be minimal to balance the nature of the play: 'The play was such an audacious statement, the way to deliver it was to do it modestly, to be reverential'. Goold and Scutt considered a Pina Bausch version: 'doing it barefoot', 'people in black suits and dresses'. Scutt also offered Goold 'a sleeping or a dead lion in a glass box altarpiece', symbolizing Elizabeth II (Scutt 2019).

In the end, Scutt gave Goold 'a very limited palette'. He created a 'cathedral-like space' in the Almeida. The bare back wall of the theatre was exposed, with a pseudo-medieval fresco running around it depicting the faces of the British people 'looking on the Royals [...] judging the events that were occurring', inspired by a fresco in the Chapter House of Westminster Abbey, the meeting place for the first incarnation of the House of Commons. Initially, Scutt thought about injecting modern elements into the fresco. Goold rejected the idea. By retaining the purity of the medieval fresco, Goold invoked a sense of history, 'a reference to the past and the present that makes it feel material'. Scutt discovered that 'the podiums that would be set out for a coronation and for when a member of the royal family is lying in state are identical'. This 'union between those ideas became the essential basis' for a bare, square, purple-carpeted podium centre stage, which formed the main playing space. The production opens with the entire cast entering holding candles while singing a requiem. This functioned as a 'ritual blessing of the room we were about to tell the story in'. Scutt argues that working in the Almeida has brought 'a real elemental kind of heft' present in Goold's work to the fore as the theatre's 'space offers that up to you' (Scutt 2019).

The production was enthusiastically reviewed the critics: 'royally entertaining' (Brown 2014); 'the most spectacular, gripping and wickedly entertaining piece of lèse-majesté that British theatre has ever seen' (Spencer 2014). Most noted the shift in Goold's directing style and approved of it: 'Goold's productions are invariably arresting. Yet here he has increased his reach, dropping his trademark video and whizzing pace' (Clapp 2014); 'Goold has refrained from going completely OTT for once' (Lukowski 2014). Goold, however, was bemused by the response: 'I always had done that, I always knew how to do that, but people were quite shocked'. It felt like, '"Now you finally graduated into being a director" or "Ah finally, he's learnt" kind of recognition' (Goold 2018d).

King Charles III was a big early success for Goold's Almeida, transferring to the West End, then to Broadway and Australia. Goold and Bartlett were also asked to make a television version for BBC2. Whereas Goold's film of *Macbeth* successfully retains the atmosphere of the original theatre production, *King Charles III* is an entirely different animal on screen. The transference to screen relocates the action of the story to naturalistic settings and is, in some sense, a realization of Goold's idea of a 'Ruritanian' staging in which the action plays out against the backdrop of an imaginary country, in this case a near-future Britain (Goold 2019b). In the theatre production, the contemporary story is framed within the context of a Shakespearean form. The tension lies between our recognition of the form and the surprise of its unexpectedly modern content. On screen, however, this is reversed. The Shakespearean verse is framed within the form of contemporary television drama, with its naturalistic presentation of both character and setting. This creates a tension between an audience's expectation of television drama's naturalistic form and the Shakespearean style of the dialogue. Though they tell the same story, the theatre and screen versions offer entirely different experiences for an audience.

The success of *King Charles III* confirmed that the work Goold was instigating at the Almeida was being noticed. Goold, however, was still trying to resolve the question of 'what did [he] want to do there?' Headlong had been 'dialectic with jazz hands' but the Almeida was still undefined. Unlike companies like the RSC and the Globe, or even Headlong, which has a touring agenda, the Almeida 'doesn't have a mission'. This, Goold argues, was 'a great liberator' because it meant that they were 'able to bring our own mission'. Goold was on the lookout for something that might give shape to what they were trying to achieve and evolve the theatre's narrative. He had a sense it might be something they could articulate through their work rather than through a mission statement: 'The repertoire and the programme can solve those problems and at the same time evolve what the thing is'. In spring 2011, Goold was invited take part in an Art Plus Drama event at the Whitechapel Gallery to raise money for its education and community projects. The event re-ignited his interest in the fine art scene. Thinking about the Almeida, he became interested in the model of the contemporary art gallery: 'Could you do the theatrical equivalent of the White Cube or the Whitechapel?' He concluded this would be 'a building that holds and curates a small number of artists in a very dedicated way, and those artists could be rather quite divergent'. This, he would argue, is what the Almeida now does 'to some extent'. There is a group of artists whose work is associated with the building: 'Anne Washburn or Sacha Wares or Robert [Icke] obviously, Rebecca Frecknall now, Ella [Hickson], Mike [Bartlett]'. While some of these artists are 'deeply political', he argues they are all linked by an interest in 'form as opposed to political interrogation' (Goold 2018d).

In trying to define the work the Almeida was looking to programme, Goold started to discuss the idea that a production needed to 'get through a number of sieves' in order to be included in a theatre's programme, with Icke and the Almeida's literary manager Jenny Worton: 'It might be the sieve of the text. It might be the sieve of the cast. It might be the sieve of the staging. It might be the sieve of the subject'. A theatre programmer would 'shake' the production to see if it can pass through the sieves: 'And if it's got through all of the sieves then you put it on'. While this is useful in making sure every aspect of a production is properly interrogated, in terms of programming it is not very 'galvanizing' (Goold 2018d). There was a need to identify exactly what the sieve that was defining programming at the Almeida was: 'If you put them into the sieve and a lot of them fell through, what was the sieve catching the things that the three of us felt like for whatever reason that's one we should do?' (Icke 2019b). Ultimately Goold came up with three guiding tenets. To be programmed, a production needed to 'put somebody new on the list, by which I mean bring an artist to the wider theatre ecology'. Alternatively, it could increase reach: 'genuinely get out of Islington. And that can be through broadcast. It could be through touring, going into schools and communities [...] It could be going to the West End, Broadway'. The final tenet was: 'Did I feel it was taking the conversation about form forward in an interesting way'? (Goold 2018d). The productions programmed through autumn 2014 and spring 2015 certainly engaged with the third tenet of form. These included: Alecky Blythe's recorded delivery account of the 2011 London riots, *Little Revolution*, directed by Joe Hill-Gibbins (Almeida 2014); a revival of David Cromer's minimalistic version of Thornton Wilder's *Our Town* (The Hypocrites 2008/Almeida 2014); a revival of Goold's Vegas *The Merchant of Venice*; Tobias Menzies in a site-specific production of Wallace Shawn's *The Fever* set in a hotel room, directed by Icke (Almeida 2015); the building of a house inside the Almeida's auditorium for an immersive production of Bartlett's *Game*, directed by Sacha Wares (Almeida 2015); and the intertwining monologues of Simon Stephens's *Carmen Disruption*, directed by Michael Longhurst (Almeida 2015).

Despite having defined some guiding tenets, Goold still felt the theatre needed something to galvanize its programming. He reflected on the work Boyd had done at the RSC, galvanizing the company through the Complete Works Festival (RSC 2006/7). *Decade* had been a 'great unifier' for Headlong, so Goold and Icke started to discuss what would be 'the big event' for the Almeida. Goold settled on the idea of Greek drama. A festival of Greek drama could act as a formal enquiry that would raise questions about the whole of drama; an 'attempt to reboot', to 'go back to the source' and really interrogate Aristotle and the *Poetics*. It was also a project that could generate other iterations: 'keep going and do a similar thing with Brecht or whatever, Ibsen. Form form form'. At first, Goold thought they could do every Greek play but he 'got nervous about selling that (Goold 2018d).' In the end they settled on three main shows: James Macdonald had an idea for a production of Euripides' *Bakkhai* (Almeida 2015) with Ben Whishaw attached; Icke was keen to do Aeschylus' *Oresteia* (Almeida 2015); and Goold knew he wanted to do Euripides' *Medea* with Kate Fleetwood (Almeida 2015).

Goold programmed a range of events around the main shows, including staged readings of Greek comedies, panel discussions, music events and one-off performances. Icke conceived the idea of including a durational reading of the *Iliad* (Almeida 2015). The plan was to split the *Iliad* up into manageable sections, each of which would be read by a different actor. The reading would be directed by Goold and Icke and live streamed so people could 'watch it for free online'. The British Museum came on board and offered themselves as a co-venue. In order to keep the readers on schedule, Icke and his team (Anthony Almeida, Daniel Raggett and Lucy Pattison) identified areas in the text that could be cut and put them in grey type, rather than black. If progress was running behind schedule, 'we would say "cut the grey" and automatically the actors would start to cut that text. And so you'd just gain a bit of time back'. Every hour, Icke would do a recap on the event's Twitter feed: 'this is where we are and this is what has happened' so online audiences dipping in and out of the live stream could catch up with the story (Icke 2019b). The event was a huge success, garnering an online and live audience of over fifty thousand ('The Making of the Iliad', 2015). Icke suggested they produce a sequel as the closing event for *The Greeks* season: 'I said we should do *The Odyssey* and we should make it an odyssey and we should travel' (Icke 2019b). *The Odyssey* (Almeida 2015) took place over multiple locations around London, including the Almeida, the London Eye, a red bus, a black cab, Islington Town Hall and on a boat on the Thames. The reading was again streamed and there were four locations on the day where a live audience could join to watch at specific times. These readings, Goold argues, were 'the highpoint of that season' (Goold 2018d).

Medea[3]

Initially Goold had a high concept for his *Medea*. Through re-engaging with the visual art world, he became interested in the question of 'is the artist visible in the work or not?'

---

[3] For production images, see https://almeida.co.uk/whats-on/medea/25-sep-2015-14-nov-2015 (accessed 2 March 2020).

Figure 12 Left to right: Georgina Lamb, Ruth Everett, Charlotte Randle, Sarah Belcher and Emily Mytton in *Medea*. Photo: Marc Brenner.

and so considered making 'a *Medea* about my own family with my own family'. While filming *True Story*, he had been away a lot and 'FaceTiming my kids'. He wondered whether there was 'a way of somehow FaceTiming my children every night in the show and doing something Pirandellian about being an artist married to a performer, but the performer destroying our children, but the artist being somehow separate'. In retrospect, it was a terrible idea: 'Thank God, I didn't make that show' (Goold 2018d).

At the time, Goold had been reading some of the writer Rachel Cusk's work and felt she had a 'really fascinating take' on contemporary feminism (Goold 2018d). He asked her to adapt *Medea*. Cusk's version of *Medea* contains echoes of Goold's initial idea but switches it around. Medea is the artist, a successful writer, and her husband Jason is the performer. The action of the story is relocated to an Islington-esque area of London. Abandonment is replaced with divorce: 'Greek tragedy by way of *Kramer vs. Kramer*' (Wolf 2015). The chorus is a host of yummy mummies, their verbal language peppered with the vocabulary of the urban upper-middle class: 'babycino' (Euripides 2015b: 10), 'Bollinger' (Euripides 2015b: 12). Unlike Medea, their priority is their family and their marriage, which they defend with hawk-like vigilance. When they first appear, wearing togas over skinny jeans, they carry their babies with them, brandishing them like status symbols. Scott Ambler created a choreographic language for the chorus drawing on everyday gestures within the parental routine: 'car keys jingling'; 'school run language' (Cork 2019). The chorus is hostile to Medea. Whereas the original Medea is an outsider because she is foreign, Cusk's Medea is foreign to these women because she prioritizes her work and struggles with motherhood. She is a woman attacked for not being womanly enough by women suffering from internalized misogyny. Critics noted the adaptation drew strongly on Cusk's personal experience of divorce, as outlined in her memoir *Aftermath* (2012). The production seemed as much an adaptation of Cusk's life as of *Medea*: 'a work that might easily have been called *Rachel*' (Lukowski 2015).

Cusk changed the ending of Medea's story so Medea did not actually kill her children, a decision Goold and the author were at 'loggerheads' about. Cusk felt that the representation of a woman killing her children on stage pandered to 'male voyeurism' as, in reality, most family annihilators are white men. She argued that 'women abandoning their children is much more common and much more of a taboo'. At the end of the play, instead of killing her children, Medea leaves them to pursue her career (a career which had been threatened by the single motherhood thrust upon her following her husband's infidelity). For Goold, however, this change was problematic as it removed the cathartic moment from the play: the 'visceral release of the murders' (Goold 2018d).

The final scenes of Goold's production blur Euripides' and Cusk's endings. They are played out against a barren icy wasteland, revealed as the back wall of the Almeida appeared to 'split open'. Medea and Jason are transformed from Islington-ites into primal warriors: 'very *Game of Thrones*' (Seymour 2019). Medea, bathed in red light, takes a spade and fills a grave with earth. This implies she has killed her children. Soon after, the audience learn she has abandoned them instead. Later still, the audience are told the children have tried to kill themselves by feeding each other with painkillers 'like fucking Smarties' (Euripides 2015b: 92), implying that rather than being physically murdered by their mother, these children have attempted self-murder as a result of the damage done to them by their parents. Critics felt 'short-changed' (Taylor 2015) by this 'closing muddle' (Cavendish 2015). While many praised the first section of the play for its effective relocation of Greek drama to a contemporary setting – 'Cusk lasers her way to the centre of Euripides' drama to come up with a coruscating 21st-century version' (Clapp 2015) – most found the ending unsatisfactory in its 'oblique and confusing' translation of Euripides' climax (Taylor 2015). Billington blamed this on the play's denial of 'cathartic satisfaction' (Billington 2015).

Richard III[4]

After the Greeks, Goold programmed revivals of two greats of naturalism, Ibsen's *Little Eyolf* directed by Eyre (Almeida 2015) followed by Icke directing Chekhov's *Uncle Vanya* (Almeida 2016). These were followed by a new Leo Butler play, *Boy*, staged on a conveyor belt by Wares (Almeida 2016). Next was Goold's first new Shakespeare in five years, *Richard III* (Almeida 2016). Goold, however, found himself struggling to find an idea for it. Goold had considered doing the play at Headlong and had previously developed a high-concept version 'about Boris Johnson with the Milibands as the princes in the tower'. Richard would

---

[4] For production images, see https://almeida.co.uk/whats-on/richard-iii/7-jun-2016-6-aug-2016 (accessed 2 March 2020).

be 'the Tory boy who can't be touched and he would refuse to die in a sort of Jarry-like way'. His ideal casting for Richard was Matt Lucas. At the same time, however, he was talking to Ralph Fiennes about playing Iago in *Othello* at the RSC. Suddenly Fiennes veered away from thinking about Iago and 'moved on to Richard'. Goold suggested the Boris idea and 'he said, "What do you mean, like a blond wig?" and I was like, "Well, maybe. . ." But then I looked across and saw like Voldemort, going, "What are you talking about, I'm playing Richard III"'. Goold backtracked: 'I thought of all the Richards I'd seen lately and I just thought, maybe we should try and make it really scary' (Goold 2018d). Instead of building the production around a concept, he decided he would build it around an actor. During rehearsals, Scott Handy, who played Clarence, noticed Goold was taking a different approach to Shakespeare than he usually did. Instead of coming in with a concept, 'he was building the vocabulary of the play in rehearsals as he went' (Handy 2019).

Despite having both Fiennes and Vanessa Redgrave on board, Goold was still concerned that he did not have an idea for the production. Then, in March 2013, a body that had been found under a Leicester car park was confirmed to be Richard III. This story sparked a connection for Goold between the idea of literal exhumation and the exhuming of a text: 'reviving the play, trying to bring it to life, to give flesh and blood to this old text'. The idea was actor-centred, in that it compared the act of recreating a Shakespearean historical character to the raising of the dead. The production would be like a 'summoning of presence, about the live-ness of the person in the room'. It raised the question of whether it was ever possible to channel the real menace the person embodied: 'Can you ever give it its true danger?' Goold knew the idea was thin, 'a gag to be honest, not really a concept even', but it gave him a way to frame the play (Goold 2018d).

Goold's production began with a pre-set. As the audience entered, an excavation was going on around a taped-off hole centre stage. Night lights shine into the hole as people in forensic white suits and masks carefully brush earth from bones and examine them. A skull is pulled out, followed by a crooked spine, which is held aloft and wondered at as the sound of a radio report heralding an extraordinary discovery is heard. Suddenly the living man, Richard III, is before us, hunchbacked in a fine blue suit. From the back, the knobby twists of Richard's spine are visible through his clothes, reminding the audience of the excavated spine. The action of the play was then played out over Richard's grave as if it had sprung from it. The characters were dressed in a mixture of medieval and modern dress, armour placed over suits. They wielded swords and mobile phones so reminding the audience of the slippage between history and myth, between the reality of the past and the story being told in the present. This mixture of the medieval and the modern was reflected in Adam Cork's score, which featured a Te Deum inspired by the music played at Richard III's coronation, 'full of medieval harmonies' but made 'more angular and modern' (Cork 2019). At the end of the play, Richard dies on the edge of the open grave, so bringing the action back to whence it sprung.

While some critics found the framing device of the exhumation 'compelling' (Taylor 2016), many found it 'marginal' (Letts 2016). Billington, like Goold himself, recognized its weaknesses: 'the references to Richard's disinterment, which bookend the evening, strike me as a red herring' (Billington 2016). Goold was praised, however, for his 'surprising restraint' (Cavendish 2016). The reviews focused on Fiennes's performance, his Richard III being seen as akin to a Voldemort Richard III, all menace and short on wit: 'He can dehumanize his gaze, chill with a reptilian smile. Vein-popping fury is a muscle-memory' (Cavendish 2016); 'a Richard III who provides not even a tiny shred of a reason to like him except for the fact you can't take your eyes off him' (Treneman 2016). For Billington, however, there was a lack of wit in Fiennes's characterization: 'he shows little delight in role-playing: he might, to all intents and purposes, be a grim-visaged banker systematically eradicating all obstacles between himself and the top job' (Billington 2016). Goold feels he let Fiennes down a little: 'I just don't think we ever quite got the gesture of what the character was'. Goold has a sense that there was something visual missing: 'I think you have to get the look, the crutches or whatever, you have to get some energy. And I couldn't quite crack it'. At the same time, he feels that he was caught between two approaches to the production, the old conceptual approach and the newer, quieter style. The production 'slightly fell between two stools of me trying to be a bit reverent to the text and not being bold enough' (Goold 2018a).

Ink[5]

The next year saw Goold directing two shows back to back, James Graham's *Ink* (Almeida 2017) and Mike Bartlett's *Albion* (Almeida 2017). The first was in the bells-and-whistles

Figure 13 The company of *Ink* (Almeida 2017). Photo: Marc Brenner.

---

[5] For production images, see https://almeida.co.uk/whats-on/ink/17-jun-2017-5-aug-2017 (accessed 2 March 2020).

style of old: 'more in the spirit of *ENRON*, incredible fun and energy'. The second was a more restrained affair and for Goold 'the emotionally richest' of all the shows he has directed at the Almeida (Goold 2018d). Between *Richard III* and *Ink*, Goold programmed two new plays, Hickson's *Oil* directed by Carrie Cracknell and Adam Brace's *They Drink It in the Congo* directed by Longhurst (Almeida 2016). These were followed by two adaptations directed by Icke, *Mary Stuart* (Almeida 2016) and *Hamlet* (Almeida 2017), and a revival of Martin Crimp's *The Treatment* directed by Lyndsey Turner (Almeida 2017).

Ink felt like 'a bit of a flashback to a Headlong' in that it was 'populist, great idea, lots of energy, vibrancy, big audience appeal'. Though Graham's play centred around a 'big idea', the relationship between the media and populism, it felt a little out of place in the Almeida's programme next to the 'very holy shows like *Oresteia* and *Vanya* that Rob [Icke] had done, and Sacha's [Wares] work' (Goold 2018d). *Ink* tells the story of the first year of *The Sun* newspaper and its battle to outsell its rival, the *Daily Mirror*. The play's set, designed by Bunny Christie, featured an 'Everest' of desks and overflowing filing cabinets. The action of the play offers a 'breezy' (Billington 2017) account of the birth of tabloid-style journalism, told through the theatrical equivalent of 'tabloid rather than the usual broadsheet principles' (McGinn 2017). *The Sun* is positioned as an underdog, and its trials and tribulations are told as a 'galloping good yarn' through a series of extended movement sequences (Williams 2017). Larry Lamb recruits his rag-bag team of journalists in pubs and saunas, getting each one to join in with a song and dance number to the strains of 'ba-da-ba' until he has a whole chorus line. In the end *The Sun* achieves its goal of outselling the *Mirror*, by winning a race to the bottom in terms of moral standards, suggesting the dubious consequences of cut-throat commercial competitiveness. Its inventive approach to spinning an attention-grabbing story is conveyed through another movement sequence in which the company act out some of the paper's most famous headlines – such as 'Man Kills Himself and Runs Away', 'Werewolf Seized in Southend' and 'Headless Man in Topless Bar'. The play cuts through this light-hearted approach, however, by portraying the human suffering behind *The Sun*'s sensational stories. For example, when the wife of proprietor Rupert Murdoch's deputy, Alick McKay, is kidnapped, the paper publishes extensively on the case, raising the question of 'did [McKay's] own newspaper reduce the chance of her being returned – alive?' (Graham 2017: 111)

The critics universally enjoyed the production: 'a rattling good evening' (Cavendish 2017). Goold's direction was identified as effectively injecting energy into the evening: 'pulses with energy, occasionally threatening to turn into a mischievous musical' (Hitchings 2017a); 'rattles along like a runaway train and the first half is a breathless, exciting and bumpy ride' (Norman 2017). He was praised for creating a production that both entertained and interrogated simultaneously: 'buoyed by his trademark appetite for asking awkward questions, it's a shrewd and absorbing look at journalistic ethics' (Hitchings 2017a). The show was 'a big hit, transferring first to the West End and then to Broadway' (Goold 2018d). Seymour remembers they also had 'good feedback from people who actually worked in newspapers', who 'said it was really accurate'. Though the show 'had a sort of cartoony element to it and it was a bit heightened, it did actually capture what the world was like at that time' (Seymour 2019).

Albion[6]

Albion, Goold's next show, was created and programmed relatively quickly. The idea for the play was born while Bartlett and Goold were working together on editing the television version of *King Charles III*. Bartlett had been thinking about writing 'the Chekhovian sort of pastoral play from the end of *Earthquakes* mixed with the garden being a metaphor for Britain and Brexit'. The play also has its roots in an image from Act Three, Scene Six of *King Charles III*, in which Charles 'talks about an Albion oak [...] an image of a tree growing that represents Britain'. Bartlett 'said to Rupert [Goold], "I think I can write this play, but it feels like it needs to go on quickly," and Goold said, "Well if you can get it to me by March, there's a slot in September"'. Bartlett, however, struggled to start writing: 'I didn't know if it was an Ayckbourn comedy or a Chekhov play'. A

Figure 14 The company of *Albion* (Almeida 2017). Photo: Marc Brenner.

---

[6] For production images, see https://almeida.co.uk/whats-on/albion/10-oct-2017-24-nov-2017 (accessed 2 March 2020).

quick consultation with Goold soon cleared the block: 'He just was like, "Chekhov, do it Chekhov". And I sort of took that instruction and started writing the next day with that sort of confidence' (M. Bartlett 2019). At the same time, Goold held his nerve and kept the slot open 'literally to the last day until he delivered' (Goold 2018a).

Albion tells the story of Audrey (Victoria Hamilton), who after the death of her son, James (Wil Coban), moves her husband and daughter out of London so she can renovate a historic garden that had once been owned by her uncle. They are regularly visited by James's ex-partner Anna (Vinette Robinson). Audrey's business starts to fail as she spends more and more time on the garden. She is eventually forced to sell up and return to London but changes her mind at the last minute, financially ruining her family but keeping her precious garden. Bartlett asked Victoria Hamilton to play the role of Audrey. The two had first met in 2012, when Hamilton played the role of Sandra in Paines Plough's production of *Love, Love, Love* at the Royal Court. It's a creative relationship Hamilton values highly: 'It is rare to find a writer you so admire and to have so many happy collaborations with them'. Before rehearsals with Goold, she spoke to a couple of actors she knew who had worked with him: 'They said he's a visionary, he always has an extraordinary concept for the play, it will look amazing. So I thought that's what I was about to meet'. What she discovered was 'they hadn't told me just how great he was in the room one to one'. She also found he had 'an ability to articulate the writing in a way that is incredibly rare'. One of the few directors who could 'articulate things to me about a character or a way to play a scene or an approach to an emotional note that genuinely hadn't occurred to me' (Hamilton 2019).

The set, designed by Miriam Buether, was an oval garden with flower beds around the edges and a lawn in the middle. For the first and fourth acts, set in the winter, the beds were bare except for a few weeds. For the second and third act, set during the summer, the beds were full of flowers, which the cast came on and planted at the end of the first act and then removed at the end of the third. At the upstage end of the lawn was a large oak tree with a semi-circular bench around its base. On a base level, the play is a metaphor for Brexit: 'A garden is a good parallel for Britain. Walls, shut the walls, shut it down, recreate something from the past' (M. Bartlett 2019). Audrey's desire to recreate a golden past reflects Brexiteers' longing for an idea of an England that was somehow better in the past. Audrey's dislike of locals entering her garden is a clear parallel for their anti-immigration stance. Audrey is presented as someone trapped in a nostalgia for the past. She describes her uncle's world as one of gentility and grace: 'the music playing, the clatter of cutlery, and then after they would retreat to their private conversations, in halls, in drawing rooms or out on summer nights, down through the private rooms of the garden to the bathing pond or the infinity walk'. This is a past she feels is rightfully hers and has been taken from her: 'I thought when I grew up that would be the world I'd inherit, but then it was the eighties, and it was all . . . destroyed' (M. Bartlett 2017: 37).

While Bartlett acknowledges the play's Brexit parallels are 'academically clever', in practice they are not great material for actually writing a play, as there needs to be 'an emotive factor' (M. Bartlett 2019). In *Albion*, this emotive factor is Audrey's grief for her dead son. On this level, *Albion* becomes a play about grief. Hamilton remembers 'the running theme of the character I played was grief for a son that she'd lost, and essentially everything she was trying to do was to cope with her grief and also push it away all the time' (Hamilton 2019). This exploration of personal grief then reactivates the Brexit metaphor, traced through Audrey's attempt to reconstruct the garden: 'Why are we so keen potentially to construct or reconstruct an imaginary idea of a country that has either gone or never existed. And it feels like you do that when you're grieving something that has been lost. When you're missing something. When your identity has been shattered, because the world has changed, and you can't recover it'. The emotional heart of the play drives its thematic brain. The grief for a lost son is paralleled with the grief for a lost notion of a country, 'a sort of national sense of identity crisis' but ultimately the garden cannot be resurrected any more than a dead loved one can be (M. Bartlett 2019). The final image of Bartlett's play is that of total destruction: '*The ground is returned to the soil. The house is destroyed*'. The final image of Goold's production, however, was more hopeful. The house is not destroyed. Instead Audrey stands cradling the single rose from which she hopes to bring the garden back to life: 'I will fix it all piece by piece, inch by inch of this garden' (M. Bartlett 2017: 122–3).

Albion received a generally enthusiastic response: 'a work of deeply absorbing emotional richness and symphonic density' (Taylor 2017). A few critics had small niggles with the play itself: 'Some of the allusions to the turbulent process of Brexit feel effortful, and several characters' actions strain credibility' (Hitchings 2017b). There was some criticism of Goold's staging of the end of Act Two in which Anna, dancing ecstatically in the rain, rubbed 'earth – and possibly cremated ashes – into her groin'. Some critics saw this as 'absurdity' (Clapp 2017), others as 'melodramatic excess' (Wolf 2017). In general, however, Goold was again praised for the subtlety and sensitivity of his direction: 'Goold's fluently orchestrated production controls the tragicomic mood with a masterly touch' (Taylor 2017).

During Goold's early years at the Almeida, he worked to redefine the public perception of the building through programming a range of formally inventive work, alongside re-imaginings of classic plays. The latter were predominantly directed by Icke. Jonathan Church argues Goold was largely successful in this endeavour: 'The transformation of the perception of that building through the work that he was doing was incredible' (Church 2018). Though Goold's remit underlying his programme is perhaps less focused than at Headlong, as an artist working within the building, Cracknell claims there is a clear sense of a narrative: 'You definitely feel like you're inside a thing. You're in the pan cooking something and it has a sort of bigger, wider importance because of the story that they're trying to make there' (Cracknell 2019). Alongside this, Goold's move to the Almeida was accompanied by a shift in his directing style, a transition which has its seeds in Goold's earlier work on *The Effect*. Scutt believes this shift is located in a combination of Goold's sense of theatre as 'holy' or as 'a ritual' and the architecture of the theatre itself: 'there's something about the space of the Almeida that I think really conjures those feelings' (Scutt 2019). While, at times, critics have seemed surprised by the shift in Goold's style, Handy argues Goold's quieter mode is 'just as much him' as his flashier mode. Critics, he theorizes, are only shocked because they 'haven't seen as much of that work' but he predicts 'they will see more of it in future' (Handy 2019).

PART II
APPROACHES TO PRACTICE

CHAPTER 6
DIRECTING

Goold identifies two different approaches to directing that have dominated at different points in his career. The first approach dominated his early work. When he started out, he felt his 'job was to have a concept or conceptually imagine something' (Goold 2019b). While at school, Goold read Jonathan Miller's book *Subsequent Performances*, in which Miller compares classical plays to damaged classical Greek sculptures, such as the Belvedere Torso. Miller argues it is impossible to authentically restore such a statue (for example, by adding arms that have been lost over the centuries): 'Far from being restored to its original state, the object has merely provided an armature on to which the modern craftsman has imposed his own ideas' (Miller 1986: 28). Therefore, Miller argues classical plays are provocations for a director's creativity rather than historical objects in need of restoration. This 'no longer reduces the director to the role of a failing archaeologist but offers actor and director alike the possibility of re-making a work of art that is essentially emergent' (Miller 1986: 75). For Goold, Miller's approach, which encouraged imbuing classical plays 'with real individual artistic sensibility', felt like 'an invitation to create' (Goold 2019a).

An example of this approach is Goold's Greenwich *Romeo and Juliet*. This production revolved around the concept of 'I'm going to invert the balcony' (Goold 2019b). Goold was fascinated with the relationship between the gallery in the original Globe and the groundlings: 'Romeo looking up to the balcony was near the groundlings, but the balcony recessed Juliet away'. In proscenium theatres, the scene is usually played side on 'so that Juliet [is] usually played on the proscenium and Romeo downstage. So Romeo [is] the central enquirer'. So Goold 'had this idea of, "What if he comes over a wall?" So he's in the middle looking down in the proscenium, which in a thrust theatre would be a great image'. Goold relocated the scene to a 'walled garden'. Romeo 'broke over the top, and then they have their scene, and then he's got to climb back over again'. In practice, however, the idea did not work: 'It was a clever idea but ultimately it never gave an obstacle' (Goold 2019a). Looking back on his earlier 'high concept' productions, Goold sees them as betraying a desire to make his work as a director visible: 'I felt that people wanted to see the directing at some level' (Goold 2019a).

Goold describes the second approach which has guided his work – the approach that came to dominate in his later career – as 'much more intuitive'. He finds this approach difficult to define. It has 'to do with space and the design, and how something feels'. Often he first becomes interested in directing a play 'because it speaks to me personally at some level rather than because of either what I can do with it or its politics'. It then takes time for a clear sense of how a production might work to develop: 'I'll sort of sniff around it a bit and go, "Oh I could see how this would work tonally at some level"'. Normally, it starts from 'a central image'. For example, 'a gathering around a fire' for *Shipwreck* (Almeida 2019). For *ENRON*, it was 'a bunch of dweeby-looking accountants conquering the world through dancing' (Goold 2019b).

A collaborative relationship between the director and the designer is vital to enable this more intuitive approach: 'It's very much working with the designer [...] beforehand although the design was absolutely a central point of it [...] I tended to probably instigate the ideas'. Goold considers several different versions of a production before settling on an approach. While one version will eventually dominate, ghosts of the imagined versions continue to live on in the production alongside it; 'those images normally will end up in the show at some level' (Goold 2019b). Tom Scutt observes that Goold usually offers him a range of 'paths we can go down'. They then 'glean from different pathways', drawing ideas from each one, aiming to deliver something in which 'the thinking of all those different strands' is visible. As they consider the overall journey of the play, they move between the different strands: 'you go on [one] journey and then at any stop on that journey you can then cross-reference and you find that you are changing lanes and referencing another one of the pathways that are in your mind' (Scutt 2019).

Goold brings his designers 'a little bag of images' as a starting point. Discussion is also an important part of the process: 'so much happens in the conversation [...] lots of talking really helps. I'll tend to free associate quite a lot with the designer' (Goold 2019b). Laura Hopkins describes her design process with him as characterized by 'dialogues in the form of both words and images going back and forth' (Hopkins 2019). Scutt notes that Goold is interested in designers who are prepared to delve deep into ideas: 'he's not really interested in a designer that's going to just offer visuals [...] It's about thorough and rigorous collaborative investigation of whatever the source material is' (Scutt 2019). Es Devlin observes that Goold puts a lot of faith in the creativity and skill of his collaborators: 'Each note is given in the spirit of, "Well, I know you'll want to do this work anyway. I know I can trust you and your art and your craft and your spirit of perfection"'. This, she argues, is 'rarer than you might think' (Devlin 2019).

A successful design, Goold argues, will not necessarily be a design that appears to directly facilitate the play in question. Miriam Buether, for example, will sometimes 'design something because she thinks it's an interesting space rather than because it's got anything to do with the play'. While this is not generally accepted practice – 'in design school they tell you that's terrible' – Goold argues that 'it can be very liberating' (Goold 2019b). Devlin argues that a set design can be a provocation for a director. For example, the small, timbered Wendy-house structure she created for *The Hunt* is in many ways 'a great big obstacle to performing a play'. Devlin recognizes this as a general approach to design in Goold's work. He knows what the 'installation' of the design is, how it functions aesthetically. The question that then needs to be grappled with in rehearsals is 'how can I make it a functioning machine for delivering the scenes?' This creates a productive tension between 'how the scenes are written and what the environment allows'. The set becomes 'a protagonist. It's another performer that you've got to cajole into being' (Devlin 2019).

Goold's productions almost always feature music and movement sequences as prominent elements. With both composers and choreographers, there tends to be less conversation than with designers. Goold's process will involve 'a lot of references rather than discussions'. He spends time 'on the internet looking for interesting composers or pieces of music or choreographic ideas'. Goold likes to work on choreography before rehearsals start. He will run choreographic workshops for a 'couple of days or even just an afternoon, even if it's only like three dancers and a choreographer a couple of weeks before I start rehearsals just to throw ideas around'. With choreography, he argues it is better 'on the whole to know what you're doing before you start with a full company'. While 'you can devise choreography' it does help 'if you've done a lot of that imaginative work beforehand' (Goold 2019b).

With composers, Goold is more hands-off. Adam Cork argues that the role of the theatrical score is to trace 'the part of the story you don't put into words. It's the narrative corners that you turn, and the states of mind and the moods that you want to either impose or encourage or bring out' (Cork 2019). When discussing a score, Goold will often 'give reference points as you would in a movie' (Goold 2019b). Goold's directions can range from the general to the very specific: 'sometimes he'll say something very specific about what he would like, and sometimes he'll say something just as vague as, "Oh I'd like some singing here"'. Often a stimulus for a specific moment will form the basis from which the whole show's sound palette is developed. A single cue can become 'a wellspring for everything else'. For Satan's fall from Heaven through the cosmos in *Paradise Lost*, Goold asked for 'a sense of the M.C. Escher drawings, where people [...] continue to walk up or down even though they are also walking in a circle'. The stimulus offered a 'formal idea', a challenge 'to try and translate something which exists in one medium in a really neat way and make it work in another'. Cork created a three-minute cue in which 'melodically we were pointing up all the time, but then with every new step the bassline would sink down another tone, another semitone'. The music produced a 'sense of striving and moving upward', even though it was actually 'going down [until] eventually you reach the bottom'. This cue then 'gave me a palette for the rest of the show'. For *ENRON*, Cork's central cue was 'The Commodities Chorus': 'the traders would come out and sing the story of what's happening to all the different commodities in the marketplace'. For this chorus he created a fugue 'with four different sections of the cast singing the same words at different intervals from each other'. Their vocal lines moved like 'a graph of stocks and shares [...] going all the way up and down as they sang'. In *Six Characters in Search of an Author*, the central cue was derived from a stage direction asking the Stepdaughter to sing '*a wailing, operatic lament*' (Pirandello 2008: 58). Cork translated this into 'a strange opera [...] jerky and puppet-like [...] based on going, "ha, ha, ha, ha" in an odd series of chords' (Cork 2019).

Goold often chooses to direct plays that have complex ideas at their heart. Despite this, he is suspicious of research. He used to do 'an enormous amount of research'. When working on a revival, this would include immersing himself 'in literature and culture from that period' and 'production histories'. Now, he is more cautious. He argues immersing yourself in research can blind you to the needs of your audience, so your production ends up 'in dialogue with [your] research, rather than with the room'. Any research 'that isn't legible to an audience can only have so much utility'. Goold aims for the complex ideas in his productions to be accessible. He uses pop culture as a conduit through which to communicate them, as pop culture 'is designed to be deeply accessible and so often when you're wrestling with deeply complicated things, pop culture references are helpful' (Goold 2019b). For example, the use of a Las Vegas casino in *The Merchant of Venice* to convey the precarious nature of merchants' investments in early capitalism or Lucy Prebble's use of the raptors in *ENRON* to convey the way shell companies operate. Goold uses physical representations to make complex ideas more accessible to his audience. Tobias Menzies observes that Goold is 'resistant to a talking head. He always looks for what is the theatrical gesture that can really open it up'. This was evident in the way Goold staged a long speech in *Arcadia* that Menzies's character, Valentine, gives about chaos theory. Goold 'wanted to find a way of physically demonstrating' the ideas and so had Menzies mark off their development in the speech using physical gestures, 'almost on a graph in 3D [...] physically articulating what I was saying. He wanted pictures that were in the theatre, in the space, that weren't just the words' (Menzies 2019).

Ultimately, Goold argues, directing is a balance between spontaneity and pragmatism: 'You've always got to really understand how your design and your aesthetic is going to work, whilst also being open to what might come out of the rehearsal room' (Goold 2019b). Cork describes this approach as a form of purposeful doubt: 'He allows himself not to always be sure about where he's heading with it, but trusts his instincts, knowing that it's heading somewhere' (Cork 2019). Deputy stage manager Lorna Seymour describes Goold's process as 'sketching in ideas and then trying another idea, just throwing things at it' (Seymour 2019). Goold extends this space to experiment to his collaborators. He is 'very happy for everyone's contributions to be in the room and to be messy'. There is permission to 'imagine things to the limit before you then rein it in and neaten it up and turn it into the final shape' (Cork 2019). This can involve 'things changing at the last minute', so Goold's collaborators need to have the capacity to 'go along with the flow of ideas and be open to it'. Enabling spontaneity in the rehearsal room means creating systems to support it. For example, Seymour has had to develop a way to practically accommodate the numerous changes that might occur to the structure of a show in the prompt book: 'There's a lot of physical cutting and pasting, sticking a whole bit of text on top or sticking a bit that comes out the bottom like a page extension with a new bit on or something like that' (Seymour 2019).

While it's useful to keep things creatively open, there are practical considerations that need to be taken into account. For Goold, a vital part of a director's skillset is about knowing how to balance the practical and the creative. A director needs to know when to make definitive choices about the practical elements of putting a production together, 'like when you build the set'. There is a delicate balance to be struck between

> managing your production manager's need to get decisions whilst also going, 'I don't know. I feel like the next time we rehearse something else might come out of this and [...] maybe all the ribbons are going to turn into birds or something, so don't start making the ribbons but can we make sure we might be able to make some birds if we needed them?'

Directing

If a directorial decision is made too late, there is a danger it will not be possible to physically achieve it within the time left. If decisions are made too soon, however, the production can lose its vitality: 'you have that rather stale thing of just building something from a design kit rather than generating it in the room' (Goold 2019b).

This need to manage a balance between spontaneity and practical demands is reflected in Goold's oscillation between doubt and certainty in his directing practice, which he sees as 'twin friends and twin enemies'. Being too doubtful makes you reluctant to make firm decisions. Being too certain, however, is also problematic as it locks the collaborators who are with you in the rehearsal room out of the creative process: 'There are some directors who are completely certain about everything and they make their choices, and good for them. But I think that really denies other creativity'. Over the years, Goold's modus operandi has developed in order to allow for doubt but to account for the practical need for certainty beyond a particular point in the production process: 'to keep everything possible as late as possible, but have a very, very strong grip and understanding of when the decision points have to be' (Goold 2019b).

Working with Actors

Goold argues that 'the thing that unites the really good [directors] is how genuinely interested they are in people'. The best directors are able to gain the confidence of their performers, 'like horse whisperers'. Despite this, Goold does not go in for social niceties during rehearsals: 'I don't do very much, "How was your weekend?" or even anecdotes in relation to the work' (Goold 2019b). Neither does he spend time on rehearsal room games. His rehearsal room, Victoria Hamilton observes, is 'very much about the work' (Hamilton 2019). Scott Handy ascribes this to Goold's heavy workload: 'He's so busy [...] he's got to go with his gut' so 'he doesn't waste time telling anecdotes' (Handy 2019). As an artistic director, Goold has 'meetings before rehearsals and on lunch breaks and afterwards and on tea breaks'. Time needs to be used effectively: 'You go, "I'd love to spend twenty minutes playing keepy-uppy, but I really should be at the finance committee meeting, so let's take this moment to stage the play"' (Goold 2019b).

Instead of creating company unity through social chit-chat or theatre games, Goold sets the company a physical task related to the show, a collective endeavour that is 'challenging but perfectible and clearly demanding of a skill set'. This often involves 'singing or a dance sequence'. This activity supports company bonding, demonstrates faith in the actors' abilities and gets them out of their heads: 'It says there's something that is difficult we expect you to get good at and be excellent at. That unifies them as a company and gets them into their body'. Many of the movement or choral sequences in Goold's shows derive from this process rather than necessarily being a vital part of the finished production: 'Many sequences in my shows were put in because of a belief that that was a necessary process. And I think in a couple of shows they probably would have been better left out'. Other tasks have focused on recreating the given circumstances of the production. He ran a rehearsal at night for *The Weir* in which the actors told their

103

ghost stories by candlelight and 'drank for real what they drank in the show'. His Arctic version of *The Tempest* was rehearsed in the middle of a heatwave, so he held a rehearsal in the walk-in freezer of a supermarket so the actors could explore 'the physicality of cold in the body'. Ultimately, these tasks bond the company through a shared mythology: 'It's a job of any production to create its own mythology at some level'. Goold aims to create a shared sense of 'piracy or rebellion' in his companies: 'you want your companies to feel like they are transgressive and almost like they're organizing a heist' (Goold 2019a).

Actors who have worked with Goold often observe that he is 'not a praiser in the room' (Hamilton 2019). He 'doesn't tend to say "well done" very often' (Handy 2019). This lack of flattery, they argue, is compensated for by the high value Goold places on actors' contributions to the creative process. For Susannah Fielding, Goold is a director who 'values your intelligence as an actor'. She argues that this bolsters confidence in a more substantial way than mere praise can: 'You gain confidence from him bothering to ask you what you mean by that and talk to you about it and come back to you and have that discussion'. Goold's lack of praise, however, makes him a 'tough parent' (Fielding 2019). This can be hard for some actors, 'who get worried or think he doesn't like what they've done'. Goold's casts, however, usually include a few actors like Handy, who work with him on a regular basis and so can provide support: 'Just make sure everyone understands how he works and that if he hasn't mentioned something it's not because he's not happy with it. Or if he's not spending a lot of time socializing with people, that doesn't mean that he is not with us' (Handy 2019).

Regardless of whether you are working on a new play or a revival, Goold argues that it is important actors feel that 'at some level they are participating in the writing' of the piece: 'their creativity is being seen as well as their performance' (Goold 2019b). Fielding notes Goold is 'willing to take ideas from actors; he doesn't see that as a weakness' (Fielding 2019). Jonjo O'Neill remembers being surprised by this when he first met Goold: 'He asked me what I thought. I was a very young actor at this point, and people didn't ask me what I thought, they told me what to do'. Whereas some directors 'want you to be happy about being in their picture', O'Neill argues Goold 'gives you the keys' (O'Neill 2019). Menzies notes Goold 'doesn't shut things down too quickly': 'Even if it's not quite clear where it might lead [...] He allows a lot of space for people to work it out, crash about a bit' (Menzies 2019). Cork observes that this approach applies to the whole company as well as the actors. Goold 'gives everyone their head, from actors to creative team members to stage management, and accepts all ideas into the room' (Cork 2019). Handy sees Goold's ability to allow actors and other creatives space to contribute as rooted in his intellectual confidence. He has 'incredibly strong ideas' that 'deliver radical propositions', which enable him to 'give a lot of practical space for me as an actor to try and join the dots' (Handy 2019). O'Neill notes, however, that Goold's offer of creative freedom is not unlimited: 'There's always a moment in the process where a director comes in and goes, "Here is the one I am selecting" and you're like, "Oh, where is the freedom? Where has it gone?"' But some directors 'turn up on day one like that. And it means they haven't seen the offers before they get to trim, to edit, to encourage'. Goold, in contrast, allows space to see what the actor can bring to the table first (O'Neill 2019).

Goold believes creating an environment in which actors can genuinely contribute to the creative process is more about 'how you run your room and less about some methodology [...] like "we're going to do this exercise or this improvisation"'. The rehearsal room is 'by nature hierarchical' with the director in charge, 'setting up the rules', but because the director sits at the top of the hierarchy 'instigating the game', they can shift the nature of the creative relationships within that space (Goold 2019b). In order to contribute creatively and confidently, Goold believes that an actor needs to feel uninhibited. When an actor is feeling inhibited, Goold argues the director's job is to enable them to 'release the inhibitor and let them show you what you might do'. Goold puts an emphasis on the actor's discoveries guiding the director's creative choices: Let them show you what *you* might do, not let them show you what *they* might do. It is 'a different thing to telling them what you think that might be' (Goold 2019b). It's about seeing what a particular actor brings and drawing inspiration from that. Fielding observes that Goold makes 'the most of what comes organically'. The final moment of Goold's production of *The Merchant of Venice*, with 'Portia dancing on the spot almost like a ballerina in a music box but with one shoe off', happened 'by accident'. One day during rehearsals, she 'didn't manage to get both shoes on, and so we kept it' (Fielding 2019). O'Neill remembers casually playing with some grapes during the tech for *Faustus*. He threw one 'as high as I could into the gods, as it were, above the stage and caught it in my mouth, and [Goold] said keep it in because he liked it. He's like, "the audience want that". They want to see something that's abnormal, something extraordinary, something that maybe they can't do, something that they wish they can do' (O'Neill 2019).

Goold argues the traditional position of the director, behind a desk with the text spread out before them, is 'very sedentary' and can prevent you from seeing clearly: 'The more clutter you have as a director (notes, research, script, bags, rehearsal ideas) the less you see what's happening in front of you'. Instead, Goold tries to direct on his feet, which allows him to be more present in the room: 'Your energy is better when you're up but also you're in the space more which can be helpful'. He avoids constantly referring to the script: 'I prefer watching and listening and seeing if that makes sense to me'. When something is not working, his practice is to examine what is happening on the floor of the rehearsal room first: 'I'll just ask the actors to keep repeating it until I hear the thing that I think is wrong' (Goold 2019b).

Goold is not, as he is sometimes reputed to be, a director who likes to ride roughshod over the text: 'I do do very detailed text work, in fact in terms of my "training" it's probably what I'm strongest at but it's as much for the writer or for me as for the actor'. He 'used to be quite thorough in uniting everything' but now his approach varies depending on the production and the nature of its rehearsal process. When analysing the text with actors, Goold employs three 'bog standard' terms: 'targets, objectives, actions'. He has his own nuanced understandings of them: 'I feel I know what I mean by those and I try and share that with [the company]' (Goold 2019b). The term 'target', in Declan Donnellan's original definition of it, is the object towards which the actor's action is focused: 'all "doing" has to be done *to* something'. The target is the something and 'can be real or imaginary, concrete or abstract' (Donnellan 2005: 17). Goold's interpretation of the term is wider as it encompasses thought as well as physical action: 'It's where the thought is heading towards. It's the directionality of the thought. Normally the line as well'. The second term Goold uses is 'objective', which he defines simply as '"I want" – what you want to achieve'. This is both the 'I want' in a particular moment and the relationship of that 'I want' from moment to moment with the larger 'I want' across the play. The final term Goold uses is 'action'. For Goold, an action is a matter of how. Whereas Stanislavski would describe an action as a verb, Goold defines an action as an adverb: 'It's the -ly word, it's the thrillingly or excitedly or anxiously'. The ability to pick effective actions is a skill Goold believes both good directors and good actors possess. They are 'able to find nuance and imagination in their actions'. While Goold uses these terms to break down the text with his actors, 'I don't really say, "This is what it's about"'. He avoids being too prescriptive about the meaning of the text itself (Goold 2019b).

When working with Shakespeare, Goold resists psychologizing it. Shakespeare, he argues, contains the action of his narrative within the play itself: 'The key action happens during the span of the play [...] backstory is utterly irrelevant, you are defined by what you do in the play, not by who you were before the play started' (Goold in Neill 2011). Instead, Goold focuses on the verse. Goold argues Shakespearean verse is often presented in a way that makes it inaccessible: 'There's a lot of cant and stuff designed to intimidate the uninitiated' (Goold 2019a). Goold follows John Barton's approach to verse speaking, which focuses on clarity. Barton encourages actors to stress the antitheses, the opposing words or ideas, in Shakespeare's sentences in order to convey the meaning of the lines clearly: 'If an actor doesn't point up antitheses, he will be hard and sometimes quite impossible to follow' (Barton 1984: 55). In Shakespeare, 'each new word in a sentence qualifies what has gone before or changes the direction of that sentence. If we don't set up one word, we won't prepare for another to qualify it. And if the next word doesn't build on the first and move the sentence on, both the audience and the actor may lose their way' (Barton 1984: 56). Focusing on antithesis brings clarity of communication. In line with Barton, Goold stresses that 'as long as you concentrate on antithesis and not over-stressing an idea and playing the argument then you don't need to worry about the iambics and the line endings and caesuras' (Goold 2019a).

Handy describes Goold's approach to directing actors as a process of getting them to 'join the dots'. Goold creates puzzles for actors to solve, setting 'these kind of impossible tasks for actors to make an idea work'. This can be both 'tricky' and 'exciting'. The trickiness is that the performance 'may not feel complete from the inside' for the actor, even though it will look 'compete from the audience'. For example, in *The Merchant of Venice*, Goold cut the scene where Antonio pursues Shylock in the street (3.3) into two shorter filmic scenes. The first showed Antonio 'at the opera being surprised' by Shylock, then arrested. The second showed 'Antonio, in the prison' talking to Solanio. Handy argues cutting the scene was impactful on the audience's relationship with Antonio: 'What it made the audience feel in terms of Antonio's journey was immeasurably greater than what they would have felt for Antonio had Antonio been chasing and appealing to Shylock'. From the inside, however, it felt tricky: 'I never got the verse expression I would have if I'd had that original scene'. Handy partly attributes this paradox, between the internal incompleteness of the actor's sense of their performance and the external completeness of the audience experience, to Goold's use of bells and whistles: 'What he's doing with colour and sound and light [...] originally the actors had to do everything, and he's bringing more items to the table and therefore the actors don't need to complete that experience'. Handy likens acting for Goold to acting for film: 'When they're taking a close-up of your foot tapping under the table [...] just tap your bloody foot because you're taking a shot' (Handy 2019). Rather than being about delivering a complete performance from inside the character, it is about trusting the totality of the elements making up the performance to convey the character's story in its entirety effectively to an audience looking in from outside. Considering this, it is no surprise that runs of the play during rehearsals are an important part of Goold's process. Goold argues that running the play helps the actors to 'knit it all together'. In order for actors to integrate and absorb the work that they have been doing on a sequence of beats or scenes or the play as a whole, they need to have 'the muscle memory of doing it'. Ideally, Goold aims to run the show every day during the final week of rehearsals: 'You might think that will be rather deathly [...] but actors, particularly if they're playing substantial roles, always find stuff by doing a run' (Goold 2019a).

Goold thinks very carefully about when the best time is to give a particular note to an actor or creative in order for them to be able to absorb and process it effectively: 'one of the most important skills, is knowing when to intervene'. Sometimes a note needs to be given immediately: 'I'll look at an actor and go, if I don't give that note tonight we're in trouble'. At other times, a note needs to be left for later: 'Equally I'll see something and think, "I'll be giving that note in three weeks' time or in the tech or during previews"'. The delaying of notes can be disconcerting for others in the rehearsal room: 'My assistant will be going, "Don't you think the way that they do that is terrible?" And you go, "Yes it is terrible, but now is not the time to change it, because they're not going to be receptive"'. Giving a note at the wrong time can make people feel 'self-conscious or judged in the wrong way', and if they cannot process the note effectively 'they won't own the choice'. For Goold, directing is 'like seasoning a stew'. It's about 'the elements you add and when you add them' (Goold 2019b). Mike Bartlett observes that Goold is extremely good at giving actors 'the right note at the right time to make their performance 50 or 100 per cent better' (M. Bartlett 2019). Hamilton concurs: 'Every single note he gave me made something clearer for me, or made me dare more, and that's very rare I think' (Hamilton 2019).

Goold observes actors will often bring the big picture to the rehearsal room: 'They do the big, dreamy character stuff on their own'. The job of a director is 'to pay attention to the detail' by bringing a 'deep close reading' (of the text) and 'a deep understanding of the grammar of acting'. Goold argues 'a performance is often a calibration of a million small moving parts within sentences', therefore a director needs the skills to be able to support the development of that (Goold 2019c). Fielding notes Goold is demanding of his actors in his pursuit of perfection: 'He really cares about every moment being the best it can be and he won't relent until it is'. While some directors 'are really interested in the accolades and the networking and the show being a success', Goold is 'fascinated with why and how you get there and the tussling and the rigorous questioning and challenging and long

The Theatre of Rupert Goold

hours and perfectionism that make something watertight and brilliant'. Fielding sees the latter approach as more productive for actors. Actors 'do like being challenged and poked and made to be better and made to look harder and work harder, because certainly for myself, that's what I'm interested in'. Goold 'won't let you act badly. He'll keep going until you do what's real or truthful' (Fielding 2019).

Ultimately, Goold argues that 'the best way to create a good atmosphere in the room is to do good work, if people create something they know is really exciting'. Goold sees this as a collaborative process. It's not just a question of 'having good ideas' as a director. It's also about 'releasing the best parts of the performers' (Goold 2019a).

The Hunt

During May and June 2019, I observed a number of Goold's rehearsals for *The Hunt*, which is an adaptation by the writer and director David Farr of Thomas Vinterberg's 2012 film of the same name. *The Hunt* tells the story of a teacher, Lucas, living in a small Danish town, who is wrongly accused of sexually abusing one of his pupils, Clara. As the investigation into the alleged abuse proceeds Lucas becomes increasingly ostracized from the community. Eventually Lucas is exonerated, but despite this many in the town remain secretly convinced of his guilt. The production was designed by Es Devlin and starred Tobias Menzies as Lucas. Cork provided the score and Botis Seva choreographed

Figure 15 The company of *The Hunt* (Almeida 2019). Photo: Marc Brenner.

Directing

the piece. This section provides an account of elements of Goold's directorial practice, based on conservations with the production's creatives and my observations in the rehearsal room.

Devlin argues that *The Hunt* picks up on concerns with 'tribal male structures'. Her initial way into the design was via thinking about these structures through music: 'In my other work I'm thinking a lot about tribal choral expression. So I had found for another piece this shouting male choir from Finland'. Reading the script, her instinct was that the 'territory where the design might lie' was a 'combination of these shouting male choirs and IKEA. And something kind of very primal versus something very benign and global' (Devlin 2019). Goold and Devlin identified a couple of different approaches to this territory: a 'Chekhov version' which could 'be set in a wood, in a birch forest'; or a version reflecting on 'the structure and geometry of a school'. While reading the script, Devlin would sketch: 'gym environment, school pegs environment, school lines environment' (Devlin 2019). Some elements of the design arose subconsciously while reading and sketching. For example, in the final design, gym markings on the floor become the lines Clara 'can't walk on' (Vinterberg and Lindholm 2019: 71). Devlin and Goold never spoke about 'that piece of text in relation to those physical lines on the floor but instinctively that must have been where they came from'. While sketching, Devlin also thinks about the design as 'a machine to deliver the scenes' (Devlin 2019).

The final design was a 'little Wendy-house timber structure' with glass windows in the centre of a raised platform with a double revolve. The edge of the platform could act as a

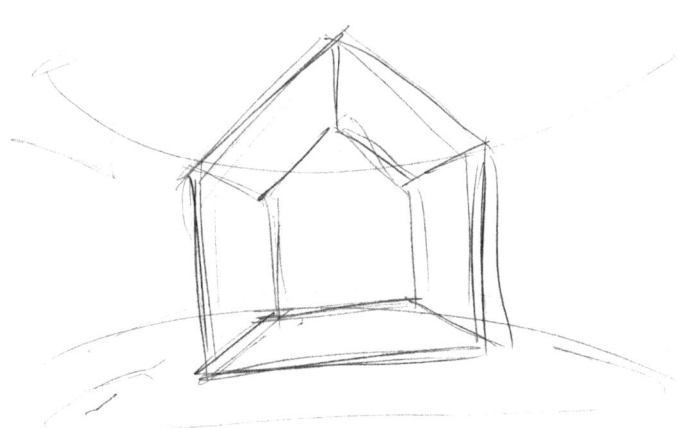

Figure 16 Design sketch for *The Hunt*. Courtesy of Es Devlin.

bench to reduce the need for furniture to come on and off. The platform was positioned on a floor with gym markings. There were pegs for coats on either side of the stage. The design drew heavily on the concept of IKEA. Devlin observes that when 'you go around IKEA, each section is a kind of design for life'. When walking around other environments, such as an airport or a shopping mall, you sometimes see an 'extract from the IKEA life is plonked slightly out of context'; for example, a children's play area in an airport. The image of the house came from the idea of 'a little design for life sponsored by IKEA that's just plonked at the Almeida'. The house had glass windows that could be opaque or clear as demanded. At other times, the design allowed the house to be filled with haze. This element of the design was inspired by Antony Gormley's installation *Blind Light* and turned the house into an 'instrument of apparition and disappearance', with people and objects magically appearing or disappearing within it, creating a sense of instability within the fabric of the play's world (Devlin 2019).

Cork's score was built on a stage direction in a draft of Farr's script that did not make it into the final production. Originally, in Act Two, Scene Four, there had been a moment when the audience hear the men of Lucas's hunting lodge beating menacingly in the trees near his house, '*Figures in the trees. A beating sound. Slow*' (Vinterberg and Lindholm 2018: 58). From this, Cork drew out the sound of 'wood on wood' as 'a percussive force' within the score. The 'heartbeat of the show' became 'simple groups of three strikes'. The men of the hunting lodge would sing, 'Ah, ah, ah. Oo, oo, oo,' and this was repeated throughout the score. Within the musical world of the production there were 'three levels'. The first drew on the idea of Denmark as 'a social democratic utopia with all social ills solved' but simultaneously suggested a 'dark underbelly' underneath. The second was a 'dreamy level' reflecting the reserved 'Lucas's interior world', which the audience are introduced to when they 'first see the house revolving and the little girl inside'. This level forms a 'place of safety from which we then depart' (Cork 2019). The third level was encapsulated by the ancient Danish hymn, 'This is Our Country', which Rune sings as he trims the hedge (Vinterberg and Lindholm 2019: 35). The song's lyrics suggest 'a blend of patriotism and violence'. For the second act, when it becomes clear 'the whole community is out to get' Lucas, Cork created a 'climactic' version of the song, which suggests 'the mask has completely fallen away and we're in a more belligerent, primitive, aggressive way of conducting ourselves in society'. At that point, Cork brought in 'older instruments' to create 'what I imagine a Viking sound would be' (Cork 2019).

The Hunt was the first time Goold and Seva had worked together. Goold had seen Seva's dance piece *BLKDOG* (Sadler's Wells 2018) and felt 'the language that I made with my company would translate into this new show'. Before rehearsals began, Goold arranged a choreographic workshop for Seva and gave him stimuli from the play. Working with his own dancers, Seva played with 'masculine movements, very heavy, dark and grungy'. Initially, Goold found the movement 'too British laddish'. Building on the initial movements, Seva shifted them: 'In choreography you can change the textures and layers of what the movement is. So the movement can still stay the same or the physical language can still stay the same, but changing the content of what it looks like'. Seva also received Cork's music before rehearsals. Hearing Cork's 'aggressive' percussion helped create the show's choreographic language, which included 'pumping of the shoulders' and 'hitting on the chest' (Seva 2019). Menzies was also wired into the creative process early on. He and Goold were in conversation, 'talking back and forward in terms of the adaptation and [...] in broader terms about what the atmosphere, the tone of it should be'. He was also present in 'early design meetings with Es Devlin' (Menzies 2019).

Once rehearsals begin, the work of other creatives is integrated into the rehearsal room from early on in the process. Goold works alongside them and defers to them when the focus shifts to their work. Seva works with the actors on choreography both on his own in a separate space and with Goold on the floor. At times Seva works with actors in part of the rehearsal room, while Goold is working with other actors on another moment in another area. For example, while Goold worked with the majority of the actors on the transition into the house/church in Act Two, Scene Five, Seva took the time to work with Menzies on his movement as he runs carrying his dead dog in his arms during the same transition. At times, Goold switches the main company's focus to another of the creatives in the room. In that same rehearsal, taking a break from staging the transition out of the church scene, Goold moved over to work with Menzies while Cork was given space to work on the climactic version of 'This is Our Country' with the rest of the company. At other times, multiple creatives work together. For example, while working on the scene in which the men from the lodge go swimming (Act One, Scene Two), Goold works on the staging at the same time as Seva works on the movement and Cork rehearses the song.

Figure 17 Design sketch for *The Hunt*. Courtesy of Es Devlin.

Early on in rehearsal, I observed Goold working from two different perspectives with the actors, encouraging them to see each scene from both inside (as the character) and outside (as the audience) simultaneously. The first internal perspective focuses on the psychological and emotional state of the characters in each scene. Given circumstances were established and the characters' immediate objectives identified. For example, in Act One, Scene Eight, Lucas waits outside the school for Clara's parents, Theo (Justin Salinger) and Mikala (Poppy Miller), while a parents' meeting about the alleged sexual abuse takes place inside. Goold first established the facts of the situation Lucas has found himself in. The time between the accusation and the scene was established as six days. Questions were raised about the nature of the investigation so far, such as 'Is the investigation confined to the school or have the police been involved?' There was an interrogation of what is new information at this point for the characters. Characters' objectives and motivations were discussed. What was Lucas trying to achieve by being present outside the school meeting? Was he being confrontational? Relationships between the characters were explored. Does Theo feel Lucas's betrayal of their previously close friendship more than the abuse of his daughter? Would Theo and Mikala's relationship with Lucas be different if the accusation related to a child other than their daughter? Goold supported the actors' investigation of these questions by offering concrete analogies for the characters' possible psychological or emotional states from both personal experience and wider culture. For example, while exploring how Lucas's supposed betrayal of Theo might feel, Goold asked Salinger how he would feel if he told a friend about a great part he wanted, only to discover later the friend had then secured themselves an audition for the part and got it.

The second external perspective focuses on exploring the metaphorical meanings of different possible stagings of each scene in discussion with the actors in them. For example, in the process of exploring the staging of Act One, Scene Eight, Goold and Menzies discussed the placing of a bench Lucas could be sitting on in relation to the scene's action in symbolic terms. Is the meeting shown inside the hut, while the bench is placed directly outside it so Lucas is proximate but separated from the meeting, communicating the beginning of his separation from the community? Is it placed further away, suggesting greater separation? Is the hut full, as if the meeting is taking place inside, or empty? Is there a less naturalistic image in the hut? Clara skipping? Clara with antlers? Metaphorical questions are raised about the overall journey. How would the image of the parents' meeting inside the house read against an image of the community in church inside the house in the second act? Should this scene be naturalistic against increasing stylization later?

Early rehearsals involve an exploration of the staging possibilities and limitations defined by the set. Devlin remembers Goold's instant response to her design as 'I know how to do it in that' (Devlin 2019). Despite this, Goold expresses doubt as to whether he can stage the play on the set in conversations I have with him immediately prior to rehearsals. Though Goold may have pre-thought staging ideas, he conveys no sense of having a definite plan for how the play will be staged in early rehearsals. The set is positioned as a question to be responded to. When looking at the scene inside the church (Act Two, Scene Five) Goold tries several staging possibilities on the floor. Theoretically

Directing

there should be thirteen actors inside the church during the scene. The limited dimensions of the house, however, force a less literal interpretation of space. First, the actors squeeze four rows of benches inside the house/church. Next the benches are placed outside the house/church. First downstage of the house/church with two benches lined up on the edge of each side of the stage. Next they move to the upstage corners of the stage. Finally, the benches are placed back in the house/church with the congregation inside. The pastor is placed on the downstage edge of the stage, his back to the congregation. When Lucas and his son Marcus (Stuart Campbell) enter the house/church, they are forced to climb onto the benches and through the tightly packed congregation inside. Their intrusion into the space and the disruption it causes are more pronounced within the unnaturally crowded space. As he stages, Goold is mobile in the room. He rarely sits, preferring to move around and view the scene from different places. He demonstrates staging possibilities physically. He makes a swaying gesture with his hands to illustrate the way Campbell should move through the congregation. When working out an exit with Menzies, he walks with him to communicate the movement he wants to try. At other times, he uses visual images to communicate staging ideas. When Lucas finds himself alone with Clara in Act Two, Scene Eight, Goold uses the image of Clara as a tiger to convey the nature of the tension between them to Menzies.

During early rehearsals, ideas are raised and options are tried but nothing feels set in stone. Different options hang in the air. For example, Theo could be a man who is quick to violence or a man who feels emasculated by the situation he is in. Theo's encounter

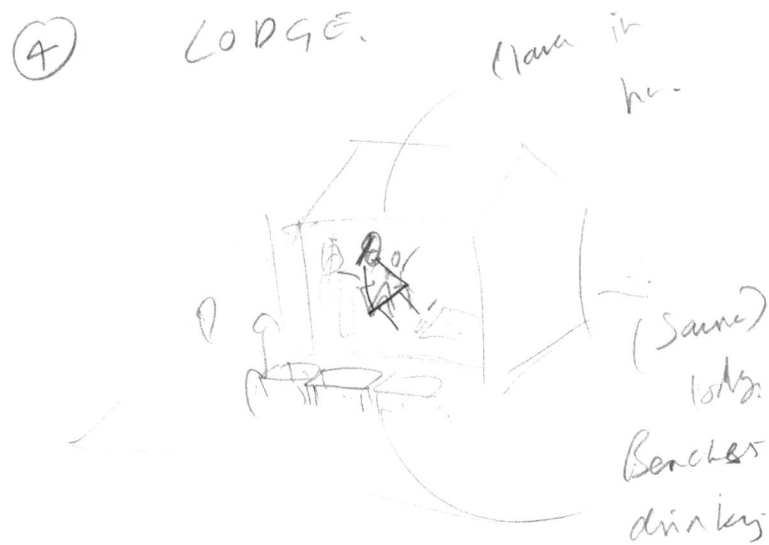

Figure 18 Design sketch for *The Hunt*. Courtesy of Es Devlin.

with Lucas outside the parents' meeting in Act One, Scene Eight could be played as 'I can't believe this is true but I hate you' or as 'I hate what you did but I love you'. Goold does, however, close some options down. For example, while discussing the given circumstances surrounding the party scene (Act Two, Scene Eight), in which Lucas appears to have been reaccepted into the community, he narrows the company's choices when the question arises of the tone of the play's ending. Is it a happy ending in which the community truly reaccepts Lucas or an ambivalent ending in which everything returns to how it was but nothing is resolved? Here, Goold leaves the exact nature of the situation open but stipulates that the ending is ambivalent because it follows the structure of a Shakespearean comedy. The world is turned upside-down, then flipped back to how it was, with all the flaws that have been exposed still seething under the surface.

CHAPTER 7
SHAKESPEARE

School plays and pantomimes aside, Goold's early experiences of theatre were predominantly of Shakespeare. There are three productions he clearly remembers seeing as a child. The first is Bill Alexander's *Richard III* (RSC 1984) starring Anthony Sher playing a spider-like Richard using crutches. The second was the same director's *The Merry Wives of Windsor* (RSC 1985), which was set in the 1950s, 'complete with hairdryers, a cocktail cabinet and Morris Minor car' ('Bill Alexander's production: The Merry Wives of Windsor'). The third was a revival of Jonathan Miller's *The Tempest* (Mermaid Theatre 1970) at the Old Vic (1988), in which the lords were white colonialists and the island's inhabitants West Indians. As a teenager, Goold found Shakespeare problematic: 'basically boring and hard to listen to'. Despite this, 'my first way into directing was thinking about what I could do with Shakespeare plays'. Looking at past performance histories while studying for GCSE and A-level, Goold realized Shakespeare was much more flexible than people are led to be believe: 'It's so much more protean. It's so much more plastic. It's so much more capable of all the wonderful individuality performers can bring to it'. Directors, he concluded, needed to give the plays 'energy' and 'open up the possibility anything could be in Shakespeare' (Goold 2019a).

Despite directing several Shakespeare plays at university, while freelancing and in Northampton, Goold's approach only became fully formed with his RSC production of *The Tempest* in 2006. Goold's early attempts at directing Shakespeare were 'typical Jonathan Miller, like we'll decontextualise it in this way'. For example, his Northampton *Othello* was built around an American actor. Goold's first challenge was 'how do we make sense of that?' so he relocated the play to 1940s Britain to make sense of the casting: there were 'black GIs coming over here. They were going to war in the Mediterranean. Often, they would develop relationships with white girls'. Although the production was a success, it was the last production Goold did in that idiom. He realized that just because 'you can make something work in eighteenth-century Istanbul' does not make it 'meaningful'. There needs to be a 'rationale' (Goold 2019a).

Preparing *The Tempest*, Goold was concerned about how he would stage the show successfully in the 'big white proscenium' Royal Shakespeare Theatre (RST). The RST was a 'famously difficult space' before its refurbishment in the late 2000s. Goold had seen several shows there 'that hadn't been vivid or muscular enough'. He thought back to the two successful Alexander shows he had seen there as a child, remembering them as 'crutches *Richard III*' and 'fifties *Merry Wives*'. He realized they could both be reduced to a 'one-word thing', and the same idea could be extended to include successful Shakespeare productions by other directors, for example Brook's 'circus *Dream*' (RSC 1970) or Miller's 'Rothschild *Merchant*' (NT 1970). At the time, Goold was trying to decide between three different approaches to *The Tempest*. He was able to reduce one of them to the 'Arctic Tempest'. It had 'the same single adjective kind of thing' (Goold 2019a).

The first step of Goold's approach to Shakespeare is to identify the most essential quality of the play: 'put a post-it note on the wall, metaphorically or literally, to say, "What's the fundamental thing you want to get right in this?"' Normally it is the simplest and most obvious thing, 'the most childlike response', something it can be 'easy to lose sight of', such as *Romeo and Juliet* should 'be romantic' or *Macbeth* 'scary'. The next step is to identify the weakest scenes by listing them 'from the best scene to the weakest'. Goold then works his way up the list, asking 'what is weak' about the weakest scenes. He may then cut some of the weaker scenes, if they are not essential to the play's basic narrative (Goold 2019a).

Goold researches performance histories to work out why certain scenes 'drag or are opaque' and to explore how to stage them, as other directors will have tried ways to solve any issues in staging the plays already: 'somebody has done a lot of research for you beforehand'. While he was preparing *Hamlet*, Goold went to the Shakespeare Centre in Stratford-upon-Avon and watched the eight most recent RSC productions of *Hamlet*: 'It's enough to show you, "Oh, that's interesting. They did that with that"'. Shakespeare's plays often present a director with a choice between two archetypal but unsatisfactory ways of staging key scenes or approaching the play as a whole that haunt their performance histories. For example, in staging *Macbeth*, a director is faced with a choice between staging the banquet scene with or without the ghost of Banquo visible. In staging *Romeo and Juliet*, you either get praised

> for doing the first half really well and they're really gorgeous and Zeffirelli-like and then it gets a bit of a slog in the second half because it's dark and gothic and you kind of go, where's Mercutio, I want to be back in the sunshine. Or you get dark, gothic productions that acknowledge the skull behind [...] the lipstick and draw on the sort of death wish of the lovers and are compelling and properly tragic but make really heavy weather of the joy of the first half.

As a director, Goold argues, 'You always think, I'm going to be the one to find the synthesis of these two things' but ultimately 'you have to acknowledge that you're going to have to be one or the other' (Goold 2019a). In his *Macbeth*, however, he did successfully encompass both approaches to the banquet scene by doing it twice.

Once he has a sense of the play's performance history, Goold looks at the 'bottom-most section' of his list of scenes. Whereas most directors 'whip through the boring stuff until we get back to the fun stuff to direct', Goold's focus is on these weaker scenes, which he tries to make 'live through design'. He argues that 'if the production can bring the bottom up, then the top should take care of itself' (Goold 2019a). During rehearsals for *Macbeth*, Scott Handy remembers Goold 'spent quite a large percentage of his creative energy on some of the smaller scenes that are really quite boring on the page and most productions either skate over or it's deeply dull to watch'. For example, the arrival of Duncan at the castle (1.6) is usually staged with 'a group of actors pretending they've just got off horseback standing looking up at invisible battlements'. Instead, Goold's company 'spent huge amounts of time learning how to choreograph this complex series of chopping and arriving in the kitchen with birds'. Instead of being dull, the scene became 'a bit of a *coup de théâtre*'. Handy argues that Goold's theatricalisation of the weaker scenes means 'you don't get this up-and-down bump that you do with a lot of other classical work' (Handy 2019). Goold's idea to set *The Tempest* in the Arctic came out of such a consideration of how to revitalize the weaker scenes of the play: 'I'd found the lord scenes, the sort of Gonzalo, Antonio, Sebastian scenes, incredibly hard work'. He decided he needed to create a more challenging environment for the lords to grapple with in order to energize their scenes: 'What if they're not just sitting around on a beach. You know, maybe they're going somewhere. What's the struggle?' In looking for a world that could be 'some sort of obstacle course', Goold drew on Zacharias Kunuk's *Atanarjuat: The Fast Runner*, a film about an Inuit desperately trying to traverse an icy Arctic landscape (Goold 2019a).

Next Goold examines the historical context of the play using secondary accounts by writers like James Shapiro alongside primary sources, such as pamphlets from the time. He tries to work out 'the social matrix [Shakespeare] was working within', for example, 'fear of Catholic supremacy or the desire for Catholic supremacy or bourgeois anxiety about property'. Goold also looks at the sources Shakespeare was adapting to 'try and get a flavour of what he'd done with [them] to try and speak to his audience then'. Then Goold uses this information to work out how the play might be revitalized for audiences now: 'essentialize what the equivalent comparator is now in that anxiety. And then I look for a social world to map that onto, which can be now but might equally be historic'. For *The Merchant of Venice*, he remembers reading accounts of how 'the influx of new world gold had led to rapid inflation'. People at the time 'couldn't understand what was going on. They thought it was some sort of witchcraft of malice, because basically a loaf of bread had cost the same for 400 years and suddenly it was twice as expensive'. This thought developed into an interest in what this first encounter with inflation meant for 'the language of value': 'If you can say this is worth something absolutely, and when that worth becomes fluid, what does that mean?' Looking at *The Merchant of Venice* within that context, 'there seems to be a big thing here about rating someone's value. How do you value them literally in the debt, but also in the way that Portia talks about Bassanio?' Although there were more obvious contemporary parallels like 'high finance', Goold decided his 'way into this play would be around the idea of value'. Preparing *The Tempest*, he came across an Elizabethan pamphlet about 'journeys to the Baltic and the Arctic', which revealed 'they thought icebergs were giant swans' and 'resonated with the new world pamphlets, the Bermuda pamphlets, the play was based on'. Relocating *The Tempest* to the Arctic did, however, cause some textual issues: 'you hit problem lines like the ground is lush and green here' (2.1.51). Such problems can be creatively productive: 'I thought, what if it is that thing where you see the grass under the ice and you have to rub it clear?' When Gonzalo brushed the snow and delivered the line, the audience laughed. The fact 'the schematic doesn't fit' can be 'fun' (Goold 2019a).

In tandem with establishing a social world for the play, Goold also establishes a poetic idiom: 'the aesthetic or poetic, the tonal world of my production' (Goold 2019a). Handy identifies this poetic idiom as a lens through which to see the social world: 'a way of seeing that unlocks it and makes it incredibly exciting' (Handy 2019). For Goold, poetic idioms are 'more intuitive'. Sometimes, they are 'a kind of performance idiom'. For example, the poetic idiom for *Hamlet* was 'Pina Bausch's work – super feminine'. His *Tempest* has a 'Beckett-like quality' in its portrayal of masters and servants. At other times, Goold will find the poetic idiom in 'one single piece of art that encapsulates – whether it's a song but normally it's a painting or sculpture – the tonality of what I'd like my production to be'. For *King Lear*, Goold found a Richard Billingham-esque 'image of two boys killing each other with plastic swords'. At other times, the poetic idiom will draw on real world events. For *Romeo and Juliet*, the poetic map was the murder of Sophie Lancaster (Goold 2019a).

At the end of this process, Goold will have a 'Jonathan Miller social relocation world' and a 'more abstracted poetic world' he can 'smash' together. Goold feels that in his less successful shows one of these aspects has dominated over the other: 'I haven't forcefully articulated both of those'. For Goold the poetic idiom tends to be 'the one that dominates', but if it dominates too much, 'you don't really get any world stakes'. The social world has to be clearly articulated: 'You have to get a lot of world information in the first two or three scenes about what Venice means or where Verona is'. The audience need to understand the way power structures operate within the world. Shakespeare productions often fail to establish 'stakes and hierarchies' and make them 'meaningful'. Audiences need to understand 'what generals are, what kings are', as 'without hierarchy, Shakespeare doesn't really work': 'the insurrection needs to have an orthodoxy to challenge' (Goold 2019a).

Goold's approach to establishing the social world is cinematic. He argues you need to think about your establishing shot as you would in a film: 'If you want to get across a certain idea, take the time to print it. Because once you've printed it, you don't need to go back'. For example, 'if you show an amazing vista of the Scottish Highlands in *Mary Stuart*, you don't really need to show any more shots of outside because we know we're there'. You need to take time to 'anchor' the audience in the world. For his RSC *Romeo and Juliet*, Goold focused on two establishing shots: 'I've got to get the first fight right and I've got to get the banquet right, because that carries the hedonism and excitement of the world and the first fight carries the danger'. Goold's banquet (1.5) included a six-minute dance sequence, full of 'fire'. The first fight (1.1) was staged not as a single fight, but as an extended running battle engulfing the entire city. Establishing shots are important because they communicate the parameters of the social world: 'like this is a martial world, or what the witches are, or how the power politics work'. Therefore, 'creating the space, often outside the text, to do that is absolutely fine' (Goold 2019a).

The development of *Macbeth* offers a good example of Goold's overall process: 'the map'. The production's starting point was an actor, Patrick Stewart. His casting had implications for the world of the production. Stewart is older 'than is normal' for Macbeth, and this raises the age of the characters generally: 'The other generals around him, the Duncans, the Banquos, they really ought to be near his generation'. This led Goold to consider 'Brezhnev and Andropov and the late Soviet period and when you had all these old generals who seemed to just replace each other'. From his historical research, Goold realized there was a parallel with the political situation at the time the play was written: '[Robert] Cecil and the post-Gunpowder Plot, sort of anti-Catholicism, secret police'. Initially, Goold was thinking about Cold War-era Soviet Russia as a parallel, but through conversations with Stewart, he realized that 'Stalin seemed a better map' (Goold 2019a). The play's Stalinism, however, is a tonal quality rather than a concrete setting, evoked through specific elements of the production, such as its 'Shostakovichian-style' score (Cork 2019). The production itself is not specifically set within that time period: 'It wasn't ever set in any one moment. If anything it felt late 1960s Cold War, even though that doesn't date Stalin quite right obviously, but it was sort of infused with that' (Goold 2019a).

In tandem with the social world of Soviet Russia, Goold had an instinct about setting the play in a kitchen. Like Stalinism, the kitchen is an imaginative space rather than a concrete setting. Goold tried to explain this in his first meeting with the designer, Anthony Ward: 'I want to do the play in a kitchen. The set's not a kitchen. The play has to happen in a kitchen'. There is a sense of performing in a space rather than being in a space. The space has 'a meaning' rather than being a 'setting'. It is the difference between getting 'everyone into a toilet together [to] do a couple of scenes' and setting the scenes in a toilet. Goold felt the kitchen space would inject an interesting dynamic into the Macbeths' relationship: 'that feeling of being in the kitchen or in the backroom with your partner during a dinner party [...] that weird intensity and arguing you can have'. This chimed with the Macbeths' relationship in the banquet scene: '"Why have you left the table?" "What do you mean why have I left the table?" "Aren't you meant to be at the fucking party?"' The combination of the two felt 'domestic in an interesting way'. Initially, Ward was concerned with the practicalities of staging *Macbeth* in a kitchen: 'Anthony [Ward] would push back and go, "But no, how are we going to do this scene?"' Goold was confident the concept would work: 'I'll figure it out, just give me kitchen'. The poetic idiom drew its inspiration from horror films: 'Talking to the video designer and sound designer, it was *Suspiria* and *Ring* I was referring to, much more than Soviet stuff'. The elements of the production feel at odds with each other, but for Goold these conflicting dynamics are productive: 'I don't think you can have too many ingredients when you cook with Shakespeare, but you need to have enough oppositional ones'. The same pattern of oppositional elements is evident in some of his other Shakespeares. For example, *The Merchant of Venice* encompasses 'social world Las Vegas, idiomatic world Britney Spears gameshow, performative map feminine trophy' (Goold 2019a).

Handy argues that Goold deliberately confounds the audience's expectations of Shakespeare in order to prevent them from being 'hijacked by memories of Shakespeare' (Handy 2019). Handy frames his theory with Anne Bogart's theory of eroticism. Bogart postulates that the attraction between audiences and actors has seven stages mirroring 'the pattern of a passionate relationship': 'Something or someone stops you in your tracks'; 'You feel "drawn" to it'; 'You sense its energy and power'; 'It disorientates you'; 'You make first contact; it responds'; 'You experience extended intercourse'; 'You are changed irrevocably' (Bogart 2003: 61–2). Handy argues Goold's approach mirrors this: 'He's not shocking for the sake of shocking; he's shocking in order to connect with something'. As actors and audiences, our expectations of Shakespeare 'are always wrong' because they are 'nothing to do with life, they're to do with Shakespeare productions'. In order to see the plays clearly 'you have to wake up first'. Goold uses oppositional elements to shock his audience awake and reconnect them with the living play: 'He'll use TV shows or he'll use horror or something you've seen in popular culture or he'll use something that he saw on the street, but it will be something to try and connect you out of that classical library with all of our memories of other Shakespeare plays' (Handy 2019).

Shakespeare has featured less in Goold's repertoire in recent years. *Richard III* is the only Shakespeare production he has directed at the Almeida. In the current climate, he feels that there are other more pressing stories to be told: 'When I think of all the stories one could tell, you know, why?' Despite this, there are still some Shakespeare plays he would like to tackle or revisit, including *Antony and Cleopatra*, *The Winter's Tale* and *Hamlet*. His rationale for why he would like to direct them is now led, however, by 'an actor I want to see do it, rather than "I've got a great take on a play"'. The Almeida's space, Goold argues, is too small for that kind of actor-led production. It favours a more conceptual approach, in the vein of his more radical adaptations of classic texts: 'At our scale, you want to take more risk'. There is one radical Shakespeare he is currently considering: 'a sort of conceptual mash-up of bits of *Twelfth Night* and *In Memoriam*, this Tennyson poem, but it's much more autobiographical and not really the play' (Goold 2019a).

CHAPTER 8
ADAPTATION

Goold's approach to adaptation is not concerned with fidelity to the source text, but rather it emerges from an interest in how moving a story from medium to medium transforms it. For Goold the process raises two major questions: 'Where do you find your stories from?' and 'What happens to a story when you put it on stage?' The adapter may not seek to change the story, but the process of shifting it into another medium with different structures innately changes its nature. Goold notes this shift is 'a transference of form rather than of idea, rather than meaning'. His final-year university dissertation examined why there had been so many stage adaptations of the story of King John during the sixteenth century. It touched on both the issue of where stories come from and how staging them transforms them. King John, who had previously always been seen as a bad king, was rehabilitated during the Reformation because, like Henry VIII, he had both stood up to the Pope and abandoned his first wife in order to marry a second. This led to the production of a range of cultural artefacts presenting John in a positive light as a Protestant monarch, including John Bale's 1538 play *King Johan*. Bale's positive portrayal of King John was then challenged by two later history plays presenting the king in a more negative light, George Peele's *The Troublesome Reign of John, King of England* (1591) and Shakespeare's *King John* (circa 1594). Goold was interested in the evolution of this story, through songs and ballads to *Foxe's Book of Martyrs* (1563) and *Holinshed's Chronicles* (1577) to the stage. One of the primary effects of staging, he argues, is a shift in the relationship of audience to character: 'there is an innate humanism in putting a character on stage'. There is 'something about the protagonist in front of the audience' that produces 'innate empathy'. This created a problem for both Peele and Shakespeare, as despite their negative portrayals of King John, their audiences still empathised with the character in front of them. This paradoxical affect stands at the heart of tragedy: 'The hero does a terrible thing, you put them on the wheel, they suffer, they should deserve what they get, but you can't help but feel complicated about that'. Goold theorizes it was not an affect 'Tudor cultural form and Tudor dramatists were able to deal with', so was disruptive to the intentions behind Peele's and Shakespeare's representations of King John (Goold 2019c).

Goold's first forays into adaptation focused on novels. The first of these was the adaptation of Graham Greene's *The End of the Affair* that he worked on with Caroline Faber. His interest in the novel derived from an interest in 'a sort of Catholic art' and the fact Greene had adapted his own personal experience: 'how the novelist applied strategies to remake a true story of his own life', as the narrative is based on Greene's real-life affair with Catherine Walston. Greene re-imagines himself through the character of Maurice and Walston through the character of Sarah. Goold argues that the novel is 'not very true' in its representation of Greene and Walston's affair; Greene has an 'agenda'. For example, in the novel Sarah's husband is unaware of the affair, whereas in real life Walston's husband knew all about it, as they had what would now be termed an open relationship. In the novel, 'Sarah is a supressed voice'. Faber and Goold were interested in 'giving Catherine [Walston] a full voice', not only through how they presented Sarah as a 'character on stage' but also through 'the potency of hearing her narrative separately'. Their adaptation thus centres around a 'battle for control of the narrative voice' between Sarah and Maurice: 'her diary is one side of the literary voice, and Maurice's inner monologue is the other'. The first section of the play is framed within Maurice's inner monologue. The second is framed by Sarah's diary entries, allowing the audience to access her version of the same events. The time afforded to Sarah's version of events is less than is afforded to Maurice's, but her version comes second, undermining his. Goold and Faber attempted to evoke 'the sense of faith' running through the novel 'through music' (Goold 2019c). Adam Cork created a 'haunting soundscape with very complex, layered choral pieces' for the piece (Faber 2019). A clear example of this use of music to invoke the spiritual comes in the final moments of the production. As Maurice rails against God for taking his lover from him, a requiem builds and swells over him, drowning out his anger (Greene 2001: 61).

Goold's next adaptation was Italo Calvino's novel *The Baron in the Trees*, which he adapted on spec and planned to direct at the Gate (Notting Hill) in 1999. The novel, set in eighteenth-century Italy, is about 'an eleven-year-old boy [who] climbs a tree. And his parents come out and say, "You've got to come down from that tree". [...] And he says, "I don't care, I'm never coming down," and then he never sets foot on land again for the rest of his life. And he sort of hops from tree to tree to tree'. Goold was attracted to the story because it had 'a sort of child's quality', while also having 'an enquiry' in that it posed the question of 'how much can the intellectual be part of society and comment on it?' Goold had met Chichita, Calvino's widow, while he was directing *Il pomo d'oro* for Batignano Opera Festival in 1998. Chichita introduced him to the novel and Goold thought 'she was warmish' about the idea of him adapting it. The official rights, however, were with the actor Richard Gere, who wanted to make a movie version. Goold tried everything to get permission for his stage version: 'I was literally on the phone every night to LA from the Gate going, look this is sixty seats [...] this notional film that has got no traction for ten years is not going to be infringed by this tiny production'. Despite this, Goold still could not get permission: 'Mick Gordon, who was running the Gate, said we can't put something on without a licence, and so even though I'd done the whole adaptation we had to pull it'. Goold still checks the rights situation every few years: 'I actually walked around [Hampstead] Heath for six hours gathering bin liners full of beautiful autumn leaves on spec that one day we might do *The Baron in the Trees*, and they rotted away' (Goold 2019c).

After *The Baron in the Trees*, Goold 'didn't really do adaptations for a while'. He came back to them in 2003 with *Paradise Lost*. Working on the adaptation with Ben Power, Goold found himself dealing with the same issue of empathetic affect he had theorized about in his university dissertation. Although 'Satan's voice is famously dominant in the Milton', the poet attempts to distance his reader from the character: 'the narrative voice in the Milton is constantly commenting on Satan's voice'. They stripped out Milton's commentary and gave 'human form' to Adam, Eve, Satan and some of the angels. As a result of their changes, they found Satan elicited more empathy than he had done on the page: 'It did remind me of that King John thing'. In attempting to convey the vast landscapes of *Paradise Lost*, Goold discovered that with stage adaptations 'dialogue forms proportionally a smaller part of the delivery mechanism of the play'. In contrast, 'image [is] greater than normal'. In adapting sources from mediums such as novels, poetry or film 'you often are interpreting visual sequences that playwrights would probably dismiss because they are not central to their characters' (Goold 2019c).

Adapting a story for the stage can present seemingly insoluble problems. For the last ten years, Goold and Power have been working on an adaptation of Jonathan Swift's *Gulliver's Travels*. For Goold, the piece has become his equivalent of Kubrick's famously unmade film *Napoleon* (Castle 2017). The mapping of the material itself is not the problem, as the text presents myriad possibilities: 'loads of interesting political resonances and sort of marginal, liminal readings and deconstructions of parts of the text, and radical relocations'. Versions they have considered include one 'set in sort of Dubai about relativism and what does relative mean between first world and third world, and what it means to feel big and small in every sense' (Goold 2019c). Robert Icke remembers being pitched a version 'about minibars and people taking out miniature-sized bottles of whisky' (Icke 2019a). The problem they always get stuck on is a practical staging problem: '"How are we going to do the big people and the small people?" which you're going to have to do at some point without it looking like *Spinal Tap*' (Goold 2019c).

In recent years, Goold has mainly worked on stage adaptations of films. While finding a way to stage cinematic visuals might enable a director to demonstrate their virtuosity, the key to producing a successful adaptation, Goold argues, is to facilitate a shift from the private to the political: 'to have an argument, to have a sense of live address to other people, rather than the sort of "How can we turn twelve chairs into a mountainscape?"' Film, he argues, is 'single character focused', whereas theatre is focused 'on community, as the audience by nature are a community'. Transferring a story from film to theatre involves opening up a private world and making it more public. For example, the original film version of *The Hunt* is 'a private enquiry into a man's sense of paranoia and isolation under community attack'. In the stage adaptation, however, the centre of the story shifts to focus on the town's response to the events and 'the community becomes more present' (Goold 2019c).

The other form of adaptation Goold engages with is the adaptation of classic plays for contemporary audiences, as exemplified by his productions of *Faustus* and *Six Characters in Search of an Author*: 'taking one kind of theatre and making another kind of theatre'. This is an extension of his approach to dealing with Shakespeare's weaker scenes; the idea of 'the director's job being to heal the broken parts of a play, to solve them'. Examining both the original Marlowe and Pirandello, Goold found parts he 'thought were bulletproof and electrifying' and parts that felt 'dated'. For example, the metatheatrical elements of the Pirandello seemed old-fashioned. The idea 'the director and all the actors are innately fake' felt like 'a trope we see all the time' so 'their scenes were the weakest'. To address this stale trope, Goold moved towards the opposite extreme: 'What if we try and make that part of the piece more real, the most real, and then argue against that about what is realer?' With the Marlowe, 'everything around Mephistopheles and Faustus seemed great, but the stuff that probably wasn't even written by Marlowe was weak' (Goold 2019c). For Goold and Power, the answer to this question was to 'rectify' the play following the model of what the Chapman Brothers had done to Goya (Grochala 2017); the idea that 'the greatest act of love for an artwork is to deface it with your own homage'. In making such radical changes, Goold argues, he is attempting to re-find the original heart of the play, as opposed to changing the play into something different: 'trying to get to what I thought was the real essence, the sort of lost essence of something. Rather than just go, "Oh it's got two wheels. Even though it's a car, I'll turn it into a bicycle"'. Goold believes classic texts are robust enough to survive any radical alterations. A director's work is 'utterly ephemeral': 'You think of Lindsay Anderson or John Dexter or Tony Richardson, the absolute giants, and yet no one's got any idea of their work compared to say Bond or Osborne'. In comparison, the playwright's work is always accessible in its original form: 'the playwright has the playtext' and so outlasts any director's take on it. To exemplify this, Goold returns to the Chapman Brothers: 'The Chapmans, they're major artists, they're hugely influential on me, but they could burn every single Goya in existence and they'd barely leave a mark on him' (Goold 2019c).

Goold understood that adaptation can be an effective way to make your mark on the industry and define a directorial voice. Early in his career, when his choice of material was more limited either because it was given to him or there was a need to put bums on seats with recognizable titles, he was able to 'smuggle in the art [he] wanted to make by the back door' through adaptation. These adaptations had the added benefit of highlighting his directorial interventions against the background of a familiar text, so conveying a clear sense of voice. Adaptation also allowed him a safe platform on which to create: 'I was craving to write something original, but I couldn't work outside of extant form'. He recognizes this tendency in other artists he meets, 'who I think are really desperate to write pure fiction, pure plays, but really intimidated or inhibited without the skeleton of the novel, the Ibsen or the Aeschylus or whatever to guide them'. For now, however, Goold has moved on: 'I've swapped the skeleton of the extant canonical material for the full body or maybe a not-quite-grown-up body of the new play' (Goold 2019c).

CHAPTER 9
NEW WRITING

Goold's first experiences of directing new writing were 'frustrating'. He worked with writers who were either 'first-time writers or inexperienced writers or quite sort of wilful or mystical' and were resistant to discussing making changes. Goold did not have the 'confidence to be assertive' so he left the plays as they were (Goold 2019c). In at least one case, *Sunday Father* (Hampstead Theatre 2003), the reviews indicate that the play would have benefited from some intervention. Paul Taylor observes the play had 'risible plot devices' and identifies one character as 'more like a dramaturgical convenience than a person' (Taylor 2003b).

Nowadays, Goold tends to be involved in the development of the new plays he directs. He often commits to a play before it is fully formed: 'many are substantially unfinished at the point I say I want to come on board' (Goold 2019a). For Mike Bartlett, Goold's ability to confidently and quickly commit to a project at a very early stage is an important vote of confidence in a writer's work: 'If someone goes, "I love it, do it, write it now" and with a sort of confidence of going, "I think you can write that idea". You come out and go, "I'd better do it then"' (M. Bartlett 2019). Goold is honest about wanting to be 'a creative voice' in the development of the new plays he directs (Goold 2019c). Robert Icke remembers script development at Headlong as a process of continual refinement: 'Big long discussions, lots of feedback, lots of emails'. The process continually questioned, pushing writers to improve what was on the page. It 'wasn't a Royal Court model', where the writer 'turned up and said, "Here are the tablets, interpret them"' (Icke 2019b). Carrie Cracknell observes that Goold thinks like a director when developing new writing. He tries 'to imagine elements of the piece and give that as an offer to the writer, which can be really thrilling but also challenging at times' (Cracknell 2019). Adam Cork argues Goold's approach to new plays is based on the idea of the director as providing an interpretation, a directorial lens through which the play is viewed: 'He never stamps on what's already there. He just supplies a sort of contrapuntal version of the play which is his take on it' (Cork 2019).

Goold believes his reputation creates 'a self-fulfilling prophecy' when it comes to new writing. His bells-and-whistles style inspires people to 'write that way and then you stage it that way and then so on'. This was particularly true of work created for Headlong: 'Both Lucy [Prebble] and Mike [Bartlett] wrote their plays aware that Headlong was putting them on and that I would probably direct them. And both *ENRON* and *Earthquakes in London* invite some lights' (Goold 2019c). Ben Power supports this view but argues certain writers saw Goold as the director who could meet their own ambitions: 'There was a generation of writers who wanted to write at scale, and write theatrically, formally ambitious work'. They 'really wanted [Goold] to direct their plays and they wrote for him': '*ENRON* and *Chimerica* and *Oil* and *Earthquakes in London* and some constituent parts of *Decade* were all written for that style and form'. This, Power argues, is a rare phenomenon: 'I don't think you can look at many artistic directors and say that their voice as a collaborator is distinct enough that you could form a whole programme of new plays around it' (Power 2018). Bartlett admits to writing with Goold in mind when working on both *Earthquakes in London* and *King Charles III*: 'Rupert has such a strong directorial style and capability that I found myself, I think with *Earthquakes* and *Charles*, writing up into that'. For Bartlett, this is as much about pushing Goold's practice as writing to his style: 'Not just playing to that director's strengths, but challenging them and kind of going, "Wouldn't it be cool if Rupert Goold directed this scene?"' (M. Bartlett 2019).

Ella Hickson, who has worked with Goold on three plays – *Boys*, *Oil* and *The Writer* (Almeida 2018) – describes developing plays with him as about a sense of endless potential rather than meeting a specific directorial style: 'The conversation was so thrilling and the intellectual offers were so huge'. During the development of her first commission for Goold, *Oil*, this was as problematic as it was exciting. The development process for the play took over five years. Each time a draft was handed in but not programmed, Hickson's instinct was to respond with more potential: 'I'll just go and make it bigger and smarter and they got more thrilled and more excited but they didn't want to put it on so I went away and made it bigger and smarter'. The play become more ambitious and more sprawling, but less stageable. In retrospect, Hickson feels she really needed someone to 'take two thirds of it out and put it on a stage'. She also partly blames her own inexperience as a writer at the time: 'The dynamism and bombasticness of notes from brilliant directors are hugely inspiring and make for incredible theatrical events, but it is your job as a writer to seek pragmatism from between that bombast and try and work out how you can build a thing that can stand up'. Despite the problems Hickson encountered, the final production was a success: 'it did a huge amount for my career'. The belief in the potential of her work enabled her to produce an epic play expressing that she was 'a writer of scale. I was interested in big ideas and I would become somebody that was thrilled by formal experimentation'. Ultimately, she says, 'it made me a serious theatre writer'. Hickson also feels she learnt how to pinpoint what might be provocative, which became 'crucial' in the development of her next play, *The Writer*: 'If you can spot the way, the particular way that everybody in the room is being polite, find it, name it, shine a light on it, and say it out loud' (Hickson 2019).

Developing New Work

Goold divides the process of supporting the development of new plays into three roles: 'One is to tease, cajole, flatter, inspire, to get the writer to have the courage to make the first offer. The second is to mop their brow and make them cups of tea through the long period of the writing. And then the third is to deliver; the midwife thing'. As with any collaborator, it is important for a director to win the writer's trust. They need to 'really feel you are beside their play, trying to make the best for their play' (Goold 2019c).

Bartlett notes that Goold feels present within the development process, even though he is 'supremely busy' and often physically absent. When he is in the room, 'he's present, very present, and he's yours [...] he absolutely gives the work the attention it deserves' (M. Bartlett 2019).

Goold argues that a director's job with regard to dramaturgy is similar to their role as regards acting: 'getting beat by beat by beat in terms of detail'. This involves 'turning over the words again and again and again and shaking them and trying to listen to them'. As with actors, it is important a director is able to judge the most productive time and way to give writers notes. It's a 'really fine balance' and one that is easily upset: 'I've seen a lot of directors who [...] go, "No, it ought to be X" and then the writer clams up'. This is because 'the director is moving too quickly'. The other extreme is equally harmful: 'The director will respectfully let the play wander around the garden and not intervene at all. And I think that's irresponsible to any writer'. Once the trust between a writer and director is broken it is hard to fix: 'The director head down ploughing on slightly relentlessly doing a load of work for no gratitude and the writer increasingly sort of hopping around about the ways their play has been misinterpreted'. It's a particularly difficult situation to manage as, usually, neither one is in the wrong: 'quite often they're both right' (Goold 2019a).

Goold's interest in classical texts influences his approach to dramaturgy. Much of his early dramaturgical work was based on allowing 'those archetypal structures and canonical forms to play out, sometimes in more personal or contemporary worlds'. Some of the themes Goold repeatedly returns to in his work with classical texts can be discerned in the content and structure of some of the new plays he has worked on: 'faith and damnation and the idea of destroying gods'. Spiritual images and metaphors are present in *ENRON*: 'There's iconography of Skilling on the cross, and the idea of faith as something underpinning the financial sector, the idea of breaking apart the kind of Godhead, in that sense the financial system'. In *Earthquakes in London*, Freya's journey through London could be read as a 'pilgrimage' paralleling the journey of Orpheus or Dante through Hell (Goold 2019c).

Goold might ask a writer to consider how the whole play would function if its structure was modelled on a specific classical structure; for example, encouraging Lucy Prebble 'to think about *ENRON* in the model of a Marlovian tragedy'. It involves applying the template of a classical scene to a contemporary scene: 'lying them under scenes and going, "Is that useful?"' (Goold 2019c). There are traces of specific classical plays woven into Prebble's commissions for Goold. *ENRON* was dubbed 'a corporate Macbeth' (Adams 2009). *The Effect* is haunted by *Romeo and Juliet*. The resonances between the latter two plays are particularly striking in the scene where Prebble's lovers meet for the first time, their hands touching as they both clasp a urine sample (Prebble 2012: 25–7), mirroring the 'palm to palm is holy palmers' kiss' moment between Romeo and Juliet when they first meet (*Romeo and Juliet*, 1.5.99). The scene where the lovers escape from the hospital and find themselves falling in love with each other has resonances of the balcony scene (2.2). *Romeo and Juliet* was used as a reference point for these scenes during rehearsals (Sheffield 2012). By structurally juxtaposing a romance which may only be a chemical reaction with Shakespeare's most famously romantic play, Prebble raises questions about our understanding of the nature of love.

Goold regularly uses Shakespeare as a reference point in rehearsals. Working on *King Charles III*, Bartlett notes that many of the conscious references to Shakespeare originated during rehearsals. During the writing phase, he had consciously inserted a few small references to specific moments in Shakespeare. For example, the tipping of the crown by Charles to show 'Nothing' at its centre in the coronation scene (M. Bartlett 2014: 122) references the image of the 'hollow crown' in *Richard II* (3.2.160). During rehearsals, more Shakespearean parallels emerged, for example, 'echoes of Lady Macbeth would come out in Kate Middleton I hadn't really anticipated'. They also used Shakespeare to 'turn the volume up' on specific scenes. Goold would observe a specific scene was similar to one in Shakespeare, and Bartlett 'would go away and read it and that would galvanize the play a little bit'. This 'was never trying to pay homage to another Shakespeare play. It was about stealing the toolkit to make our play better' (M. Bartlett 2019).

Goold finds Shakespeare useful partly because of the centrality of argument in his work, both in the speeches and in the structure of the plays themselves: 'The basic thesis, antithesis, synthesis structure [...] You start with a proposition, you counter it ("to be or not to be") and unpack it'. Working on new plays, he will 'try to find the play's thesis and then its antithesis' (Goold 2019a). Goold argues dialectical structure is fundamental to theatre. An effective piece of theatre does a 'sort of dance along the razor's edge of conflicting ideas'. It's about something unsettled and complex: 'about social anxiety, not about polemic'. Polemic is theatrically unengaging: 'I'm not sure I've seen a piece of theatre that was really effective that just said something we all know and believe with great passion. Because where's the surprise?' It's 'not going to sustain you through the evening'. Dialectical theatre is both engaging and politically productive: 'Your job is just to try and keep an audience bewildered about the fact that they are dancing back and forwards in terms of sympathy emotionally or intellectually until the end of the evening. And so, if you've really stirred that pot, then they go and think about what they feel'. Polemic might make an audience feel, but argument provokes them to reflect on those feelings (Goold 2019c).

Directing New Writing

When directing revivals, Goold does 'stacks of research', but when directing new writing, he 'never does any research'. With a new play, his job is not 'to interpret the research'; it is 'the opposite. It's to kind of go, "I'm the audience, I know nothing," so if I can't understand it, the audience won't'. Goold also pays less attention to the text on the page than other directors might: 'I'm not a great believer [...] in the play as written down'. He argues there's too much 'holiness' around punctuation. Goold believes it is more important to listen to the text as spoken in the room: 'I just try to listen and go, "I can't hear that, can't hear that, why can't I hear it?" And if I get really stuck, I'll look back and go, "Oh, it's not punctuated that way"'. Often, however, he finds issues with an actor's delivery are 'more to do with the actor not quite connecting with where the stress is' than not adhering to punctuation (Goold 2019c).

During the rehearsal process, Goold stresses the need for clear and responsive communication between the director and the writer: 'It is incumbent upon you to be really timely in your correspondence with the writer, be that in the pub or on email or whatever'. If a writer is up all night working on rewrites then the director may also need to stay up: 'You have to accept that you are not going to sleep doing a new play because you will be up all night thinking about all the things the writers have to write and are thinking about as well'. You might need to be up emailing a writer into the small hours and then wake early in the morning to read cuts: 'That's where you put the work in. It's being really responsive and keeping as positive and as energized as possible in the process' (Goold 2019c).

It can be helpful to discuss the text in the rehearsal room: 'If you run a room properly you should be able to have collective discussions about choices'. These discussions should encompass both 'the performance of the piece' and 'why the text is as it is in the way that it is'. Goold argues that discussing the text promotes 'maximum buy-in from the performers' as it enables them to, 'on a deep level, understand why text choices are being made'. In order to enable the play to be 'properly interrogated', however, the director needs to manage conversations around the text with the company: 'You are the gatekeeper in the room'. At times, 'you have to pull the drawbridge up if somebody is inappropriately invading or being unhelpful', while at other times you need to 'lower it down quickly, if there's a pause and somebody's imagination might really enlighten it'. Managing discussions effectively is important, as some writers find the interrogation of their work in the rehearsal room challenging (Goold 2019c).

Bartlett initially found Goold's way of working 'a complete culture shock': 'I'd come from the Royal Court so I was used to, you go into the rehearsal room and if anyone wants to change a comma, they take you outside and sit you down with a stiff cup of coffee and go, "Look, we just wondered if we might be able to change this comma"'. With Rupert, 'You'd rehearse the scene once, he'd look around to you with a cheeky smile and say, "Hmm, it's a bit long" or "That's not working, is it?" and do it in front of all the actors'. Goold's approach took Bartlett 'a few weeks to get used to': 'it requires you as a writer to have real confidence not just in your own ideas, but the ability to marshal collaboration'. During the first week, Bartlett remembers Goold doing exercises which involved 'getting the cast to design the play, getting them to talk about which scenes they like and which scenes don't work'. This was 'incredibly exposing'. Goold's more collaborative approach raised questions for him about how to deal with the ideas that he was receiving: 'What ideas do you accept? What ideas do you not accept? How do you accept ideas but without offending the person or reject ideas without offending the person that gave them?' During rehearsals for *Earthquakes in London*, there was 'a lot of re-writing, restructuring, changing of the play' but by the end of the process Bartlett was a convert to Goold's collaborative approach: 'I went from being quite annoyed about it to loving it. And loving that what we ended up with was a really collaborative thing, not just with Rupert but with the actors as well' (M. Bartlett 2019).

The process taught Bartlett how useful actors are as advocates for characters: 'When you've got a massive play with a big structure and loads of characters, it's hard to hold all those journeys in your head and to keep them all authentic and truthful'. An actor is entirely focused on their character's journey and so 'often their response of "this scene doesn't work for me" is "this doesn't work for my character" and should be listened to' (M. Bartlett 2019). A clear example of this occurred with Victoria Hamilton during rehearsals for *Albion*. The play originally ended with Audrey leaving: 'She went to London. She left the garden where her son was buried'. When they rehearsed the final scene, however, 'We got to that moment and I just went, "I can't leave, I can't move, I don't know how to play leaving because this entire journey has been about protecting the memory of my son who I'm in denial about grieving. And my child is in the earth around me and we wouldn't be leaving"'. They realized it would be 'perverse' for Audrey to leave her son, so Bartlett reworked the ending (Hamilton 2019).

Both Bartlett and Hickson credit Goold with helping them to push their practice as writers to a new level. For Bartlett, working on *Earthquakes in London* taught him how to write 'bigger plays' and 'to structure these big casts and big ensemble things' (M. Bartlett 2019). For Hickson, the takeaway was about courage. She identifies herself as a writer with a tendency to want to be 'incendiary'. Goold provides a supportive space for the development of provocative work. He 'encourages bravery and then meets that bravery, whatever it is'. To date, he is her first port of call for provocative ideas: 'If I write something that I know is going to be incendiary, I'll send it to Rupert. I trust that he'll read it like I wrote it' (Hickson 2019).

CHAPTER 10
OPERA

Goold's first experience of directing opera came in 1998, when he was invited to direct a production of Antonio Cesti's *Il pomo d'oro* (1668) at the Batignano Opera Festival, Musica nel Chiostro, in Italy. Batignano was set up by Adam Pollock, who was a theatre designer and successful interior designer in the Swinging Sixties. In 1969 he relocated to Tuscany: 'Like lots of people did, I dropped out'. He 'bought this derelict monastery' with no electricity or running water. Initially, it 'was just somewhere to live', 'milking the goat and all that, planting lettuces'. Someone, however, suggested staging opera there. Pollock had become friends with a singer who had experienced vocal problems while performing at the Wexford Festival. He decided to take the plunge: 'I said, "Would you come to Batignano and sing for nothing and we'll do *Dido and Aeneas*?"' The resulting performance in 1974 was a great success. The mayor of the town decided to contribute some money towards it so it happened again the next year 'and then another year, another year, another year and it grew' into an annual opera festival, which he ran for thirty years (Pollock 2019).

Pollock came to see Goold's Greenwich *Romeo and Juliet* and was taken with Goold's work. He invited him to direct *Il pomo d'oro* at Batignano. Pollock had 'this great track record for finding opera directors and designers' (Goold 2019c). Other directors who worked at the festival early in their career included Richard Jones, Tim Albery and Graham Vick. Pollock describes Batignano as a 'trampoline'. It was a stamp of quality that 'meant you were at a certain level and could do whatever you were depended on to do well' (Pollock 2019). Goold had not directed opera before and knew nothing about Batignano. He remembers going out there 'having no idea what it was'. When he arrived, he quickly realized it was 'amazing' (Goold 2019c).

Batignano had begun simply with friends working and living together to enjoy making music theatre. That spirit remained even when Goold was directing there in the 1990s and 2000s. The festival 'didn't have any money' so the performers and the creatives offered their services for free, doing 'it as a sort of a holiday'. The company and creatives were offered catered accommodation and travel expenses. People slept in dormitories, in tents in the olive grove and in the former monks' cells. The structure of the company was 'unhierarchical' (Goold 2019c). This was unusual within the opera world, where people doing different jobs often never meet each other: 'Singers don't really know what orchestras do, who do not know electricians, who do not know prop makers' (Pollock 2019). The company did menial chores together, like the laundry and the washing-up, and were encouraged to mix: 'You'd be sitting at lunch and you'd be next to the props maker or the guy who was building the fence or the prima donna' (Goold 2019c). It was 'a place where everyone mucked in together'. The festival's approach was 'much more in tune with the seventies than now, that kind of hippy, communal living that's very rough around the edges, but it does wonders to develop company spirit' (Thicknesse 2004). Goold liked the festival's ethos, especially as it felt 'a world away from the flock wallpaper and red velvet of opera houses and garden opera' (Goold 2019c).

Days were organized to give time for both rehearsals and relaxation: 'You rehearse in the morning, in the afternoon you go to the beach, then you come back and rehearse in the evening'. In the run-up to the performance, the schedule shifted to allow for technical rehearsals, which had to happen at night so the lighting could be integrated as the performance was outdoors. The monastery was full of activity: 'Little string quartets would form and be practising and doing different kinds of music, and you'd hear the singers warming up'. The performances were 'either in the round or environmentally staged' (Goold 2019c). Initially, Pollock's idea was for the performances to be site-specific, 'to use the building' with 'no scenery at all', but as the festival developed set elements were added depending on the nature of the show. Props, costumes and materials from previous productions were sometimes reused to create the new productions. The tickets were relatively cheap and the operas were sung in Italian so they were accessible to the locals: 'Everybody, from the villagers to the shepherdess who lived down the hill to whoever it was, had to be able to understand us' (Pollock 2019). The audience was very mixed: Italian intellectuals, people on holiday along the coast and serious opera buffs. Sometimes, there were international celebrities. Goold remembers one night where 'Alan Rickman, Donatella Versace, Kate Moss' were in the front row (Goold 2019c).

Pollock describes *Il pomo d'oro* as 'the grandest opera there is' (Pollock 2019). The piece is based on the Greek myth of the golden apple. Paris, a Trojan prince, is asked to judge which of three goddesses, Hera, Athena and Aphrodite, is the most beautiful and therefore deserves to win the golden apple. The opera includes twenty-four different sets, a horse ballet and a fireworks display. It was Goold's first experience of directing on such a large scale. The cast of the opera was huge, 'like 120 people'. The opera was staged 'inside the old monastery and then outside in the olive grove'. Despite the fact the festival had no money, the company were good at finding the resources needed to create the requisite spectacular effects. If you said, '"Could we have a World War II Jeep turn up?" someone would turn up with a World War II jeep to drive onstage'. If you had a bucolic scene, they would ask 'Nella, the old shepherdess from down the hill, to escort her flock of sheep through the olive grove during the aria' (Goold 2019c). Characters rode in on horses. One entered on a red scooter. Paris appeared on a boat, swaying, with 'Gene Kelly sailors all swaying with him'. Pollock even remembers 'a great friend seeing if there were circuses nearby' to investigate whether they could secure an elephant, as there had been elephants in the original production (Pollock 2019). The prologue to the piece involves 'the marriage of words and music to create opera'. Goold realized 'about a week before we were due to open' that they 'didn't have anyone left' to play these non-speaking roles. Pollock suggested Kate Fleetwood and Goold himself play the roles, so Goold ended up acting in the first opera he directed (Goold 2019c).

After *Il pomo d'oro*, Pollock had planned to wind up the festival: 'I told everybody at the end of the season that that was going to happen and they were all a bit glum'. Goold wrote Pollock a letter encouraging him to continue, saying 'this is the most fantastic thing and you can't stop'. Pollock remembers 'it was one of those very well-argued letters so I thought, "All right, we'll go on"' (Pollock 2019). The festival carried on for another five years as a result. Goold returned to Batignano to direct twice more: a production of Stephen Storace's *Gli equivoci* (1786) in 1999; and Florian Gassmann's *L'Opera seria* (1769) in 2004, the festival's final year. Goold positions Batignano as a 'formative' experience for several reasons. Firstly, it was the place he 'learned to do opera' (Goold 2019c) and 'made me at last *love* opera' (Goold 2004e). Secondly, the festival's ethos changed his understanding of opera: 'I associate opera as much with Batignano and the art form and the scratchiness of the surroundings and the purity of the music. I feel like it was a very pure experience'. Finally, it provided him with an opportunity to develop his work at a time when he was struggling to forge a career as a director, 'faced with the impossibility of getting on anywhere' (Goold 2019c). In a letter he sent to Pollock on his retirement, Goold emphasises the impact Batignano had on all his work as a director: 'It set me on a whole new path of creativity, exploration and adventurism and still inspires me hugely' (Goold 2004e).

Turandot

After Batignano, Goold directed a couple more opera projects, including a studio production of *On Thee We Feed* (English National Opera 2001), a new opera by Richard Chew and Rufus Norris 'about nineteenth-century seances and female hysteria' (Goold 2019c) and a production of Gioachino Rossini's comic opera *Le comte Ory* (Garsington 2005). In 2009, he was asked to direct Giacomo's Puccini's *Turandot* (1926) at the English National Opera (ENO). *Turandot* is based on a story from Nizami Ganjavi's Persian epic poem *Haft Peykar*. Set in China, it tells the story of a prince who falls in love with a princess, Turandot, but has to solve three impossible and potentially deadly riddles to win her hand.

In directing *Turandot*, Goold faced two challenges. The first was the opera's representation of race. The opera is a 'sort of orientalist Gothic fantasia' written by an Italian, often still performed in yellowface. Goold found the idea of using yellowface 'offensive'. Instead, he wanted to 'make a production that challenges that and looks at what appropriated oriental culture is'. Goold became intrigued by the kind of people who would frequent the late-night restaurants in Chinatown. For Goold, 'the chinoiserie of [Puccini's] music' resonated with the atmosphere of these restaurants, so he relocated the action of the opera to the dining room and kitchen of a Chinese restaurant 'in a slightly cyberpunk world'. He populated his chorus with a wild variety of late-night Chinese restaurant customers: 'Marilyn Manson, three Elvis impersonators, a group of people on a hen night, a wrestler'. As with the kitchen in *Macbeth*, this was not a literal setting but more a sense of what it would be like to perform *Turandot* in a late-night Chinese restaurant. As well as flagging the opera's orientalism, the location gave the opera a more quotidian feeling. Puccini's music is 'overblown', 'so huge' that there is a danger of putting 'a hat on a hat' if you match 'epic staging with epic music and epic slightly melodramatic acting'. Goold wanted it to feel more like Lars von Trier's musical film *Dancer in the Dark*, 'where you have your songs but in this factory' (Goold 2019c).

The second issue Goold faced was the fact that Puccini died before he finished the opera. The opera was completed after his death by Franco Alfano, who added its conveniently romantic ending. Originally, Goold wanted to use Puccini's music up to the moment it finishes and then have the 'rest of it silent because there wasn't any more music'. The ENO said no: 'I lost that fight'. Instead he decided to represent Puccini in the figure of the Writer (Scott Handy) and stage his murder by Turandot (Kirsten Blanck) at the point where Puccini's music finishes, flagging to the audience the moment at which Puccini loses control of his narrative, so staging both a literal and a Barthian death of the author (Goold 2019c). Michael Billington notes that, as in *Six Characters in Search of an Author*, it was as if the characters had taken control of their own narratives: 'Calaf and Turandot finally destroying the on-stage figure of the writer as if achieving creative autonomy' (Billington 2009). Placing a Puccini figure within the production also enabled Goold to clearly position the opera as a vision of China through Western eyes, written by 'a writer figure who was writing influenced by China' (Goold 2019c).

Despite the fact Goold thought he had made 'interesting choices', the production was 'absolutely hammered' by the opera critics, who 'thought it was trivial' and felt he was 'belittling this great tragic tale' (Goold 2019c). The critic Andrew Clements accused Goold of striving 'to make a garish impact, never trusting the music to make any points without the help of totally redundant stage business, piling one irrelevance on another' (Clements 2009). The tone of the bad opera reviews is reminiscent of the tone of bad theatre reviews of Goold's work: 'The simultaneous bullshit about what singing is reminds me of the pomposity of people who talk about verse, and indeed the sanctimony around certain ideas of new writing as well' (Goold 2019c). Pollock observes that opera critics can be 'very isolated', and this lack of exposure to other cultural forms means they are slow to move with the times, so will attack 'something which in five years' time would be perfectly normal' (Pollock 2019). Billington's was the only positive critical voice. He praised Goold's production, arguing that 'it captures the element of barbaric fantasy in Puccini's opera, ingeniously addresses the problem of its incompletion and, for all its excesses, is theatrically alive'. Billington accused the opera reviewers of a prejudice against 'pesky, tin-eared theatre directors invading the world of opera' (Billington 2009). This, he argues, is the underlying reason for Goold's bad reviews. Handy agrees that prejudice played a role in the production's failure: 'It divided people and some of the people regarded opera as their area'. They thought, 'how dare he muck around with it' (Handy 2019).

Directing Opera

Opera poses a set of specific challenges for a director. The first is the fact the 'repertoire is so canonical'. This means there is often a demand for a director to leave their mark on the text: 'the Jonathan Miller-esque kind of "Oh, what have they done with it?"' The second is a lack of action: 'particularly baroque opera, where the arias are very static and you often get verse and chorus repeated many times'. During these moments there is 'almost no character development, and so you're basically staging. You're having to make a story up around music'. This means 'you can't sit down and action the whole thing, you have to create'. The third challenge is temporal. Time moves differently in opera than in theatre: 'Everything moves more slowly. People just don't speak with the same speed, or sing with the same speed of thought, and so you're constantly trying to make sense of longer paragraphs of emotion'. Therefore, the staging needs to help make 'an audience oblivious of the fact that it's taken someone an incredibly long time to say "I love you" or "I think I'm going to go"' (Goold 2019c).

Singers and actors are 'different'. Actors can never be entirely sure of their skill: 'There's no way of proving Judi Dench is better than you or me empirically'. This means actors are more doubtful in rehearsal. They question their choices. This also means they have a level of humility. Singers are more certain of their skill: 'If you can sing, everybody knows it and so you know': 'They're kind of bulletproof'. Singers are also less questioning: 'Whatever you ask them to do they'll probably do'. They have, however, 'none of the humility'. As a result, Goold finds opera rehearsal room culture 'less collaborative' and more competitive: 'The first run-through in opera is gladiatorial. The chorus watching the singers fail. The bar is set so high. There's nowhere near as much generosity in the room'. There is, however, a clear appreciation of skill: 'If someone succeeds, if the bar is cleared, the acclaim is really meaningful'. Opera singers live 'in constant fear of technical failure'. Therefore, the most vital part of an opera director's job is 'to create the conditions in which they can deliver technically, and give them that confidence, and then plot everything else in'. The atmosphere in an opera rehearsal room can be exciting in a way a theatre rehearsal room rarely is. Goold ascribes this to the proximity of the singers: 'You're seeing it close up and the voice is not supported by the whole orchestra so it's more exposed'. To be in a rehearsal room when a singer is performing an aria can be 'extraordinary' (Goold 2019c).

CHAPTER 11
ARTISTIC DIRECTION

Goold has served as an artistic director since 2002 in three successive but very different organizations: a regional theatre, a touring theatre company and a high-profile London theatre. Being an artistic director involves taking responsibility for guiding the direction of an institution both artistically and strategically. Surprisingly, as Goold observes, there is little to no training available to learn how to do this: 'We're not really taught any of it'. Instead, directors have to learn how to be artistic directors by 'witnessing' the work of other artistic directors while they are embedded in organizations (Goold 2018b). Goold has a passion for working out their structures: 'I find the Rubik's cube of putting [an organization] back on its feet or giving it the best possible version of itself, endlessly fascinating' (Goold 2019b). Robert Icke describes Goold as a master strategist when it comes to planning both his own career and the future of the institutions he runs: 'His strategic thinking is second to none'. He has an 'ability to see the chessboard and work out how to make space for himself or his venue' (Icke 2019b).

Artistic director roles vary from one institution to another. This is partly because organizations vary in character. For example, leading an arts organization in London is very different to leading a regional one. In a regional theatre, finding a regular local audience is 'essential', so it's important to understand the specifics of what your community needs. In contrast, London has an established audience, but competition for their attention is high so leading an organization is more about maintaining a presence in people's minds. Goold sees the London theatres as 'like boats on a river, and you're all bobbing along. If you want to be talked about or be in the conversation you can't slip behind in that race, so you're looking for fast water' (Goold 2019b).

The role of an artistic director also varies from one institution to another because their position within different organizations varies. For example, while Goold has been a joint chief executive at the Almeida and Headlong, at Northampton he was only senior management. Goold argues that artistic directors should be chief executives 'because it makes them financially responsible':

> This back-scratching indulgent culture where you employ a sort of sensitive, talky executive director who hires or has under them or beside them a totally wild, eccentric artist who is there as a gorgeous strange orchid who is there to come up with ideas and dream, and then is interpreted by the organization, I think it's bullshit, it's really unhealthy.

It is also potentially disastrous: 'All theatres I've seen like that have gone to the wolves'. The person leading artistic policy should be fully aware of the theatre's resources: 'Ideally you want the person in overall charge of the economics to be the person who is giving the artistic notes' (Goold 2019b). Icke argues that Goold is as concerned with the financial health of the institutions he runs as with their artistic health. Whenever Goold takes over an institution, 'he's actually quite bothered about having the organization in the black in a year. He doesn't like spending, he doesn't like debt'. For example, while Goold was pleased with *Decade* artistically, 'he really hated what it did to the finances of Headlong' (Icke 2019b).

When starting at a new organization, Goold argues, an artistic director should prioritize working out how it functions. This involves understanding: 'what the challenge is'; 'what success might look like'; 'what the function of the theatre is in its community'; and 'how that feeds into the national theatre ecology' (Goold 2018b). In order to do this, you need to 'think really hard' about 'the means of production, the location, who the audience might be, what other resources you might need to make the work you want to make, what's going on in the conversations that you need to have, be that in the sandwich shops in Northampton, or up and down the country on the road for Headlong' (Goold 2019b). A consideration of these factors enables you to both shape policy and effectively communicate the theatre's identity, 'articulate the narrative' (Goold 2018b).

Carrie Cracknell notes Goold has 'an astonishingly innate sense' of organizational story. This is helpful for audiences as it gives them a sense of both what an organization is and the character of its work: 'It makes audiences really bold because they can understand in some way what each piece feels like before they go and see it. They can understand how each experience fits into the story' (Cracknell 2019). In terms of defining the ethos of an organization, Goold believes it is best to keep it simple: 'normally three-ish main ideas'. While at the RSC, Goold learnt from Michael Boyd's approach to organizational messaging: 'He just kept hitting the same three messages all the time. One was new work, another was international – relations with international theatres – and the third was long ensembles' (Goold 2019b).

Goold remembers his three key words for Northampton being 'playful, theatrical and cross-artform', the latter encompassing the fact the organization was both a large-scale commercial receiving house with a varied programme and a subsidised producing theatre. Of the three, Goold felt playfulness was the most important as the town seemed to lack 'a sense of imaginative freedom, which was bound up in all sorts of things about how Northampton self-identified itself'. At Headlong, there were initially just two ideas: 'dialectical interrogation married with bells-and-whistles showmanship'. These reflected the company's desire 'to talk about things', 'to be unafraid of argument and a sort of boldness that asks of the audience'. At the same time, they wanted to make 'very total theatre'. A third idea, 'contemporary', was added after the first year as the company realized they wanted to make work 'about the world that we live in now', which 'inevitably was going to push towards new work', catalysing the 'defining sea change of my time as artistic director at Headlong'. At the Almeida, Goold's three ideas take the form of questions. Firstly, whether the work 'can get outside Islington', which is related both to the relatively small size of the theatre and the perception of it as a bastion of the upper-middle classes. Secondly, whether 'it introduces someone new onto the list', by which Goold means whether it can enable an emerging artist to establish themselves. Finally, 'are the plays doing something that is pushing the form of theatre-making in a different way?'. Looking back, across his aims for all of the three organizations, Goold can see them linked by a 'consistent desire to do surprising theatrical things' (Goold 2019b).

Goold argues that clarity around messaging 'helps internally as well as externally'. His three ideas for each company are equally derived from both the specific challenges they face as organizations and the needs of their audiences. Northampton's messaging was shaped by 'the identity and context of that town' but also by the fact the organization was dealing with how to encompass two venues that were 'culturally very different'. At Headlong, the messaging was shaped by both the challenges of creating an audience for the company's work on the mid-scale touring circuit and the financial necessity of co-producing, which involved reconciling Headlong's artistic aims with the needs of their co-producers: 'If we're going to producing theatres, how can you bring them shows that expand their programmes but also that they want to do?' At the Almeida, the messaging was born out of challenges related to 'not having a studio space', 'the relatively small size of the audience' and the theatre's 'location' (Goold 2019b).

Programming is extremely important: 'programme is everything'. It involves both a consideration of the 'financial framework' the institution is working within and whether the work will 'find an audience'. In Goold's experience, 'really excellent work does tend to find an audience', but when programming, you still need 'to be aware of where you are making it'. A successful artistic director understands both their current audience and the audiences they might be able to reach. They 'have their eyes and ears open about what is going on in their community' and, in an ideal world, are 'ahead of it'. Shifting a programme towards a new style of work needs careful consideration. Sometimes you need to 'tiptoe your way'. At other times, you might be able to spot an opportunity to try something new and 'really exploit it'. You need to pay careful attention to the audience's response: 'If you have a warning note you have to really interrogate why something has not done well and pull your horns in accordingly'. When establishing themselves and their work within an organization, Goold recommends an artistic director initially direct the bulk of the programme because 'the clearest way for an organization and a community to understand what you are trying to do is your work on stage'. Your shows 'will immediately give a sense of direction' (Goold 2019b).

Beyond that, Goold agrees with Richard Eyre that 'policy is who you work with'. Goold recommends making space within the programme to 'genuinely celebrate other people's work more than your own' (Goold 2019b). Jonathan Church argues that being an artistic director has allowed Goold 'to pursue his vision of what theatre should be'. He doubts Goold 'could have had the same control over a narrowing of the focus to what he believes in, had he not been running a building'. The vision, however, is not a single vision. Alongside developing his own work, Goold 'has managed to enable a group of artists around him and inspired and influenced them to push work forward, that's not the same, but in the same palette, the same DNA'. This, Church argues, is what makes him remarkable as an artist. He has not only 'delivered dazzling work' but he has also made an 'investment in other artists'. In addition to being a great director, he is also 'a great artistic director' (Church 2018).

CHAPTER 12
TALENT DEVELOPMENT

Jonathan Church argues Goold has 'a gift for enabling other artists' (Church 2018). Goold's approach to developing artists draws on his own experience of both artist development and, at times, a lack of support during his early years as a director. When Goold first started out, he got lucky: 'I got these two bursaries when I first began'. He was particularly lucky with his Regional Theatre Young Directors Scheme (RTYDS) bursary as he was placed at Salisbury Playhouse with Church, who would become his long-term champion and mentor: 'someone who consistently backed me, not just at Salisbury but at Hampstead, Birmingham, was my referee when I went to Northampton'. When Goold arrived at Salisbury, Church was careful to work out exactly where the emerging director was in his trajectory and exactly what support he needed at that point. He discerned there was 'no point in [Goold] assisting' as he had already done a lot of assisting at the Donmar. Instead, he encouraged Goold to 'try and learn about running a theatre'. Goold believes that having a champion and a mentor, as he did with Church, is 'priceless' for an emerging director. Goold argues the best mentor for an emerging director is someone who might employ them in the near future. In choosing people to mentor at the Almeida, Goold feels it is most useful to focus on 'the people who might possibly get a job in the next two or three years here and therefore are ready for it'. This policy, however, has to be balanced with the need to also 'bring in really grassroots people' (Goold 2019a).

Though Goold's career started promisingly, it hit a rut after Salisbury. Up until his Greenwich *Romeo and Juliet*, Goold feels the work he did was 'really good'. He felt he had 'proved' himself as a director but then could not 'find a route to move on': 'I lost my way and my confidence and didn't pick it up again until my early thirties'. He observes that a similar thing can happen to writers after the first play: 'How do you get the second play and the third play and all that?' Goold compares being spun out as an artist to the difficulty professional athletes have recovering from a major injury: 'Footballers who get an injury at nineteen and they come back a year later and it should be fine, but they've missed a crucial year of development' (Goold 2018a). This discarding of emerging artists just as they emerge happens partly because theatre is 'vampiric': 'it feeds off new actors, designers, directors, writers' (Goold 2019a). Talent development, at times, facilitates this process by providing a continual supply of new artists for the industry rather than enabling artists to build sustainable careers. He argues all major theatre organizations are to a lesser or greater extent 'culpable on this front' (Goold 2018a).

There are two main routes for an emerging director. Goold identifies both as unsatisfactory. The first is the assistant director route: 'this idea that you give your time, you learn'. This route is problematic as many assistant directors are never given the opportunity to actually direct. The other route is for a director to just do 'their own thing' and make 'their own work the best way they can'. This, however, requires the director to be able to access the resources to produce their own work.

Even when an emerging director is feted by the industry, their future is still uncertain. Every generation has directors who the industry identify as 'the next thing'. Even with all the excitement and support being the 'anointed person' entails, these rising directors still often fail: 'nine times out of ten they don't work, or burn out very, very quickly'. It is 'staggering the way directors are jettisoned'. Once an emerging director has been 'spun out, it's very, very hard to come back in'. Goold sees himself as lucky to have been spun out so early in his career, which meant 'when I came back in at thirty-two, I was very tenacious about trying to stay'. Goold claims this tendency to spin young talent out is understandable. In an industry with limited opportunities to make work, more established directors can feel threatened 'when you see thrusting young talent moving into your very competitive area' (Goold 2018b). The irony is, 'those kids who are assisting you and starting out will be the artistic directors of the future'. They are the people who can 'give you the jobs when you're old' (Goold 2019a).

Developing Directors

Goold argues that his reputation is for 'not so much discovering talent' as rather for supporting the speedy, fast-track people I believe in'. At the Almeida, Goold currently runs a resident directors' scheme, where ten emerging directors are selected to be part of the Almeida's pool for a year: 'They get workshops and masterclasses and free tickets for the shows here, and they're the pool from which the directors pull for their own assistants'. In choosing these directors, Goold often has to rely on an 'intuitive sense of why somebody is worth investing in'. He is often swayed by 'some small piece of social behaviour they're probably completely oblivious of', which betrays a level of 'humility' and 'sensitivity'. These are traits Goold sees as consistent among the directors he's championed (Goold 2019a).

Support needs to come at the right point in an emerging artist's career: 'where they are emerging enough that they can really accelerate in a meaningful way, but equally they're not so junior their practice isn't strong enough for them to withstand' the pressure. With writers, Goold feels he often reads their work too soon: 'You go, "There's probably something here, but I've read it now"'. The script he needed to read was 'the next one or the one after which would have been more assertive about where you're going to go as an artist'. He advises directors not to invite him to a show unless they are certain it will be their best work, 'because however tolerant and willing I want to be, you can't unsee the show you're disappointed in'. At the same time, however, Goold looks for the 'peaks rather than the mean' in emerging artists' work: 'If somebody does one scene that is really breathtakingly effectively achieved as a director, and the rest of it is garbage, I'll be more interested in them than someone who's done a really solid show across the board' (Goold 2019a).

Goold believes in setting the artists he supports big challenges: 'It's fine to set people really high bars, and if they pass them or sail over them, keep lifting the bar exponentially until they bump' (Goold 2019a). Mike Bartlett sees these challenges as more productive than the 'baby step' some other organizations offer: 'To say to me at the age of twenty-seven, having only written one play, "Write a massive play with a big cast," that has an impact. The confidence of someone giving you that opportunity and having that level of belief in you means you are far more likely to rise to that occasion and do something remarkable' (M. Bartlett 2019). Tom Scutt remembers how Goold fought for him to design his RSC *Romeo and Juliet* while he was still a relatively unknown designer. The RSC were 'adamant I wasn't going to design it. They were just like, "Who is this person? No, no, no, no"'. Goold, however, 'pushed and pushed and pushed and pushed and pushed' (Scutt 2019). Robert Icke observes that Goold prioritizes the quality of an emerging artist's work over their age or level of experience: 'The second you prove yourself he's happy to take you off an emerging directors list and put you on a directors list'. Goold supported Icke by programming his work from early on and continuing to programme it. By providing him with 'a platform to direct', Goold gave him 'the most valuable thing you can offer a director in our culture' (Icke 2019b).

Goold believes emerging directors benefit from being supported by an artistic director who continues to develop their own practice and is able to spend time with them in the rehearsal room. He argues that, in the current climate, the artistic director role is 'becoming such a big job' that it makes it difficult for artistic directors to direct. Rather than being 'director artistic directors', they are becoming 'dramaturg artistic directors'. This has an impact on an artistic director's ability to support the development of emerging directors. As an emerging director, Goold remembers appreciating notes from more senior directors: 'It's exhilarating to have an artistic director who you respect come in and give you a load of notes in late-stage rehearsals'. These notes, Goold argues, can be 'transformative to the work'. As an artistic director, 'it's hard to do that if you're not carrying experience and integrity and credibility from the rehearsal room' (Goold 2019a).

Goold has been involved in running a number of schemes supporting emerging directors. Lindsey Alvis argues talent development was central to Goold's regime at Headlong: 'We were all passionate about nurturing artists to make their most ambitious work. Providing an environment where people feel comfortable and vulnerable and can work really hard, letting their guards down, so that they can make the best show' (Alvis 2019). In 2007, Headlong launched the New Directions Award with the Gate (Notting Hill), hoping to discover new artists who were not on anybody's list. It grew out of a 'weird anxiety' that 'because there are so few opportunities for directors, are there people in cottages in Gloucestershire who might be the next Lepage who we don't know about' (Goold 2019a). Headlong were looking to partner with 'a slightly smaller organization that could be an interesting launch pad moment or mid-career moment for some of the directors they were talking to'. The Gate felt there was a 'synchronicity' between the two companies at the time. Headlong 'were making the most ambitious and the wildest theatre in the UK at that moment, and that's what we were aspiring to do on a smaller scale'. Both organizations were looking for 'authorial directors': 'people coming to classic texts and really trying to print their own identity onto them both through adaptation and direction' (Cracknell 2019).

Initially, New Directions was an open scheme. Applications were based on a pitch for a radical version of a classic play, picked from a list of selected authors. The judging panel initially judged the winner purely on the quality of the pitch, rather than on CVs. They thought they might 'find someone from a standing start' (Goold 2019a). The director Natalie Abrahami, Carrie Cracknell, Goold and Ben Power would sit in the basement of the Gate, 'where there were rats creeping around in the ceiling, and drips, and there was never any coffee' and meet promising-sounding directors. The first show they produced as part of the scheme was . . . *SISTERS*, adapted from Chekhov by Chris Goode (Headlong/Gate 2008), an artist Cracknell rates as 'one of the most original voices in British theatre'. The scheme's parameters, however, were narrowed after the second show, Dylan Tighe's *Medea/Medea* (Headlong/Gate 2009), was poorly received. Cracknell thought the show was 'an interesting provocation', though 'it was definitely much further towards live art than maybe any of us had anticipated' (Cracknell 2019). While the critic Andrew Haydon tried to argue Tighe's multimedia adaptation of the Medea story worked if an audience considered it 'more as an installation than what we British tend to think of as theatre' (Haydon 2009b), Lyn Gardner pronounced it 'banal and pretentious' (Gardner 2009c) and gave the Gate their 'best ever review quote' (Cracknell 2019) when she noted: 'Halfway through, the canary gets immolated. How I envied it' (Gardner 2009c). Cracknell remembers the Gate's relationship with its audience was always a delicate balance: 'There was constant tension between trying to lead and direct an audience to be surprised and confident and to be bold in the things that they would buy into, but also taking them on a journey where they would have confidence in the programming. *Medea/Medea* 'pushed those tensions out to their most extreme edge' (Cracknell 2019). Both the Gate and Headlong became more cautious and started to 'take people's CVs into account' (Goold 2019a). The final show in the scheme was Anna Ledwich's *Lulu* (Headlong/Gate 2010). This was a happier experience as 'it felt very connected to the story of both companies in that moment'. Abrahami and Cracknell were excited 'to see a female lead artist working on a female protagonist play in that way and it felt like there was some really interesting reclaiming of the sexual landscape of that piece' (Cracknell 2019).

At Headlong, Goold also ran a scheme enabling emerging directors to direct a mid-scale tour of a classic play. Power describes the structure of the scheme as taking 'a director who doesn't yet have a huge number of credits. Give them a play we're excited about. And let them take it forward' (Power 2019). Henny Finch argues that the scheme's focus on classic texts enabled the company to both satisfy the needs of regional theatres and allow 'the directors to really shine and demonstrate their skills rather than being hidden behind the writer' (Finch 2018a). The scheme also gave emerging directors the opportunity to work in the main houses of regional theatres, enabling them to work on a larger scale. As Alvis notes, emerging directors often 'struggle to get out of studio spaces' (Alvis 2019). The scheme had advantages for the core Headlong team as well. As a touring company, Headlong were committed to delivering a certain number of 'touring weeks' (Grainger 2018). Supporting emerging directors to deliver the classic touring shows meant the core company could focus on new writing, which they were more passionate about (Goold 2018c). Directors who took part in the scheme included Abrahami, Blanche

McIntyre, Steve Marmion and Ben Kidd. While the scheme was an opportunity for an emerging director to offer their take on a classic play, there was an extent to which the approach the directors took was 'guided by Rupert's aesthetic' (Finch 2018b). As Cracknell notes, of directing for Goold at the Almeida, 'there's a sense of a house style'. There's a level on which 'you want to hold that and honour that, but in another way you're also just trying to retain your sense of self and your own confidence in the making of the work' (Cracknell 2019).

Simon Godwin directed a production of *The Winter's Tale* as part of the scheme in 2009. Godwin was re-emerging at the time after 'he'd had a break from directing for several years'. *The Winter's Tale* 'was his second show back' so 'it was really emergent' (Power 2019). After working with Goold at Northampton, Godwin had been inspired to develop his own practice further, to 'discover how I could find my voice in the way that Rupert had'. Godwin went to study at the London International School of Performing Arts. He found the course very productive, but when he returned to directing in his early thirties, he found it difficult to re-establish himself: 'I was really up against the wall in terms of money and in terms of status'. His profile was 'very low'. Godwin was offered a job running a small arts centre in Scotland: 'I don't think it even had a producing budget. But it was a salary, it was a venue, it was a building'. He emailed Goold to ask his advice. Goold sent back 'an amazingly focused and passionate and detailed email going, "This will be a disaster to you. Say no, and if you say no come and see me when I'm back and let's find a show for you to do at Headlong"'. Based on that promise, Godwin said no to the job. He then directed a production of *The Winter's Tale* as part of the emerging directors scheme, which 'put me back on the regional mid-scale circuit and revived and breathed new life into my career'. Following the tour, Godwin was offered work at the Bristol Old Vic, where he would later become an associate director (Godwin 2019).

Icke took part in the scheme in 2012. Initially, he had planned to direct *Julius Caesar*, but after the RSC announced it would be doing a production of the play around the same time, he switched to *Romeo and Juliet*. Icke had a theory the play was about coincidence: 'that you could tie your shoelaces at the wrong time and miss meeting your soulmate'. Icke had directed the play at university but was dissatisfied with his production as he'd not succeeded in turning his 'theory about the play into a three-dimensional stage reality'. Instead, he had done 'a fairly standard production in which I'd told the actors, "It's about coincidence" without any evidence of that on the stage'. With the Headlong production, he pursued the same idea but was still concerned he 'might not be able to get the paint on the canvas'. Icke was 'struggling with how I was going to get this idea [that] there were two versions of the same scene. There was a version of the party where they didn't see each other and then another version where they did'. He noticed the play had lots of moments in it where a character tells you exactly when things are happening: 'You always know what day of the week it is. You always know exactly where you are on a literal timeline'. He realized the key to his multiple possibilities version of *Romeo and Juliet* was to 'timestamp it', a technique which would become a repeating feature in his later work. Goold encouraged Icke to push his ideas about the production further: 'His notes were basically, "If your production is really about coincidence and these missed opportunities, go further"'. He gave Icke a list of places he 'could put in another one of his "either/ors"'. He 'put a hand on my back and shoved me further in the direction I was already walking'. During previews, Icke added two more either/or moments, one from Goold's list and one of his own (Icke 2019a).

While Goold pushes emerging artists to fully realize their artistic potential, he is more pragmatic when it comes to advising them how to live successfully. Goold asks emerging artists to think about their art within the context of the rest of what they want from their lives: 'If you want to have kids, for example, or own a flat or a house, or live in London, whatever it is you want. The thing you go, "Whatever else, I'd like to be doing that"'. Goold argues you have to make peace between art and life: 'If you're one of those people who doesn't need material things, and really know that about yourself' then 'keep going at your craft and don't compromise'. Equally, if you 'want to go on holiday once a year, then accept doing a bit of teaching or whatever'. Goold does not see compromising as a crime: 'I've done work I've done for the money [. . .] It's fine'. It's more important for an emerging artist to be 'realistic' about their earning capacity and the lifestyle it is likely to afford: 'The chances are one in a hundred that the lifestyle you want with the career you want are going to come together. Probably miles less than that' (Goold 2019a).

Goold argues that success has two key ingredients. The first is ability: 'how good you are or your potential to be good'. The second is hard work. It frustrates him when people assume it is possible to achieve success without it: 'Do you know how literally ripped emerging directors' fingernails are from desperately climbing up the cliff face?' Though the struggle to establish yourself as an artist can be long and brutal, Goold sees it as formative: 'You don't just parachute in knowing how to do it [. . .] You're formed in the struggle. Your practice is formed in the struggle'. The people Goold tends to champion are not afraid of hard work. They 'graft at the important point, really put their shoulder to the wheel'. With emerging directors, however, the hard work can sometimes be misplaced, which can cause them to run out of steam during the most important part of rehearsals: 'Often I find directors exhausted at the point they really have to have their energy, in the endgame of the production, because they've put so much work into the prep and the first week or two' (Goold 2019a).

As an artistic director, it can be difficult to build a viable production with an emerging director, partly because emerging directors often pitch the wrong things. Sometimes it is 'the canonical *Hedda Gabler*s and *Woyzeck*s'. These are tricky because 'everybody's pitching those' and, although major actors are keen to play those roles, 'they'll want more experienced directors'. At other times, emerging directors 'pitch plays where literary estates won't grant an unknown person those rights'. New plays are a possibility 'if they've got a relationship with the writers'. Writers, however, will tend to request established directors: 'You'll say, "Who do you want?" They'll go, "Ivo [van Hove] and then Peter Stein and then, if I had to, Ian Rickson"'. Goold advises emerging directors to 'hustle, and develop relationships with literary agents' so they are in a better position to secure rights, alongside thinking about other things they could turn into a production: 'They don't have to come from a text; they could be conceptual ideas or devised ideas' (Goold 2019a).

Goold argues a director's legacy can consist of the 'slate of artists who have come through' under their regime. As an artistic director, he argues, 'for every five years' you should ideally put five new artists 'on the list'. Even though he has no doubt that 'my directing has suffered for being an artistic director', he is 'kind of cool with that, if that other thing is true, that people are coming through'. He identifies his proudest moment at the Almeida as 'the reception of *Summer and Smoke*' directed by Rebecca Frecknall (2018). At the beginning of 2018, none of the press round-ups of 'what are we looking forward to next year' mentioned *Summer and Smoke*: 'it wasn't on a single person's radar'. By December, it was in 'every single end-of-the-year top ten' (Goold 2019a). Goold's skill at and commitment to talent development is best demonstrated by the success of the artists he has supported. Power argues Goold does not get 'anywhere near enough credit as a producer, mentor, nurturer of talent. Very, very few artistic directors come close to his pedigree' (Power 2019). Icke notes Goold gets real pleasure from being able to spot future talent: 'He really enjoys that bit of it, of being able to go, "That's the one in five years you're going to want to watch"' (Icke 2019b).

AFTERWORD

The theatrical landscape has changed considerably in both positive and negative ways since Goold started his career in the mid-1990s. While Goold was on the young directors' scheme at Salisbury, Tony Blair was voted into power. Blair's Labour government brought with them a raft of extra funding for the arts, which had been ravaged by years of funding cuts under the outgoing Conservative government. An injection of funding into regional theatre in the early 2000s supported Goold's development of both the repertoire at Northampton and his own work. In 2010, however, in the wake of the financial crisis, austerity hit. Theatres faced cuts, or if they were lucky standstill funding (essentially still a cut). Theatres today are, therefore, less able to take the risks Goold was able to take at Northampton and Headlong. In a tight financial climate, they need to ensure bums on seats.

In an economic sense, things are also much harder for young artists starting out now than they were for Goold, especially if they come from less privileged backgrounds. Ticket prices have risen to combat falling funding, making it harder for young artists to see work. The rising cost of rents in London has made it harder for artists to develop a career, particularly as many are also saddled with large amounts of student debt:

> I think student loans, the rents, arts funding being cut (people not growing the pie so the pie is shrinking meaning less opportunities), more graduates, the general horror of wealth imbalance in this country have created desperation in the industry. I've got people working here, commuting three hours a day from where they can afford to live on the outskirts of London, earning not nearly enough, angry.
>
> (Goold 2018d)

Whereas artists working in other art forms (such as musicians and visual artists) can move out to other, cheaper urban centres, most theatre artists need to be where the theatres are, the majority of which are in London. For Goold, in the 1990s, the situation was easier. Rent and the general cost of living were lower. He was also privileged in that his family already lived in London, allowing him to live rent-free at home for a couple of years early on. He had more space to focus on developing his artistic practice and a secure platform to do this from.

The nature of political theatre has also shifted as a result of shifts in British politics. The 2000s was an age of liberal consensus in politics. Within this context, it felt possible to make provocative statements as an artist, to challenge 'liberal lazy thinking':

Like Enron, we know they were arseholes, but what if they were driven and compelling? Or climate change, we know it's terrible but what if it's just generational conflict? And we know the Royal Family are kind of redundant and we know that verse drama is an old form but what if it's not? What if both of them are still alive and part of our national identity? And what if actually Rupert Murdoch is a more complex figure that just a cartoon villain? And let's do a Brexit play that is actually trying to be perceived from the Brexiteers' mindset at some level.

Though Goold's more political shows 'ultimately came down on the liberal side, their starting point was to, at some level, get into bed with enemy ideas'. Within the current political climate, this formerly playful approach to political theatre feels dangerous. With the rise of figures such as Nigel Farage and Jeremy Corbyn, the political landscape has become more polarized. Right-wing parties and populist politicians have increasingly gained support, not only in the UK, but in the USA, Brazil, Hungary and Poland, causing the left to move further to the left or to be seen as increasingly left-wing in the context of the right. As a result of this, it feels more difficult, as an artist whose politics sit within the centrist left, to make work attempting to understand the right: 'Who wants to humanize Donald Trump? How can you? It's grotesque. You wouldn't humanize Hitler in the 1930s if you were running a theatre company' (Goold 2018d).

On a more positive note, the theatre industry has become more inclusive. Many more major British theatre companies are now run by women or people of colour or both. Goold notes that the rise of intersectional identity politics within the wider public sphere has been 'the defining feature of my time, particularly the second half of my time, at the Almeida' (Goold 2019b). This has, however, left Goold with a conundrum: 'Right now I'm sort of anti the narrative because I'm a white middle-aged man from public school, who went to Cambridge' (Goold 2018b). He is aware that 'somebody like me isn't the voice people want to hear on the political argument because we've heard enough of those voices'. Goold is also aware of his need to re-examine the past in terms of his privilege:

> thinking back to your own work and thinking, it was a different time then, but does that justify choices? Like a show like *Rough Crossings*, I look back on that and I remember thinking we've got to have a lead artist who's black on this, so getting Caryl [Phillips] was good. But actually was it even appropriate for me as a white man to make that piece?

He feels a need to go back through past work and try to identify 'where was I guilty of received power, lazy thinking?' This shift is troubling for Goold, as someone who has always seen himself as 'trying to challenge orthodoxies'. He has now come to realize that, as a middle-class white man, he is part of the orthodoxy. This has left him with an impossible question to answer: 'I've slammed into not realizing I embody it. And how far ever truly can I challenge it if I embody it?' Moving forward, both as an artist and as a producer of other artists, Goold also has a more practical question to address: 'What do I do about that? Both as an artistic director, but also as a director' (Goold 2018d).

In addition to acknowledging his own privilege, Goold has also had to deal with the Almeida's reputation as an 'uber-bourgeois venue' (Goold in Atkinson-Lord 2019). These layers of privilege raise questions around how the Almeida as an institution can 'meaningfully address diversity'. In order to change this, Goold has had to redefine the Almeida's programming. He argues this is no easy task as the theatre's limited programming capacity, producing only five or six shows a year, makes it difficult for the venue to 'be all things to all people'. Despite this, Goold has been asking himself 'as a programmer, how do I make space for other people to lead where those conversations go?' (Goold 2019b). The theatre's programming has shown a significant shift towards greater inclusivity over the last few years. The number of female directors and writers whose work is included in the main programme has significantly improved. Between December 2017 and June 2020, eight of the sixteen in-house productions in the main programme were directed by women. Seven productions were either written or adapted by female writers. In addition, there were productions directed by black British and British-Iranian directors. One of the productions was written by a black American writer.[1] While BAME (Black, Asian and Minority Ethnic) artists are still underrepresented as writers and directors, their inclusion is an improvement. Prior to autumn 2018, they had been absent from the main programme since Lynn Nottage's *Ruined* was produced at the Almeida in 2010. Goold has also noticed a shift in his own position within the theatre: 'My identity as a director has been increasingly subsumed in my identity as a producer' (Goold 2018d).

As well as programming work by artists from a diverse range of backgrounds, Goold has also programmed a variety of plays that deal with issues related to diversity. In early 2018, he produced a season of three productions which engaged with issues related to #MeToo. It included Clare Barron's *Dance Nation* directed by Bijan Sheibani (Almeida 2018), which explores ideas around women's tendency to negate themselves and their relationships with their bodies through a story about a troupe of competitive teenage dancers. It also included a revival of Sophie Treadwell's *Machinal* directed by Natalie Abrahami (Almeida 2018), which tells the story of a young woman who killed her husband after struggling to conform to the restrictive role society assigned her. The most explosive of the three productions was Ella Hickson's *The Writer* directed by Blanche McIntyre, which tells the story of a female writer trying to write a play and forge a career. In the first scene, a young woman finds herself trying to explain to a male artistic director why she does not see herself represented in his theatre. Next, in a post-show talk, a director railroads the writer, speaking for her rather than allowing her space to speak for herself. The writer then returns home to her house-husband boyfriend, who is keen to force marriage and motherhood on her. She escapes to a Greek idyll, where she luxuriates and recuperates in the company of women. After this, she undergoes a script meeting with the director in which they discuss what artists need to feel safe. In the final scene,

---

[1] Two of these productions – Jeremy O. Harris's *'Daddy'* directed by Danya Taymor and Beth Steel's *The House of Shades* directed by Blanche McIntyre – originally programmed for Spring 2020 were later postponed due to the COVID-19 pandemic.

the now successful female writer finds herself becoming the 'male' aggressor with her new female partner. The gender politics of the play are complicated by the idea that the whole play is a play-within-a-play staged by the male director.

After *Oil*, Hickson was given an open commission by the Almeida. At the time, as a woman working within the theatre industry, she was feeling exhausted: 'I was weary with a sense of powerlessness'. This led her to consider the true nature of provocation in the theatre: 'What's the thing no one wants to say?' Hickson decided the most taboo thing she could write about was the industry's treatment of female writers. Hickson wrote the play quickly while on a residency in the USA in 2017: 'There had been no permission to say it at that point [...] MeToo wasn't even on the landscape. So it just felt like the most unsayable thing' (Hickson 2019). Hickson's script arrived at the Almeida 'out of the blue' around the time the Harvey Weinstein scandal broke (Goold 2018d). Goold programmed it immediately, giving it a slot in March 2018. It was a brave piece of programming in that the play could be read as 'critical of the Almeida'. In performance at the Almeida, the play links Goold with the figure of the artistic director by association. As Andrzej Lukowski notes, the staging of the production within the Almeida suggests 'a rebuke of the Almeida's own Rupert Goold' (Lukowski 2018). As Hickson acknowledges:

> The theatre was in an extraordinary position of trying to support me and trying to put the play on, but the play in a sense felt like it was attacking the theatre. So it was a very difficult thing for them to be loyal to me about. It was a hard position for everyone to be in to put that play on.
>
> (Hickson 2019)

Politically the play was a huge success, receiving polarized reviews ranging from one star to five stars, selling out and dividing audiences, while also raising conversations about the position of women within the industry.

For most of 2018, Goold was working on a feature film, *Judy* (2019), which also addressed issues relating to the #MeToo movement. Based on Peter Quilter's play *End of the Rainbow*, *Judy* tells the story behind Judy Garland's concerts at the Talk of the Town nightclub in London in the winter before her death from an accidental overdose in 1969. The action in 1968/9 is intercut with action from Garland's experiences as a young film actress in the late 1930s, around the time she was filming *The Wizard of Oz* (1939). These scenes connect Garland's later issues with substance abuse to the pressures exerted on her as a young actress. Garland is depicted as subjected to a harsh routine in order to maintain her appearance. She is forbidden from eating and given pills both to stave off hunger and to help her sleep. Unsurprisingly, she starts to rebel; stuffing a hamburger into her mouth at a press call and jumping into a swimming pool after she's been told not to get her hair wet. After this moment of disobedience, Judy is pulled into a barn on set by producer Louis B. Mayer. Placing his hand on her chest, he then comments on her appearance, making it clear there are prettier girls who could take her place. Through such moments, the film captures the ways in which women are coerced and abused by the men in power over them. The implicit understanding is that unless a woman does as she is told and puts up with the abuse, she will lose any chance of having the career that she wants. The film is told from Judy's perspective. The first shot is a completely black screen. Young Judy then opens her eyes, her face filling the screen. The shot places the audience in an oscillating position. They are both in Judy's shoes, seeing the world through her eyes as suggested by the way in which their eyes open with hers, while at the same time gazing on Judy and scrutinising her as the object of their gaze. The latter position puts the audience in the same place as Mayer, so positioning them simultaneously as the victim and the abuser.

In 2019, Goold directed two productions at the Almeida, *Shipwreck* and *The Hunt*. The latter production also engaged with the #MeToo movement but from a different perspective. The play explores the story of a man falsely accused of abusing a young girl. Tobias Menzies, who starred in *The Hunt*, was initially nervous about producing the show within the context of the rise of the #MeToo movement: 'I was nervous about that and said, "Are you sure this is the time we should be telling the story of a white male victim of a female accuser?"' For Goold, however, the show was pertinent in that it raised a discussion, not about the act of abuse itself but about our response to it: 'It was more looking at what do we do with these moments. What do we do with these events, these traumas, to our social contract? How do we hold them? And how do we talk about them?' Menzies argues Goold has an ongoing interest in 'what's not allowed to be talked about'. He sees both his job and the role of theatre as 'to articulate the taboos of our society'. Theatre remains 'one of the few safe places left in which we can tease [an issue] apart and look at it in a slower, more meditative and more considered way'. This is the result of the fact an audience sits together in a room to watch theatre, which 'makes the conversation fundamentally different. And I think therefore it is the place to talk about stuff that is hard to talk about'. Within this context, Goold's programming of *The Hunt* can be seen as a way of opening up difficult conversations around the #MeToo movement (Menzies 2019).

The critics, while generally praising the show, were mixed in their response to its narrative. As David Jays observed: 'Programming the tale of a wrongly accused man is provocative in the thick of #MeToo' (Jays 2019). Ava Wong Davies notes that choosing to present the nuanced figure of a man falsely accused of abuse raises questions as to why we are 'still averse to having an equally tender, nuanced, empathetic depiction of an abuse victim on our stages' (Wong Davies 2019). Others, however, praised *The Hunt* for its effective exploration of the way in which a community can scapegoat its own: 'in its depiction of the way a false accusation can spread like a virus, the play is undeniably chilling' (Billington 2019); '*The Hunt* offers a sobering reminder of how quickly aggression can be stirred up, how readily we take sides and how easy that is to exploit' (Hemming 2019a).

Goold's other production in 2019, Anne Washburn's *Shipwreck*, addresses both the current political situation and explores issues around race. *Shipwreck* tells the story of a group of middle-aged, middle-class friends living in and around New York, who head upstate to spend the weekend with their friends who have bought a farmhouse in the middle of the countryside. Once there, they get snowed in and discover that one of their number voted for Donald Trump. These scenes alternate with fantastical scenes reimagining meetings between Trump and both George W. Bush and the director of the FBI, James Comey. The play, like her earlier *Mr Burns*, is interested in the myths America creates for itself. The set designed by Miriam Buether accentuated this concept. The round platform forming the main playing area had audience members seated at it as if at a table, so invoking the dinner table which sits at the heart of many classic American plays, whose structure weaves political issues with family celebrations such as Thanksgiving. Behind the platform, a bearskin and a Chapman Brothers-style totem pole featuring a hamburger and a figure holding a remote control suggest America's repackaging and cultural appropriation of its past. In its depiction of a group of stranded wealthy liberals insulated by their privilege sitting around a campfire and telling stories about Trump while doing nothing, the play theorizes that the current political moment 'springs in part out of liberal complacency' (Hemming 2019b). The stories the liberals tell then form the basis for the mythic depiction of Trump within the play.

The play is framed by a series of scenes in which a young African man, Mark, who was adopted by the white farming family who previously lived in the house, recounts his search for an identity and his decision to vote for Trump. The play reveals that the white characters are supposedly a fantasy conjured up by Mark: 'This, at any rate, is how I imagine them. The strangers who are living now in my house' (Washburn 2019: 134). As Chris Bennion notes, this framing concept is not fully articulated within the play and as such 'doesn't tie in too satisfactorily' when introduced in the final moments (Bennion 2019). The framing device is also problematic in terms of ownership. The play is positioned as a narrative told by a black man but is written by white woman. Goold's programming for 2020 addresses this lack of BAME voices telling their own stories within the Almeida's main programme by importing black American writer Jeremy O. Harris's play, *'Daddy'*, about the relationship between a young black artist and his white art dealer sugar daddy, so reopening the space for black voices within the theatre's programme.

While Goold recognizes the need to make space for underrepresented voices within his programme, he argues against the idea of 'single-issue theatres'. Theatre should be 'inclusive and discursive and consensual'. At the heart of the best theatre, Goold believes, is a 'robust, entertaining exchange of ideas, and a belief in humanism, a belief in what unites people through suffering and hope and dreaming'. It is through this, he argues, theatre can best address the rise in 'intolerance' both in British society and beyond in recent years (Goold 2018d).

As Goold notes in the foreword to this book, his work is very much a product of its times. In his development of his work, he is aware that he benefited from both a more supportive economic climate and a more stable political environment than currently exists for emerging artists in the UK, as well as from his privileged position as an educated, white, middle-class man. Despite this, his path to prominence was not as meteoric as is often portrayed, and when he was spun out of the industry in his early twenties it took several years of hard work for him to re-establish himself. For all his reputed flashiness, Goold's approach to directing is rooted in a deep examination and consideration of the text and aims to both overturn cultural clichés around the performance of classic texts and make these texts accessible and vital for contemporary audiences. His radical re-imaginings of classic plays at Northampton, the RSC and Headlong in the 2000s have been a major influence on younger British directors and, alongside increased access to the work of European directors, have played a role in a shift in how British directors approach classic texts over the last decade. As Matt Trueman notes, the 'current vogue for interventionist adaptations, from Marianne Elliott's gender-flipped *Company* to Robert Icke's recent post-truth spin on *The Wild Duck*, can be traced back to Headlong's heyday' (Trueman 2019). In more recent years, shifting his focus towards new writing, Goold has supported emerging British playwrights in the development of breakthrough works including Lucy Prebble's *ENRON*, Mike Bartlett's *King Charles III* and Hickson's *Oil*. As a supporter of emerging talent, he has played a significant role in nurturing the work of several major British theatre artists, including Icke, Ben Power and, most recently, Rebecca Frecknall. In his work as both a director and an artistic director he has had a significant impact on the nature of contemporary British theatre and merits consideration as a major British theatre artist, alongside figures such as Katie Mitchell and Simon McBurney.

BIBLIOGRAPHY

'A Fresh Twist on a Theatre Classic'. 2002. *Northampton Chronicle and Echo*. https://www.northamptonchron.co.uk/news/a-fresh-twist-on-a-theatre-classic-1-943925 (accessed 13 June 2019).
Abdulla, Sara. 1995. 'Time Out Review: Mud'. *Theatre Record*. 15, 262.
Abrahami, Natalie (Dir.). 2018. *Machinal*. [theatre production] Almeida.
Abrams, J. J., Jeffrey Lieber and Damon Lindelof (Creators). 2004. *Lost*. [TV series] Bad Robot.
Adams, Tim. 2009. '"I hate to be told somewhere is out of bounds for women." Enter Enron …' *The Guardian*, 5 July. https://www.theguardian.com/stage/2009/jul/05/lucy-prebble-playwright-interview-enron (accessed 25 February 2020).
Aeschylus. 2015. *Oresteia*. Adapted by Robert Icke. London: Oberon.
Alberge, Dalya. 2012. 'Theatre Turns to Facebook to Bring a Younger Audience through the Doors'. *The Guardian*, 22 April. https://www.theguardian.com/stage/2012/apr/22/theatre-turns-to-facebook (accessed 1 January 2019).
Alexander, Bill (Dir.). 1984. *Richard III*. [theatre production] RSC.
Alexander, Bill (Dir.). 1985. *The Merry Wives of Windsor*. [theatre production] RSC.
Alexander, Bill (Dir.). 2002. *The Importance of Being Earnest*. [theatre production] Northampton Royal & Derngate.
Allfree, Claire. 2012. 'Metro Review: The Effect'. *Theatre Record*. 32, 1214.
Alvis, Lindsey. 2019. Personal Interview.
Apollonios, son of Nestor. 100AD. *The Belvedere Torso*. [sculpture].
Argento, Dario (Dir.). 1977. *Suspiria*. [film] Seda Spettacoli.
Atkinson-Lord, Rebecca. 2019. 'The Legacy Tapes: Rupert Goold'. *Exeunt*. http://exeuntmagazine.com/podcasts/legacy-tapes-rupert-goold/ (accessed 3 November 2019).
Ayckbourn, Alan. 2001. *House and Garden*. London: Faber.
Bale, John. 1974. *King Johan*. Edited by Barry B. Adams. San Marino: Huntington Library Publications.
Barboza, David. 2002. 'Enron's Many Strands: Fallen Star; From Enron Fast Track to Total Derailment'. *New York Times*, 3 October. https://www.nytimes.com/2002/10/03/business/enron-s-many-strands-fallen-star-from-enron-fast-track-to-total-derailment.html (accessed 25 October 2019).
Barron, Clare. 2018. *Dance Nation*. London: Oberon.
Bart, Lionel. 1989. *Oliver!* London: Lakeview Music Ltd.
Barthes, Roland. 1977a. 'Death of the Author' in *Image, Music, Text*, translated by Stephen Heath, 142–8. London: Fontana Press.
Bartlett, Kim. 2019. 'Personal Email: Rupert Goold Book'.
Bartlett, Mike. 2010. *Earthquakes in London*. London: Methuen.
Bartlett, Mike. (Dir.) 2012. *Medea*. [theatre production] Headlong.
Bartlett, Mike. 2014. *King Charles III*. London: Nick Hern.
Bartlett, Mike. 2015. *Game*. London: Nick Hern.
Bartlett, Mike. 2017. *Albion*. London: Nick Hern.
Bartlett, Mike. 2019. Personal Interview.
Barton, John. 1984. *Playing Shakespeare*. London: Methuen.
Bassett, Kate. 1998. 'Daily Telegraph Review: Romeo and Juliet'. *Theatre Record*. 18, 134–5.

Bibliography

Bassett, Kate. 2004. 'Independent on Sunday Review: Faustus'. *Theatre Record*. 24, 1436.
Bassett, Kate. 2005. 'Observer Review: Hamlet'. *Theatre Record*. 25, 384.
Bassett, Kate. 2007. 'Independent on Sunday Review: Rough Crossings'. *Theatre Record*. 27, 1108.
Bassett, Kate. 2008a. 'Independent on Sunday Review: The Last Days of Judas Iscariot'. *Theatre Record*. 28, 371–2.
Bassett, Kate. 2008b. 'Independent on Sunday Review: Six Characters in Search of an Author'. *Theatre Record*. 28, 836.
Bassett, Kate. 2008c. 'Independent on Sunday Review: King Lear'. *Theatre Record*. 28, 1300.
Bassett, Kate. 2011. 'Independent on Sunday Review: Decade'. *Theatre Record*. 31, 950–1.
Bate, Jonathan and Kevin Wright. 2008. 'The Director's Cut: Interviews with Peter Brook, Sam Mendes and Rupert Goold' in Bate, J. and Rasmussen, E. (Eds), *The Tempest*. Basingstoke: Macmillan, Basingstoke, 125–41.
Bean, Richard. 2008. *The English Game*. London: Oberon.
Beckett, Samuel. 2012. *Waiting for Godot*. London: Faber.
Benedict, David. 1998. 'Save the Arts: A true Shakespearian fight for survival'. *The Independent*. http://www.independent.co.uk/news/save-the-arts-a-true-shakespearian-fight-for-survival-1144131.html (accessed 17 May 2019).
Benedict, David. 2007. 'The Tempest'. *Variety*. https://variety.com/2007/legit/reviews/the-tempest-15-1200509930/ (accessed 8 September 2019).
Bennion, Chris. 2019. 'Shipwreck'. *The Times*. https://www.thetimes.co.uk/article/review-shipwreck-at-the-almeida-theatre-n1-zd3q0sdfs (accessed 3 November 2019).
Betteridge, Natasha (Dir.). 2001. *House and Garden*. [theatre production] Northampton Royal & Derngate.
'Bill Alexander's production: The Merry Wives of Windsor'. *RSC*. https://www.rsc.org.uk/the-merry-wives-of-windsor/past-productions/in-focus-bill-alexander-1985 (accessed 18 July 2019).
Billington, Michael. 2003. 'Guardian Review: Othello'. *Theatre Record*. 23, 1485.
Billington, Michael. 2005. 'Guardian Review: Hamlet'. *Theatre Record*. 25, 382–3.
Billington, Michael. 2007. 'Guardian Review: Macbeth'. *Theatre Record*. 27, 653–4.
Billington, Michael. 2008a. 'Guardian Review: The Last Days of Judas Iscariot'. *Theatre Record*. 28, 371.
Billington, Michael. 2008b. 'Guardian Review: Six Characters in Search of an Author'. *Theatre Record*. 28, 1037.
Billington, Michael. 2008c. 'Guardian Review: King Lear'. *Theatre Record*. 28, 1298.
Billington, Michael. 2009. 'Does Rupert Goold's Turandot Really Show Him Up?'. *The Guardian*, 12 October. https://www.theguardian.com/stage/theatreblog/2009/oct/12/turandot-rupert-goold (accessed 22 August 2019).
Billington, Michael. 2010. 'Guardian Review: Romeo and Juliet'. *Theatre Record*. 30, 311.
Billington, Michael. 2011a. 'Guardian Review: The Merchant of Venice'. *Theatre Record*. 31, 530.
Billington, Michael. 2011b. 'Guardian Review: Decade'. *Theatre Record*. 31, 949–50.
Billington, Michael. 2011c. 'The RSC – Who Should Take over?' *The Guardian*, 17 October. https://www.theguardian.com/stage/theatreblog/2011/oct/17/who-should-take-over-rsc (accessed 29 July 2019).
Billington, Michael. 2012. 'D is for Director's Theatre'. *The Guardian*, 3 January. https://www.theguardian.com/stage/2012/jan/03/d-director-s-theatre-modern-drama (accessed 8 February 2020).
Billington, Michael. 2015. 'Guardian Review: Medea'. *Theatre Record*. 35, 977.
Billington, Michael. 2016. 'Guardian Review: Richard III'. *Theatre Record*. 36, 695–6.
Billington, Michael. 2017. 'Guardian Review: Ink'. *Theatre Record*. 37, 696.
Billington, Michael. 2019. 'The Hunt'. *The Guardian*, 27 June. https://www.theguardian.com/stage/2019/jun/27/the-hunt-review-almeida-thomas-vinterberg-rupert-goold (accessed 3 November 2019).

Blythe, Alecky. 2014. *Little Revolution*. London: Nick Hern.
Bogdanov, Michael (Dir.). 1980. *Hiawatha*. [theatre production] NT.
Bogdanov, Michael. 2015. *Hiawatha*. London: Samuel French.
Bogart, Anne. 2003. *A Director Prepares: Seven Essays on Art and Theatre*. London: Routledge.
Bond, Edward. 2006. *Restoration*. London: Methuen.
'Boss Quits Royal & Derngate', 2005. *BBC*, 18 July. http://www.bbc.co.uk/northamptonshire/content/articles/2005/07/18/boss_quits_royal_and_derngate_feature.shtml (accessed 13 June 2019).
Brace, Adam. 2016. *They Drink it in the Congo*. London: Faber.
Brantley, Ben. 2010. 'Titans of Tangled Finances Kick Up Their Heels Again'. *New York Times*, 28 April. https://www.nytimes.com/2010/04/28/theater/reviews/28enron.html (accessed 28 July 2019).
Brantley, Ben. 2016. '"American Psycho" Hits Broadway, So Smooth, So Rich, So Ruthless'. *New York Times*, 22 April. https://www.nytimes.com/2016/04/22/theater/review-american-psycho-hits-broadwayso-smooth-so-rich-so-ruthless.html (accessed 20 July 2019).
Brighouse, Harold. 1992. *Hobson's Choice*. Oxford: Heinemann.
Brook, Peter. 1990. *The Empty Space*. Penguin, London.
Brook, Peter (Dir.). 1970. *A Midsummer Night's Dream*. [theatre production] RSC.
Brown, Georgina. 2007. 'Mail on Sunday Review: Macbeth'. *Theatre Record*. 27, 655.
Brown, Georgina. 2008. 'Mail on Sunday Review: King Lear'. Theatre Record. 28, 1299–1300.
Brown, Georgina, 2014. 'Mail on Sunday Review: King Charles III'. *Theatre Record*. 34, 360–1.
Büchner, Georg. 2008. *Woyzeck* in *Danton's Death, Leonce and Lena, Woyzeck*, edited by Victor Price. Oxford: OUP.
Buford, Bill. 1992. *Among the Thugs*. London: Arrow.
Burrows, Abe, Frank Loesser and Jo Swerling (Dirs). 1950. *Guys and Dolls*. [theatre production] 46th Street Theatre.
Butcher, Justin. 2002. *Scaramouche Jones*. London: Methuen.
Butler, Leo. 2016. *Boy*. London: Methuen.
Calvino, Italo. 2019. *The Baron in the Trees*. London: Vintage.
Camus, Albert. 2005. *The Myth of Sisyphus*. London: Penguin.
Carnegy, Patrick. 2011. 'Spectator Review: The Merchant of Venice'. *Theatre Record*. 31, 532–3.
Carroll, Lewis. 2003. *Alice's Adventures in Wonderland and Through the Looking Glass*. London: Penguin Classics.
Castle, Alison (Ed.). 2017. *Stanley Kubrick's Napoleon*. Cologne: Taschen.
Cavendish, Dominic. 2003. 'Telegraph Review: Othello'. *Theatre Record*. 23, 1485–6.
Cavendish, Dominic. 2004a. 'Telegraph Review: Paradise Lost'. *Theatre Record*. 24, 174.
Cavendish, Dominic. 2004b. 'Telegraph Review: Insignificance'. *Theatre Record*. 24, 578.
Cavendish, Dominic. 2004c. 'Telegraph Review: Faustus'. *Theatre Record*. 24, 1436.
Cavendish, Dominic. 2009. 'Daily Telegraph Review: King Lear'. *Theatre Record*. 29, 109.
Cavendish, Dominic. 2015. 'Daily Telegraph Review: Medea'. *Theatre Record*. 35, 976.
Cavendish, Dominic. 2016. 'Daily Telegraph Review: Richard III'. *Theatre Record*. 36, 696.
Cavendish, Dominic, 2017. 'Telegraph Review: Ink'. *Theatre Record*. 37, 696–7.
Chapman, Jake and Dinos Chapman. 1999/2000. *Hell*. https://jakeanddinoschapman.com/works/hell/ (accessed 7 February 2020).
Chapman, Jake and Dinos Chapman. 2003. *Insult to Injury*. http://jakeanddinoschapman.com/works/insult-to-injury/ (accessed 7 February 2020).
Chase, David (Creator). 1999. *The Sopranos*. [TV series] HBO.
Chekov, Anton. 2013. *The Seagull*. Adapted by John Donnelly. London: Faber.
Chekov, Anton. 2016. *Uncle Vanya*. Adapted by Robert Icke. London: Oberon.
Church, Jonathan. 2018. Personal Interview.
Clapp, Susannah. 2007a. 'Observer Review: Macbeth'. *Theatre Record*. 27, 656.
Clapp, Susannah. 2007b. 'The Observer Review: Rough Crossings'. *Theatre Record*. 27, 1108.

Bibliography

Clapp, Susannah. 2008. 'Observer Review: King Lear'. *Theatre Record*. 28, 1300–01.
Clapp, Susannah. 2009. 'Observer Review: ENRON'. *Theatre Record*. 29, 852.
Clapp, Susannah. 2011a. 'Observer Review: The Merchant of Venice'. *Theatre Record*. 31, 531.
Clapp, Susannah. 2011b. 'Observer Review: Decade'. *Theatre Record*. 31, 951.
Clapp, Susannah. 2013. 'Observer Review: American Psycho'. *Theatre Record*. 33, 1147.
Clapp, Susannah. 2014. 'Observer Review: King Charles III'. *Theatre Record*. 34, 360.
Clapp, Susannah. 2015. 'Observer Review: Medea'. *Theatre Record*. 35, 977.
Clapp, Susannah. 2017. 'The Observer Review: Albion'. *Theatre Record*. 37, 1089–90.
Clements, A. 2009. 'Turandot'. *The Guardian*, 9 October. https://www.theguardian.com/music/2009/oct/09/turandot-opera-review-andrew-clements (accessed 22 August 2019).
Collins, Phil. 1981. 'In the Air Tonight'. [single] Virgin.
Cook, Mark. 2013. 'Sunday Express Review: American Psycho'. *Theatre Record*. 33, 1148.
Cork, Adam. 2019. Personal Interview.
Cracknell, Carrie (Dir.). 2016. *Oil*. [theatre production] Almeida.
Cracknell, Carrie. 2019. Personal Interview.
Crimp, Martin. 2017. *The Treatment*. London: Nick Hern.
Cromer, David (Dir.). 2008. *Our Town*. [theatre production] The Hypocrites.
Cromer, David (Dir.). 2014. *Our Town*. [theatre production] Almeida.
Cumming, Tim. 2002. 'Stuff and Nonsense'. *The Guardian*, 13 February. https://www.theguardian.com/culture/2002/feb/13/artsfeatures.arts (accessed 17 October 2019).
Cusk, Rachel. 2012. *Aftermath*. London: Faber.
de Jongh, Nicholas. 1998. 'Evening Standard Review: Romeo and Juliet'. *Theatre Record*. 18, 134.
de Jongh, Nicholas. 2007. 'Evening Standard Review: Rough Crossings'. *Theatre Record*. 27, 1107–8.
de Jongh, Nicholas. 2008. 'Evening Standard Review: Six Characters in Search of an Author'. *Theatre Record*. 28, 834.
Delgado, Maria and Dan Rebellato (Eds.). 2010. *Contemporary European Theatre Directors*. Routledge: London.
Devlin, Es. 2019. Personal Interview.
Donnellan, Declan. 2005. *The Actor and the Target*. London: Nick Hern.
Doran, Gregory (Dir.). 2008. *Hamlet*. [theatre production] RSC.
Doran, Gregory (Dir.). 2009. *Hamlet*. [film] Illuminations.
Dunnett, R. 2004. 'Independent Review: Insignificance'. *Theatre Record*. 24, 668.
Duran Duran. 1982. 'Hungry Like the Wolf'. [single] EMI.
Edwardes, Jane. 2006. 'Time Out London Review: Speaking Like Magpies'. *Theatre Record*. 26, 181–2.
Edwardes, Jane. 2011. 'Sunday Times Review: The Merchant of Venice'. *Theatre Record*. 31, 533.
Elliott, Marianne (Dir.). 2003. *The Sugar Syndrome*. [theatre production] Royal Court.
Ellis, Bret Easton. 2014. *American Psycho*. London: Pan Macmillan.
Escher, M. C. 1960. *Ascending and Descending*. [lithographic print].
Euripides. 2012. *Medea*. Adapted by Mike Bartlett. London: Methuen.
Euripides, 2015a. *Bakkhai*. Translated by Anne Carson. London: Oberon.
Euripides, 2015b. *Medea*. Adapted by Rachel Cusk. London: Oberon.
Eyre, Richard (Dir.). 2013. *Ghosts*. [theatre production] Almeida.
Eyre, Richard (Dir.). 2015. *Little Eyolf*. [theatre production] Almeida.
Faber, Caroline. 2019. Personal Interview.
Fielding, Susannah. 2019. Personal Interview.
Finch, Henny. 2018a. Personal Interview.
Finch, Henny. 2018b. Personal Interview with Henny Finch, Rupert Goold, Jenni Grainger and Ben Power.
Fleming, Victor (Dir). 1939. *The Wizard of Oz*. [film] MGM.

Fornes, Maria Irene. 1986. *Plays: Mud, The Danube, The Conduct of Life, Sarita*. New York: PAJ Publications.
Foxe, John. 1851. 'King John' in *Foxe's Book of Martyr*, edited by John Cumming, 1563 edition, 342–57. London: George Virtue.
Franks, Philip (Dir.). 2007. *Twelfth Night*. [theatre production] Chichester Festival Theatre.
Frecknall, Rebecca. 2018. *Summer and Smoke*. [theatre production] Almeida.
Gardner, Lyn. 2002. 'Arcadia'. *The Guardian*, 23 October. https://www.theguardian.com/stage/2002/oct/23/theatre.artsfeatures1 (accessed 14 June 2019).
Gardner, Lyn. 2003. 'Guardian Review: Waiting for Godot'. *Theatre Record*. 23, 229.
Gardner, Lyn. 2004. 'Guardian Review: Insignificance'. *Theatre Record*. 24, 578.
Gardner, Lyn. 2006. 'Guardian Review: Speaking Like Magpies'. *Theatre Record*. 26, 181.
Gardner, Lyn. 2009a. 'The Goold Standard for British Theatre Directors'. *The Guardian*, 6 October. https://www.theguardian.com/stage/theatreblog/2009/oct/06/goold-theatre-directors (accessed 7 February 2020)
Gardner, Lyn. 2009b. 'Guardian Review: King Lear'. *Theatre Record*. 29, 109–10.
Gardner, Lyn. 2009c. 'Guardian Review: Medea/Medea'. *Theatre Record*. 29, 721.
Godber, John. 2017. 'Bouncers' in *Plays One*. London: Methuen.
Godwin, Simon (Dir.). 2002. *The Seagull*. [theatre production] Northampton Royal & Derngate.
Godwin, Simon (Dir.). 2009. *The Winter's Tale*. [theatre production] Headlong/Schtanhaus/Nuffield Southampton.
Godwin, Simon. 2019. Personal Interview.
Goode, Chris (Dir.). 2008. *SISTERS . . .* [theatre production] Headlong/The Gate Notting Hill.
Goold, Rupert (Dir.). 1992. *Fool for Love*. [theatre production] Corpus Playroom.
Goold, Rupert (Dir.). 1993. *Othello*. [theatre production] Cambridge University European Theatre Group.
Goold, Rupert (Dir.). 1994. *Twelfth Night*. [theatre production] ADC America Tour.
Goold, Rupert (Dir.). 1995. *Mud*. [theatre production] Ectetera Theatre.
Goold, Rupert (Dir.). 1996. *Bouncers*. [theatre production] Salisbury Playhouse.
Goold, Rupert (Dir.). 1997a. *The End of the Affair*. [theatre production] Salisbury Playhouse/Bridewell Theatre.
Goold, Rupert (Dir.). 1997b. *Travels with My Aunt*. [theatre production] Salisbury Playhouse.
Goold, Rupert (Dir.). 1998a. *Il pomo d'oro*. [opera production] Batignano Opera Festival.
Goold, Rupert (Dir.). 1998b. *Romeo and Juliet*. [theatre production] Greenwich Theatre.
Goold, Rupert (Dir.). 1998c. *Summer Lighting*. [theatre production] Salisbury Playhouse.
Goold, Rupert (Dir.). 1999a. *The Colonel Bird*. [theatre production] Gate Notting Hill.
Goold, Rupert (Dir.). 1999b. *Gli equivoci*. [opera production] Batignano Opera Festival.
Goold, Rupert (Dir.). 2001a. *On Thee We Feed*. [opera production] ENO: The Knack Course End of Year Show.
Goold, Rupert (Dir.). 2001b. *Scaramouche Jones*. [theatre production] Rebbeck Penny.
Goold, Rupert (Dir.). 2002a. *Arcadia*. [theatre production] Northampton Royal & Derngate.
Goold, Rupert (Dir.). 2002b. *Betrayal*. [theatre production] Northampton Royal & Derngate.
Goold, Rupert. 2003a. 'Director's Notes' in *Theatre Programme: The Weir and Waiting for Godot*. Northampton Royal & Derngate.
Goold, Rupert (Dir.). 2003b. *Othello*. [theatre production] Northampton Royal & Derngate.
Goold, Rupert (Dir.). 2003c. *Sunday Father*. [theatre production] Hampstead Theatre.
Goold, Rupert (Dir.). 2003d. *Waiting for Godot*. [theatre production] Northampton Royal & Derngate.
Goold, Rupert (Dir.). 2003e. *The Weir*. [theatre production] Northampton Royal & Derngate.
Goold, Rupert (Dir.). 2004a. *Faustus*. [theatre production] Northampton Royal & Derngate.
Goold, Rupert (Dir.). 2004b. *Insignificance*. [theatre production] Northampton Royal & Derngate.
Goold, Rupert (Dir.). 2004c. *L'Opera seria*. [opera production] Batignano Opera Festival.

Bibliography

Goold, Rupert (Dir.). 2004d. *Paradise Lost*. [theatre production] Northampton Royal & Derngate.
Goold, Rupert. 2004e. Letter to Adam Pollock.
Goold, Rupert (Dir.). 2005a. *Le comte Ory*. [opera production] Garsington Opera.
Goold, Rupert (Dir.). 2005b. *Hamlet*. [theatre production] Northampton Royal & Derngate.
Goold, Rupert (Dir.). 2005c. 'Rupert's Q&As' in *Theatre Programme: Hamlet*. Northampton Royal & Derngate.
Goold, Rupert (Dir.). 2005d. *Speaking Like Magpies*. [theatre production] RSC.
Goold, Rupert (Dir.). 2006a. *Restoration*. [theatre production] Headlong/Bristol Old Vic.
Goold, Rupert (Dir.). 2006b. *The Tempest*. [theatre production] RSC.
Goold, Rupert (Dir.). 2007a. *The Glass Menagerie*. [theatre production] Apollo Theatre.
Goold, Rupert (Dir.). 2007b. *Macbeth*. [theatre production] Chichester Festival Theatre.
Goold, Rupert (Dir.). 2007c. *Rough Crossings*. [theatre production] Headlong/Birmingham Rep/Liverpool Everyman and Playhouse/West Yorkshire Playhouse/Lyric Hammersmith.
Goold, Rupert (Dir.). 2008a. *King Lear*. [theatre production] Headlong/Liverpool Everyman and Playhouse/Young Vic.
Goold, Rupert (Dir.). 2008b. [theatre production] *The Last Days of Judas Iscariot*. Headlong/Almeida.
Goold, Rupert (Dir.). 2008c. [theatre production] *No Man's Land*. Gate Dublin.
Goold, Rupert (Dir.). 2008d. [theatre production] *Oliver!* Drury Lane.
Goold, Rupert (Dir.). 2008e. *Six Characters in Search of an Author*. [theatre production] Headlong/Chichester Festival Theatre.
Goold, Rupert (Dir.). 2009a. *ENRON*. [theatre production] Headlong/Chichester Festival Theatre/Royal Court.
Goold, Rupert (Dir.). 2009b. *Time and the Conways*. [theatre production] NT.
Goold, Rupert (Dir.). 2009c. *Turandot*. [opera production] ENO.
Goold, Rupert. 2009d. 'NT Platform: Rupert Goold talks to Daniel Rosenthal'.
Goold, Rupert (Dir.). 2010a. *Earthquakes in London*. [theatre production] Headlong/NT.
Goold, Rupert (Dir.). 2010b. *Macbeth*. [film] Illuminations.
Goold, Rupert (Dir.). 2010c. [theatre production] *Romeo and Juliet*. RSC.
Goold, Rupert (Dir.). 2011a. *Decade*. [theatre production] Headlong/Chichester Festival Theatre.
Goold, Rupert (Dir.). 2011b. *The Merchant of Venice*. [theatre production] RSC.
Goold, Rupert (Dir.). 2012a. *Richard II. The Hollow Crown*. [TV series] BBC.
Goold, Rupert (Dir.). 2012b. *The Lion, the Witch and the Wardrobe*. [theatre production] Three Sixty Productions.
Goold, Rupert (Dir.). 2012c. *Falling Headlong*. [video] Headlong. https://www.youtube.com/watch?v=YNH6ANbLsnA (accessed 7 February 2020).
Goold, Rupert (Dir.). 2012d. *The Effect*. [theatre production] Headlong/Almeida.
Goold, Rupert (Dir.). 2013. *American Psycho*. [theatre production] Headlong/Almeida.
Goold, Rupert. 2014a. Personal Interview with Rupert Goold and Ben Power.
Goold, Rupert (Dir.). 2014b. *King Charles III*. [theatre production] Almeida.
Goold, Rupert (Dir.). 2015a. *Medea*. [theatre production] Almeida.
Goold, Rupert (Dir.). 2015b. *True Story*. [film] Plan B/Regency Enterprises.
Goold, Rupert (Dir.). 2016. *Richard III*. [theatre production] Almeida.
Goold, Rupert (Dir.). 2017a. *Albion*. [theatre production] Almeida.
Goold, Rupert (Dir.). 2017b. *Ink*. [theatre production] Almeida.
Goold, Rupert (Dir.). 2017c. *King Charles III*. [film] BBC.
Goold, Rupert. 2018a. Personal Interview, 7 November.
Goold, Rupert. 2018b. Personal Interview, 23 October.
Goold, Rupert. 2018c. Personal Interview with Henny Finch, Rupert Goold, Jenni Grainger and Ben Power.
Goold, Rupert. 2018d. Personal Interview with Rupert Goold, 27 November.

Goold, Rupert. 2019a. Personal Interview, 14 January.
Goold, Rupert. 2019b. Personal Interview, 11 March.
Goold, Rupert. 2019c. Personal Interview, 28 January.
Goold, Rupert (Dir.). 2019d. *The Hunt*. [theatre production] Almeida.
Goold, Rupert (Dir.). 2019e. *Judy*. [film] Twentieth Century Fox.
Goold, Rupert (Dir.). 2019f. *Shipwreck*. [theatre production] Almeida.
Goold, Rupert and Robert Icke (Dirs). 2015a. *The Iliad*. [theatre production] Almeida.
Goold, Rupert and Robert Icke (Dirs). 2015b. *The Odyssey*. [theatre production] Almeida.
Goold, Rupert and Ben Power. 2008. *Faustus: After Christopher Marlowe*. London: Nick Hern Books.
'Goold Unveils Headlong's 2010, Reworks *Gulliver*'. 2009. *Whats on Stage*. https://www.whatsonstage.com/west-end-theatre/news/goold-unveils-headlongs-2010-reworks-gulliver_15821.html (accessed 28 July 2019).
Gore-Langton, Robert. 2006. 'Sunday Telegraph Review: Restoration'. *Theatre Record*. 26, 1050.
Gore-Langton, Robert. 2009. 'Mail on Sunday Review: ENRON'. *Theatre Record*. 29, 852.
Gormley, Antony. 2007. *Blind Light*. [installation] Hayward Gallery.
Goss, John. 2003. 'Sunday Telegraph Review: Othello'. *Theatre Record*. 23, 1486.
Goya, Francisco. 1810–20. *The Disasters of War*. [print series]
Graham, James. 2017. *Ink*. London: Methuen.
Grainger, Jenni. 2018. Personal Interview with Henny Finch, Rupert Goold, Jenni Grainger and Ben Power.
Grainger, Jenni. 2019a. Personal Interview, 4 June.
Grainger, Jenni. 2019b. Personal Interview, 19 September.
Greene, Graham. 1996. *Travels with My Aunt*. Adapted by Giles Havergal. London: Oberon.
Greene, Graham. 2001. *The End of The Affair*. Adapted by Rupert Goold and Caroline Butler. London: Samuel French.
Grochala, Sarah. 2017. 'Controversial Intentions: Adaptation as an act of iconoclasm in Rupert Goold and Ben Power's Faustus (2004) and the Chapman Brothers' Insult to Injury (2003)' in Reilly, Kara (Ed.), *Contemporary Approaches to Adaptation in Theatre*, 295–316. London: Palgrave Macmillan.
Guirgis, Stephen Adly. 2002. *Jesus Hopped the 'A' Train*. London: Methuen.
Guirgis, Stephen Adly. 2006. *The Last Days of Judas Iscariot*. New York: Farrar, Strauss and Giroux.
Halliburton, Rachel. 2006. 'Rupert Goold: Interview'. *Time Out London*. https://www.timeout.com/london/theatre/rupert-goold-interview-1 (accessed 23 July 2019).
Halliburton, Rachel. 2007. 'Raising the Bard'. *Time Out*. 12 September, pp.36–8.
Hamilton, Victoria. 2019. Personal Interview.
Handy, Scott. 2019. Personal Interview.
Hart, Christopher. 2008. 'Sunday Times Review: Six Characters in Search of an Author'. *Theatre Record*. 28, 1038–9.
Haydon, Andrew. 2009a. 'Time Out London Review: King Lear'. *Theatre Record*. 29, 110.
Haydon, Andrew 2009b. 'Time Out London Review: Medea/Medea'. *Theatre Record*. 29, 721.
Haydon, Andrew. 2013. 'Theatre in the 2000s' in Rebellato, Dan (Ed.), *Modern British Playwriting: 2000-2009*, 40–98. London: Methuen.
Hemming, Sarah. 2019a. 'Financial Times Review: The Hunt'. *Theatre Record*. 39.
Hemming, Sarah. 2019b 'Financial Times Review: Shipwreck'. *Theatre Record*. 39.
Hickling, Alfred. 2004. 'Faustus'. *The Guardian*, 12 November. https://www.theguardian.com/stage/2004/nov/12/theatre1 (accessed 8 February 2020).
Hickson, Ella. 2012. *Boys*. London: Nick Hern.
Hickson, Ella. 2016. *Oil*. London: Nick Hern.
Hickson, Ella. 2018. *The Writer*. London: Nick Hern.
Hickson, Ella. 2019. Personal Interview.

Bibliography

Hill-Gibbons, Joe (Dir.). 2014. *Little Revolutions*. [theatre production] Almeida.
Hitchings, Henry. 2010a. 'Evening Standard Review: Romeo and Juliet'. Theatre Record. 30, 311.
Hitchings, Henry. 2010b. 'Evening Standard Review: Earthquakes in London'. Theatre Record. 30, 879.
Hitchings, Henry. 2017a. 'Evening Standard Review: Ink'. Theatre Record. 37, 697.
Hitchings, Henry. 2017b. 'Evening Standard Review: Albion'. Theatre Record. 37, 1087.
Hopkins, Laura. 2019. Personal Interview.
Ibsen, Henrik. 2002. *Hedda Gabler*. Translated by Michael Meyer. London: Methuen.
Ibsen, Henrik. 2015. *Little Eyolf*. Adapted by Richard Eyre. London: Nick Hern.
Ibsen, Henrik. 2013. *Ghosts*. Adapted by Richard Eyre. London: Nick Hern.
Icke, Robert (Dir.). 2012a. *Boys*. [theatre production] Headlong.
Icke, Robert (Dir.). 2012b. *Romeo & Juliet*. [theatre production] Headlong/Nuffield Southampton/Nottingham Playhouse.
Icke, Robert (Dir.). 2014. *Mr Burns*. [theatre production] Almeida.
Icke, Robert (Dir.). 2015. *The Fever*. [theatre production] Almeida.
Icke, Robert (Dir.). 2016a. *Uncle Vanya*. [theatre production] Almeida.
Icke, Robert (Dir.). 2016b. *Mary Stuart*. [theatre production] Almeida.
Icke, Robert (Dir.). 2017. *Hamlet*. [theatre production] Almeida.
Icke, Robert. 2019a. Personal Interview, 14 June.
Icke, Robert. 2019b. Personal Interview, 24 June.
Icke, Robert and Duncan Macmillan (Dirs). 2013a. *1984*. [theatre production] Headlong.
Icke, Robert and Duncan Macmillan. 2013b. *1984*. London: Oberon.
Jarecki, Andrew (Dir.). 2003. *Capturing the Friedmans*. [film] Magnolia Pictures.
Jays, David. 2019. 'The Hunt'. *Sunday Times*. https://www.thetimes.co.uk/article/the-hunt-review-tobias-menzies-is-superb-in-a-story-of-abuse-in-the-danish-forest-pbs3wcvsc (accessed 3 November 2019).
John, Emma. 2005. 'A Bomb in the Basement'. *The Guardian*, 27 September. https://www.theguardian.com/stage/2005/sep/27/rsc.theatre (accessed 18 December 2019).
John, Emma. 2008. 'Going for Goold'. *The Guardian*, 28 September. https://www.theguardian.com/stage/2008/sep/28/theatre (accessed 1 November 2019).
Johnson, Terry. 1993. *Insignificance* in *Plays One*. London: Methuen.
Jones, Jonathan. 2003. 'Look What We Did'. *The Guardian*, 31 March. http://www.theguardian.com/culture/2003/mar/31/artsfeatures.turnerprize2003 (accessed 21 February 2015).
Jones, Richard (Dir.). 2001. *Six Characters in Search of an Author*. [theatre production] Young Vic.
Jonze, Spike (Dir.). 2002. *Adaptation*. [film] Columbia Pictures.
Kavanaugh, Rachel (Dir.). 2008. *The Music Man*. [theatre production] Chichester Festival Theatre.
Kennedy, Laurence. 1995. 'What's On Review: Mud'. Theatre Record. 15, 262.
Kingston, Jeremy. 2003. 'Times Review: The Weir/Waiting for Godot'. Theatre Record. 23, 229.
Kirkwood, Lucy. 2013. *Chimerica*. London: Nick Hern.
Kramer, Daniel (Dir.). 2007. *Angels in America*. [theatre production] Headlong/Glasgow Citizens/Lyric Hammersmith.
Kubrick, Stanley (Dir.). 1980. *The Shining*. [film] Warner Bros.
Kunuk, Zacharias (Dir.). 2001. *Atanarjuat: The Fast Runner*. [film] Isuma Igloolik Productions.
Kushner, Tony. 2007. *Angels in America: Part One Millennium Approaches & Part Two Perestroika*. London: Nick Hern.
Landy, Michael. 2001. *Break Down*. [installation] London.
Lawson, Mark. 2014. 'Why the Almeida Is a Little Wonder'. *The Guardian*, 18 April. https://www.theguardian.com/stage/2014/apr/18/almeida-theatre-olivier-awards-mark-lawson-history (accessed 30 July 2019)
Ledwich, Anna. 2010. *Lulu*. Headlong/Gate Notting Hill.

Lee, Veronica. 2011. 'Sunday Telegraph Review: The Merchant of Venice'. *Theatre Record*. 31, 533.
Letts, Quentin. 2008. 'Daily Mail Review: The Last Days of Judas Iscariot'. *Theatre Record*. 28, 370–1.
Letts, Quentin. 2016. 'Daily Mail Review: Richard III'. *Theatre Record*. 36, 697.
Lewis, C. S. 2009. *The Lion, the Witch and the Wardrobe*. London: Harper Collins.
Lister, David. 1995. 'This is a Job for the Arts Council'. *The Independent*. http://www.independent.co.uk/arts-entertainment/this-is-a-job-for-the-arts-council-1601980.html (accessed 5 August 2019).
Lloyd, Jamie (Dir.). 2010. *Salome*. [theatre production] Headlong.
Logan, Brian. 1997. 'Guardian Review: The End of the Affair'. *Theatre Record*. 17, 1499.
Longhurst, Michael (Dir.). 2015. *Carmen Disruption*. [theatre production] Almeida.
Longhurst, Michael (Dir.). 2016. *They Drink It in the Congo*. [theatre production] Almeida.
Luketic, Robert (Dir.). 2001. *Legally Blonde*. [film] MGM.
Lukowski, Andrzej. 2011. 'Rupert Goold Talks Decade'. *Time Out London*. https://www.timeout.com/london/theatre/rupert-goold-talks-decade (accessed 1 November 2019).
Lukowski, Andrzej. 2013. 'Time Out London Review: American Psycho'. *Theatre Record*. 33, 1148.
Lukowski, Andrzej. 2014. 'Time Out London Review: King Charles III'. *Theatre Record*. 34, 258.
Lukowski, Andrzej. 2015. 'Time Out London Review: Medea'. *Theatre Record*. 35, 977–8.
Lukowski, Andrzej. 2018. 'The Writer'. *Time Out London*. https://www.timeout.com/london/theatre/the-writer-review (accessed 2 November 2019).
Macaulay, Alastair. 1998. 'Financial Times Review: Romeo and Juliet'. *Theatre Record*. 18, 135.
Macdonald, James (Dir.). 2015. *Bakkhai*. [theatre production] Almeida.
'The Making of the Iliad'. 2015. *Almeida Theatre*. https://almeida.co.uk/the-making-of-the-iliad (accessed 1 October 2019).
Marlowe, Christopher. 1631. *Doctor Faustus*. London: John Wright.
Marlowe, Christopher. 1986a. *Doctor Faustus* in *The Complete Plays*. London: Penguin, 263–339.
Marlowe, Christopher. 1986b. *Tamburlaine the Great: Part One* in *The Complete Plays*. London: Penguin, London, 101–78.
Marlowe, Sam. 2003. 'Times Review: Othello'. *Theatre Record*. 23, 1487.
Marlowe, Sam. 2004. 'Times Review: Faustus'. *Theatre Record*. 24, 1435–6.
Marlowe, Sam. 2006. 'Times Review: Restoration'. *Theatre Record*. 26, 1049–50.
Marlowe, Sam. 2007. 'The Times Review: Macbeth'. *Theatre Record*. 27, 654.
'The Marlowe Society'. n.d. *Camdram*. https://www.camdram.net/societies/the-marlowe-society (accessed 5 July 2019).
Marmion, Steve (Dir.). 2009. *Edward Gant's Amazing Feats of Loneliness*. [theatre production] Headlong/Nuffield Southampton.
Marshall, Neil (Dir.) 2005. *The Descent*. [film] Celador Films.
Maxwell, Dominic. 2009. 'The Times Review: ENRON'. *Theatre Record*. 29, 849–50.
Maxwell, Dominic. 2013. 'The Times Review: American Psycho'. *Theatre Record*. 33, 1145.
McBurney, Simon (Dir.). 1999. *Mnemonic*. [theatre production] Complicite.
McGinn, Caroline. 2011. 'Time Out London Review: Decade'. *Theatre Record*. 31, 952.
McGinn, Caroline. 2017. 'Time Out London Review: Ink'. *Theatre Record*. 37, 697–8.
McGuinness, Frank. 2005. *Speaking Like Magpies*. London: Faber.
McIntyre, Blanche (Dir.). 2013. *The Seagull*. [theatre production] Headlong.
McIntyre, Blanche (Dir.). 2018. *The Writer*. [theatre production] Almeida.
McNulty, Charles. 2008. '21st Century Macbeth'. *LA Times*, 9 April. https://www.latimes.com/archives/la-xpm-2008-apr-09-et-macbeth9-story.html (accessed 1 November 2019).
McPherson, Conor. 2001. *The Weir*. London: Nick Hern.
Mendes, Sam (Dir.). 1994. *Oliver!* [theatre production] London Palladium.
Mendes, Sam (Dir.). 1995a. *Company*. [theatre production] Donmar.
Mendes, Sam (Dir.). 1995b. *The Glass Menagerie*. [theatre production] Donmar.

Bibliography

Menzies, Tobias. 2019. Personal Interview.
Miller, Jonathan (Dir.). 1970a. *The Merchant of Venice*. [theatre production] NT.
Miller, Jonathan (Dir.). 1970b. *The Tempest*. [theatre production] Mermaid Theatre.
Miller, Jonathan. 1986. *Subsequent Performances*. London: Faber.
Milton, John. 2003. *Paradise Lost*. London: Penguin.
Milton, John. 2006. *Paradise Lost*. Adapted by Ben Power. London: Oberon.
Moore, Rich (Dir.). 1993. 'Cape Feare'. *The Simpsons*. [TV programme] Twentieth Century Fox.
Murphy, Siobhan. 2013. 'Metro Review: American Psycho'. *Theatre Record*. 33, 1147.
Nakata, Hideo (Dir.). 1998. *Ring*. [film] Ringu/Rasan Production Committee.
Naylor, Ben (Dir.). 2003. *Tamburlaine the Great*. [theatre production] Rose Theatre Bankside.
Neill, Heather. 2011. 'Rupert Goold Directs Romeo and Juliet'. *Theatre Voice*. http://www.theatrevoice.com/audio/rupert-goold-directs-romeo-and-juliet/ (accessed 8 September 2019).
Neilson, Anthony. 2009. *Edward Gant's Amazing Feats of Loneliness!* London: Methuen.
Norman, Neil. 2011. 'Daily Express Review: Decade'. *Theatre Record*. 31, 950.
Norman, Neil. 2017. 'Daily Express Review: Ink'. *Theatre Record*. 37, 698.
Nottage, Lynn. 2010. *Ruined*. London: Nick Hern.
Nunn, Trevor and John Caird (Dirs). 2004. *Les Misérables*. [theatre production] Queens Theatre.
O'Neill, Jonjo. 2019. Personal Interview.
Orr, Jake. 2012. 'Theatre Thought: The Rise of the Digital Theatre'. *A Younger Theatre*. http://www.ayoungertheatre.com/theatre-thought-the-rise-of-the-digital-theatre/ (accessed 1 October 2019).
'Oxford Stage Company is One of the Leading National Touring Theatre Companies'. 2010. *What's On Stage*. https://www.whatsonstage.com/west-end-theatre/news/oxford-stage-company-is-one-of-the-leading-nationa_24862.html (accessed 23 July 2019).
Peele, George. 2016. *The Troublesome Reign of John, King of England*. Edited by Charles R. Forker. Manchester: MUP.
Peter, John. 2005. 'Sunday Times Review: Hamlet'. *Theatre Record*. 25, 383–4.
Pinter, Harold. 1991. *Betrayal*. London: Faber.
Pinter, Harold. 2007. *The Hothouse*. London: Faber.
Pirandello, Luigi. 1989. *Six Characters in Search of an Author*. London: Methuen.
Pirandello, Luigi. 1994. *The Rules of the Game*. London: Oberon.
Pirandello, Luigi. 2008. *Six Characters in Search of an Author*. Adapted by Rupert Goold and Ben Power. London: Nick Hern.
Pollock, Adam. 2019. Personal Interview.
Power, Ben. 2014. Personal Interview with Rupert Goold and Ben Power.
Power, Ben. 2018. Personal Interview with Henny Finch, Rupert Goold, Jenni Grainger and Ben Power.
Power, Ben. 2019. Personal Interview.
Prebble, Lucy. 2003. *The Sugar Syndrome*. London: Methuen.
Prebble, Lucy. 2009. *ENRON*. London: Methuen.
Prebble, Lucy. 2012. *The Effect*. London: Methuen.
Presley, Elvis. 1960. 'Are You Lonesome Tonight?' [single] RCA.
Priestley, J. B. 2000. *Time and The Conways* in *An Inspector Calls and Other Plays*. London: Penguin, 7–82.
Puccini, Giacomo. 2004. *Turandot*. Milan: Casa Ricordi.
Quilter, Peter. 2005. *End of the Rainbow*. London: Methuen.
Ramsden, Timothy. 2002. 'Betrayal'. *Reviews Gate*. https://reviewsgate.com/betrayal/ (accessed 13 June 2019).
Reiner, Rob (Dir.). 1984. *This Is Spinal Tap*. [film] Goldcrest.
Riches, Chris. 2008. 'Daily Express Review: King Lear'. *Theatre Record*. 28, 1299.
Roberts, Clióna. 2019. Personal Email: Rupert Goold Book.

Rourke, Josie (Dir.). 2018. *Mary Queen of Scots*. [film] Studiocanal/Working Title/Perfect World.
Rubasingham, Indhu (Dir.). 2010. *Ruined*. [theatre production] Almeida.
Sater, Steven and Duncan Sheik. 2007. *Spring Awakening*. New York: Theatre Communications Group.
Schama, Simon. 2004. *Landscape and Memory*. London: Harper Perennial.
Schama, Simon. 2007. *Rough Crossings*. Adapted by Caryl Phillips. London: Oberon.
Schama, Simon. 2009. *Rough Crossings: Britain, the Slaves and the American Revolution*. London: Vintage.
Schiller, Friedrich. 2016. *Mary Stuart*. Adapted by Robert Icke. Reprint edition. London: Oberon.
Scola, Ettore (Dir.). 1983. *Le Bal*. [film] Almi Classics.
Scutt, Tom, 2019. Personal Interview.
Service, R. 2005. *Stalin: A Biography*. Cambridge, Massachusetts: Harvard University Press.
Seva, Botis (Choreographer). 2018. *BLKDOG*. [dance production] Far from the Norm/Sadler's Wells.
Seva, Botis. 2019. Personal Interview.
Seymour, Lorna. 2019. Personal Interview.
Shakespeare, William. 1995. *Antony and Cleopatra*. Edited by John Wilders. London: Arden Shakespeare.
Shakespeare, William. 1998. *Julius Caesar*. Edited by David Daniell. London: Arden Shakespeare.
Shakespeare, William. 2002. *Richard II*. Edited by Charles R. Forker. London: Arden Shakespeare.
Shakespeare, William. 2005a. *Hamlet*. Rehearsal Script. Northampton Royal & Derngate.
Shakespeare, William. 2005b. *Hamlet*. Edited by Ann Thompson and Neil Taylor. London: Arden Shakespeare.
Shakespeare, William. 2008. *Twelfth Night*. Edited by Keir Elam. London: Arden Shakespeare.
Shakespeare, William. 2010. *The Winter's Tale*. Edited by John Pitcher. London: Arden Shakespeare.
Shakespeare, William. 2011. *The Tempest*. Edited by Alden T. Vaughan and Virginia Mason Vaughan. London: Arden Shakespeare.
Shakespeare, William. 2012. *Romeo and Juliet*. Edited by Rene Weis. London: Arden Shakespeare.
Shakespeare, William. 2014. *Macbeth*. Edited by Sandra Clark and Pamela Mason. London: Arden Shakespeare.
Shakespeare, William. 2016. *Othello*. Edited by E. A. J. Honigmann. London: Arden Shakespeare.
Shakespeare, William. 2017. *Hamlet*. Adapted by Robert Icke. London: Oberon.
Shakespeare, William. 2018. *King John*. Edited by John Tobin and Jesse Lander. London: Arden Shakespeare.
Sharp, Rob. 2011. 'From Big Names to Fringe Venues, Cuts Hit Hundreds of Arts Bodies'. *The Independent*. http://www.independent.co.uk/arts-entertainment/art/news/from-big-names-to-fringe-venues-cuts-hit-hundreds-of-arts-bodies-2257885.html (accessed 1 October 2019).
Shawn, Wallace. 1991. *The Fever*. London: Faber.
Shebani, Bijan (Dir.). 2018. *Dance Nation*. [theatre production] Almeida.
Sheaffer, Anna, 2009. 'Writing as Exorcism'. *The Virginia Quaterly Review*. https://www.vqronline.org/authors/writing-exorcism-luigi-pirandello-vqr (accessed 26 July 2019).
Sheffield, Audrey, 2012. 'The Effect: Rehearsal Diary Week 4'. *Headlong*. https://headlong.co.uk/productions/the-effect/explore/effect-rehearsal-diary-week-4/ (accessed 20 July 2019).
Sheik, Duncan and Robert Aguirre-Sacasa. 2016. *American Psycho*. Milwaukee: Hal Leonard Corporation.
Shepherd, Sam. 1984. *Fool for Love*. London: Faber.
Shuttleworth, Ian. 2008a. 'Financial Times Review: Six Characters in Search of an Author'. *Theatre Record*. 28, 836–7.
Shuttleworth, Ian. 2008b. 'Financial Times Review: King Lear'. *Theatre Record*. 28, 1299.
Shuttleworth, Ian, 2010. 'Financial Times Review: Romeo and Juliet'. *Theatre Record*. 30, 313–14.
Spencer, Charles. 2005. 'Daily Telegraph Review: Hamlet'. *Theatre Record*. 25, 383.

Bibliography

Spencer, Charles. 2007a. 'Beamed to a Better Ship'. *The Telegraph*. https://www.telegraph.co.uk/culture/theatre/drama/3663504/Beamed-to-a-better-ship.html (accessed 8 November 2019).
Spencer, Charles. 2007b. 'Daily Telegraph Review: Macbeth'. *Theatre Record*. 27, 654.
Spencer, Charles. 2007c. 'Daily Telegraph Review: Rough Crossings'. *Theatre Record*. 27, 1107.
Spencer, Charles. 2008a. 'Daily Telegraph Review: The Last Days of Judas Iscariot'. *Theatre Record*. 28, 370.
Spencer, Charles. 2008b. 'Daily Telegraph Review: King Lear'. *Theatre Record*. 28, 1298–9.
Spencer, Charles. 2009. 'ENRON'. *The Telegraph*. http://www.telegraph.co.uk/journalists/charles-spencer/5893217/Enron-at-Minerva-Theatre-in-Chichester-review.html (accessed 30 January 2016).
Spencer, Charles. 2010a. 'Daily Telegraph Review: Romeo and Juliet'. *Theatre Record*. 30, 312.
Spencer, Charles. 2010b. 'Daily Telegraph Review: Earthquakes in London'. *Theatre Record*. 30, 883.
Spencer, Charles. 2011a. 'Daily Telegraph Review: The Merchant of Venice'. *Theatre Record*. 31, 530.
Spencer, Charles. 2011b. 'Daily Telegraph Review: Decade'. *Theatre Record*. 31, 949.
Spencer, Charles. 2012. 'Daily Telegraph Review: The Effect'. *Theatre Record*. 32, 1212–3.
Spencer, Charles. 2013. 'Daily Telegraph Review: American Psycho'. *Theatre Record*. 33, 1145–6.
Spencer, Charles, 2014. 'Daily Telegraph Review: King Charles III'. *Theatre Record*. 34, 359.
Stephens, Simon. 2015. *Carmen Disruption*. London: Methuen.
Stoppard, Tom. 1993. *Arcadia*. London: Samuel French.
Stratton, Kate. 1998. 'Time Out London Review: Romeo and Juliet'. *Theatre Record*. 18, 135.
Supple, Ruth. 2002. 'Tempted out by Royal's Arcadia'. *Northampton Chronicle and Echo*. https://www.northamptonchron.co.uk/news/tempted-out-by-royal-s-arcadia-1-943992 (accessed 13 June 2019).
Szalwinska, Maxie. 2011. 'Sunday Times Review: Decade'. *Theatre Record*. 31, 952.
Taylor, Paul. 2003a. 'Independent Review: Othello'. *Theatre Record*. 23, 1486–7.
Taylor, Paul. 2003b. 'Sunday Father'. *The Independent*. http://www.independent.co.uk/arts-entertainment/theatre-dance/reviews/sunday-father-hampstead-theatre-london-96618.html (accessed 22 July 2019).
Taylor, Paul. 2004. 'Independent Review: Paradise Lost'. *Theatre Record*. 24, 172–3.
Taylor, Paul. 2006. 'The Tempest'. *The Independent*. http://www.independent.co.uk/arts-entertainment/theatre-dance/reviews/first-night-the-tempest-royal-shakespeare-theatre-stratford-upon-avon-411147.html (accessed 8 September 2019).
Taylor, Paul. 2007. 'Independent Review: Macbeth'. *Theatre Record*. 27, 655.
Taylor, Paul. 2008. 'Independent Review: Six Characters in Search of an Author'. *Theatre Record*. 28, 834–5.
Taylor, Paul. 2011. 'Independent Review: The Merchant of Venice'. *Theatre Record*. 531–2.
Taylor, Paul. 2015. 'Independent Review: Medea'. *Theatre Record*. 35, 978.
Taylor, Paul. 2016. 'Independent Review: Richard III'. *Theatre Record*. 36, 695.
Taylor, Paul. 2017. 'Independent Review: Albion'. *Theatre Record*. 37, 1086–7.
Taymor, Danya (Dir.). (forthcoming). *Daddy*. [theatre production] Almeida. Programmed for 2020 but postponed due to COVID-19 outbreak.
'The Tempest: Rehearsal Note 1'. 2006. RSC Archives. RSC/SM/2/206/85
'The Tempest: Stage Management Notes'. 2006. RSC Archives. RSC/SM/2/206/85
Tennyson, Alfred. 2003. *In Memoriam*. Edited by Erik Gray. New York: W. W. Norton & Company.
Thatcher, Margaret. 1979. 'Remarks on Becoming Prime Minister'. *Margaret Thatcher Foundation*. https://www.margaretthatcher.org/document/104078 (accessed 27 July 2019).
Thatcher, Margaret. 1987. 'Interview for Woman's Own'. *Margaret Thatcher Foundation*. https://www.margaretthatcher.org/document/106689 (accessed 27 July 2019).

Thicknesse, Robert. 2004. 'A Tuscan Love In'. *The Times*. https://www.thetimes.co.uk/article/a-tuscan-love-in-jgbgnwpblmt (accessed 21 August 2019).
Tighe, Dylan (Dir.). 2009. *Medea/Medea*. [theatre production] Headlong/Gate Notting Hill.
Treadwell, Sophie. 1993. *Machinal*. London: Nick Hern.
Treneman, Ann. 2016. 'The Times Review: Richard III'. *Theatre Record*. 36, 696.
Trueman, Matt. 2019. 'Headlong: The Little Theatre Company that Changed the Course of British Drama'. *The Telegraph*. https://www.telegraph.co.uk/theatre/what-to-see/headlong-little-theatre-company-changed-course-british-drama/ (accessed 27 July 2019).
Turin, Victor (Dir.). 1929. *Turksib*. [film] Vostokkino.
Turner, Lyndsey (Dir.). 2013. *Chimerica*. [theatre production] Headlong.
Turner, Lyndsey (Dir.). 2017. *The Treatment*. [theatre production] Almeida.
Tynan, Kenneth. 2002. *The Diaries of Kenneth Tynan*. London: Bloomsbury.
Unitt, Chris. 2012. 'Falling Headlong: A Theatre Trailer Case Study'. *www.chrisunitt.co.uk*. https://www.chrisunitt.co.uk/2012/04/falling-headlong-a-theatre-trailer-case-study/ (accessed 1 October 2019).
Vinterberg, Thomas (Dir.) *The Hunt*. [film] Zentropa.
Vinterberg, Thomas and Tobias Lindholm. 2018. *The Hunt: Delivery Draft*. Adapted by David Farr.
Vinterberg, Thomas and Tobias Lindholm. 2019. *The Hunt*. Adapted by David Farr. London: Faber.
von Trier, Lars (Dir.). 1996. *Breaking the Waves*. [film] Zentropa.
von Trier, Lars (Dir.). 2000. *Dancer in the Dark*. [film] Zentropa.
von Trier, Lars (Dir.). 2003. *Dogville*. [film] Zentropa.
Wachowski, Lana and Lilly Wachowski. 1999. *The Matrix*. [film] Warner Bros.
Walker, Tim. 2008. 'Sunday Telegraph Review: The Last Days of Judas Iscariot'. *Theatre Record*. 28, 373.
Wares, Sacha (Dir.). 2016. *Boy*. [theatre production] Almeida.
Wares, Sacha (Dir.). 2015. *Game*. [theatre production] Almeida.
Washburn, Anne. 2014. *Mr Burns*. London: Oberon.
Washburn, Anne. 2019. *Shipwreck*. London: Oberon.
Wedekind, Frank. 2001. *Lulu*. Adapted by Nicholas Wright London: Nick Hern.
Wilde, Oscar. 1968. *Salome*. Translated by Lord Alfred Douglas. New York: Dover Publications.
Wilde, Oscar. 2011. *The Importance of Being Earnest:* London: Samuel French.
Wilder, Thornton. 2014. *Our Town*. London: Samuel French.
Williams, Holly. 2017. 'Independent Review: Ink'. *Theatre Record*. 37, 696.
Williams, Tennessee. 2009a. 'Summer and Smoke' in *Baby Doll and Other Plays*, 111–92. Penguin Classics.
Williams, Tennessee. 2009b. *The Glass Menagerie*. London: Penguin.
Wodehouse, P. G. 2008. *Summer Lightning*. London: Arrow.
Wolf, Matt. 2015. 'International New York Times Review: Medea'. *Theatre Record*. 35, 978.
Wolf, Matt. 2017. 'International New York Times Review: Albion'. *Theatre Record*. 37, 1088–9.
Wong Davies, Ava. 2019. 'The Hunt'. *Exeunt*. http://exeuntmagazine.com/reviews/review-hunt-almeida-theatre/ (accessed 3 November 2019).
Wyver, John. 2019. Personal Interview.

INDEX

Note: Page numbers in italic denote images. Page numbers in the format 1 n.1 refer to footnotes.

Abdulla, Sara 11
Abrahami, Natalie 142, 148
ACE *see* Arts Council England
acting and actors
    directing new writing 128–30
    directing opera 135
    gender issues 149
    Goold on 3, 57–8, 62–3, 80
    Goold on directing 103–8, 112
    and new writing 127–30
adaptation 4, 43, 121–4
Adaptation (film) 50
Adès, Thomas 9
Aeschylus, *Oresteia* 88, 93
Aguirre-Sacasa, Roberto 75, 82
Albion (Bartlett) 67, 92, 94–6, *94*, 130
Alexander, Bill 3, 17, 115
Almeida, Anthony 88
Almeida Theatre 79–96
    Albion 94–6
    American Psycho 81–4
    artistic direction 136, 137, 138
    Goold's arrival 79–81, 84
    The Hunt 2 n.2, 4, 100, 108–14, 123, 150
    inclusivity 148, 149, 150
    Ink 92–3
    King Charles III 84–8, 94, 128
    The Last Days of Judas Iscariot 4, 34, 46–8, 79
    Medea 88–90
    The Merchant of Venice 70, 87
    programming 87–8, 96, 148, 151
    Richard III 90–2
    Shipwreck 100, 150–1
    talent development 139, 140, 143
    theatre mission 86–7
    theatre space 96, 120
Alvis, Lindsey 33, 39, 60, 74, 80, 83, 141, 142
Ambler, Scott 58, 60, 72, 73, 89
American Psycho (Ellis adaptation) 75, 78, 79, 80, 81–4, *82*
Angels in America (Kushner) 34, 38
Arcadia (Stoppard) 17–18, 23, 25, 29, 102
argument 4, 128
Aristotle, *Poetics* 88
art 25–6, 70, 87, 144

artistic direction 4, 136–8, 140, 141, 144, 145
Arts Council England (ACE) 16, 31, 32, 33, 39, 78, 81
assistant directors 139, 140
Attenborough, Michael 79, 80–1
Ayckbourn, Alan 16, 17, 20, 23

Bale, John, *King Johan* 121
BAME (Black, Asian and Minority Ethnic) artists 147, 148, 151
The Baron in the Trees (Calvino) 122
Barron, Clare, *Dance Nation* 148
Bart, Lionel, *Oliver!* 47, 58
Barthes, Roland, 'Death of the Author' 49
Bartlett, Kym 74
Bartlett, Mike
    Albion 67, 92, 94–6, *94*, 130
    Decade 73
    Earthquakes in London (*see Earthquakes in London*)
    Game 87
    Goold and actors 107
    Goold and new writing 1, 125, 126, 127, 128, 129, 141, 152
    King Charles III 84–8, *85*, 94, 126, 128, 152
    Love, Love, Love 95
    Medea adaptation 75
Barton, John 3, 36, 106
Batignano Opera Festival 122, 131–3
Bausch, Pina 27–8, 30, 85, 118
BBC (British Broadcasting Corporation) 26, 42, 70, 86
Bean, Richard, *The English Game* 47, 78
Beckett, Samuel, *Waiting for Godot* 18–19, 23, 29
Benedict, David 14
Bennion, Chris 151
Betrayal (Pinter) 18, 23
Betteridge, Natasha 17
Billington, Michael
    on Almeida plays 91, 92, 150
    on Goold for RSC 79
    on Headlong plays 42, 47, 61, 65
    on opera 134
    on Shakespeare plays 29, 42, 65, 92
Black, Asian and Minority Ethnic (BAME) artists 147, 148, 151

Index

Blair, Tony 72, 146
Blythe, Alecky
   Decade 73
   Little Revolution 87
Bogart, Anne 119
Bogdanov, Michael 9
Bond, Edward, *Restoration* 34, 37–9
Bouncers (Godber) 13
Boy (Butler) 90
Boyd, Michael 35, 79, 88, 137
Boys (Hickson) 75, 126
Boytchev, Hristo, *The Colonel Bird* 17
Brace, Adam, *They Drink it in the Congo* 93
Brantley, Ben 62, 83
Brayben, Katie *82, 85*
Brecht, Bertolt 66, 88
Brexit 94, 95, 96, 147
Bridewell Theatre, London 14
Bristol Old Vic 21, 22, 143
British theatre 1, 3, 12, 151–2
Broadway 42, 61, 62, 83–4, 86, 93
Brook, Peter 36, 85, 115
Brown, Georgina 42
Buether, Miriam 67, 74, 76, 95, 100, 151
Buford, Bill, *Among the Thugs* 53
Butler, Leo, *Boy* 90

Cadle, Giles 52
Calvino, Italo, *The Baron in the Trees* 122
Cambridge University 10–11, 12, 18, 20, 44
Campbell, Stuart 113
Camus, Albert, *The Myth of Sisyphus* 28
Capturing the Friedmans (documentary) 48–9
Carlton Television 12
Carmen Disruption (Stephens) 87
Carnegy, Patrick 69
Cavendish, Dominic 20, 22, 23
Cesti, Antonio, *Il pomo d'oro* 122, 131, 132
CFT *see* Chichester Festival Theatre
Chapman Brothers 1 n.1, 25–6, 124
Charles III see King Charles III (Bartlett)
Cheek by Jowl 79
Chekhov, Anton 66–7, 94–5, 109, 142
   The Seagull 17, 78
   Uncle Vanya 90, 93
Chew, Richard 133
Chichester Festival Theatre (CFT) 32, 39–42, 50, 51, 58, 62
   ENRON 2, 58–63
   Macbeth 3, 39–44, 51, 55, 118–19
   Six Characters in Search of an Author 2, 48–51
Chimerica (Kirkwood) 75, 78, 79, 80, 125
choreography 72, 73, 89, 100–1, 110–11
   see also dance
Christie, Bunny 93

Church, Jonathan
   Chichester Festival Theatre 39, 42
   on Goold 3, 96, 138, 139
   and Headlong 39, 42, 59
   Salisbury Playhouse 12–13, 14
cinema *see* films
classic texts 99, 123–4, 127, 141, 142–3
Clements, Andrew 134
Cohen, Danny 75
The Colonel Bird (Boytchev) 17
Company (musical) 12, 152
composers 100–1
   see also music
co-productions 33–4, 55, 79, 138
Cork, Adam
   Decade 73
   The End of the Affair 13–14, 122
   ENRON 73, 101
   on Goold 2, 3–4, 101, 102, 104, 125
   Hamlet 28
   The Hunt 2 n.2, 108, 110, 111
   Macbeth 119
   Medea 89
   Othello 20
   Paradise Lost 22, 101
   Richard III 91
   Rough Crossings 45
   Six Characters in Search of an Author 101
   The Tempest 36
   Time and the Conways 56, 57
Cracknell, Carrie 93, 96, 125, 137, 141, 142, 143
creativity 102, 103, 104, 105
Crimp, Martin, *The Treatment* 93
Cromer, David 87
Cusk, Rachel
   Aftermath 90
   Medea adaptation 89–90

'Daddy' (Harris) 148 n.1, 151
dance 72, 73, 76–7, 100–1, 110–11
Dance Nation (Barron) 148
Dancer in the Dark (film) 24, 134
Decade (Headlong play) 70–6, *71*, 77, 88, 126, 137
de Courcey, Jamie *27*, 28
de Jongh, Nicholas 14, 44
Derngate 16, 17
   see also Royal & Derngate, Northampton
The Descent (film) 43
Devlin, Es
   American Psycho design 82–3, 84
   Goold on directing 100, 109–12
   The Hunt design 108–13
dialectical theatre 128
directing 99–114
   adaptation 124
   artistic direction 136–8

167

Index

directing opera 134–5
emerging directors 14–15, 139–40
Goold on 29–30, 67, 80
Goold's directing style 1–5, 151–2
The Hunt 108–14
new writing 128–30
notes 107, 126, 127, 141
overview 4, 99–103
talent development 139–40
working with actors 103–8
diversity 81, 147–8
Doctor Faustus (Marlowe) 1 n.1, 23–4, 25, 37, 123, 124
Donmar Warehouse 12, 139
Donnellan, Declan 79, 105
Doran, Gregory 42
dramaturgy 1, 4, 72, 127
Dromgoole, Dominic 31–2, 37
D'Silva, Darrell *21*, 22
Dumezweni, Noma *49*, 50, 51
Dunne, J. W. 55, 56
Dunnett, Roderic 23

Earthquakes in London (Bartlett) 55, 66–8, 77, 94, 125–7, 129–30
Edward Gant's Amazing Feats of Loneliness (Neilson) 47
The Effect (Prebble) 75, 76–8, 80, 85, 96, 127–8
Eldridge, David 66
Elliott, Marianne 152
Ellis, Bret Easton, *American Psycho* 75, 81–4
The End of the Affair (Greene) 13–14, 15, 121–2
The English Game (Bean) 47, 78
English National Opera (ENO) 47, 61, 133, 134
ENRON (Prebble)
    Goold on 2, 67, 77, 100–2
    Headlong 47, 55, 58–63, 66, 71, 78
    image *59*
    new writing 125, 127, 152
    sound design 73
Euripides
    Bakkhai 88
    Medea 88–90
Everyman (play) 18
Eyre, Richard 80, 90, 138

Faber, Caroline
    in *The End of the Affair* 13, 121, 122
    on Goold 9
    in *King Lear* 52
    in *Mud* 11
    in *Paradise Lost 21*, 22
faith 4, 34, 64, 127
Falling Headlong (video trailer) 75
Farr, David
    The Hunt 2 n.2, 4, 100, 108–14, 123, 150
    Paradise Lost adaptation 21, 22

Faustus (Goold and Power play) 2, 3 n.3, 23–7, *24*, 29, 34, 38, 105, 123, 124
Fenwick, Oliver 38
The Fever (Shawn) 87
Fielding, Susannah
    in *American Psycho* 82, *82*, 83
    Goold's directing style 104, 105, 107–8
    in *The Merchant of Venice* 69, 105
Fiennes, Ralph 91–2
films
    adaptation to stage 123
    Faustus 26
    female artists 149
    Goold's directing style 3, 107
    Hamlet 42
    horror films 40, 43, 119, 120
    King Charles III 86
    Macbeth 40, 42–4, 47, 61, 70, 86, 119
    Othello 19
    Richard II 70
    Time and the Conways design 56
    True Story 80, 89
Finch, Henny
    Goold and talent development 142, 143
    Goold departure from Headlong 78, 79, 80
    Headlong early years 31, 32, 33–4, 39, 47, 51, 73
    Headlong later years 55, 78, 79, 80
Fleetwood, Kate 19, 40, 70–1, 88, 132
Fool for Love (Shepard) 10
Fornés, María Irene, *Mud* 11
Frecknall, Rebecca 1, 87, 145, 152
funding of theatre 31, 39, 78, 81, 136–8, 146

Gale, Mariah 36, *63*, 64, 75
Game (Bartlett) 87
Ganjavi, Nizami, *Haft Peykar* 133
Gardner, Lyn 18, 19, 23, 142
Garland, Judy 149–50
Gassman, Florian, *L'Opera seria* 133
Gate Theatre, Notting Hill 14, 122, 141, 142
gender issues 147, 148, 150
The Glass Menagerie (Williams) 12, 38
Gli equivoci (Storace) 133
Globe Theatre 86, 99
Godber, John, *Bouncers* 13
Godwin, Simon 14–15, 16–18, 20, 143
Goode, Chris, . . .*SISTERS* 47, 142
Goodman-Hill, Tom 76, 77
Goold, Rupert
    on actors 57–8, 62–3, 103–8
    adaptation 4, 121–4
    Almeida 4, 79–96
    artistic direction 4, 136–8
    on directing 3, 4, 9–11, 13, 29–30, 67, 80, 99–114, 124
    early life and education 9–11

168

Index

Headlong early years (2005–2009) 31–54
Headlong later years (2009–2013) 55–78
new writing 4, 58, 62–3, 67, 125–30
Northampton 4, 16–30
opera 4, 131–5
overview 1–5, 146–52
reputation 1, 2, 47, 151–2
Royal Shakespeare Company (RSC) 4, 35, 36, 38, 53, 61, 63–5, 68–70, 79, 115–16, 137 (*see also* Royal Shakespeare Company)
Salisbury Playhouse 12–15
Shakespeare 4, 79, 90–2, 106, 115–20, 127–8
talent development 4, 139–45
Gordon, Mick 122
Gormley, Antony, *Blind Light* 110
Goya, Francisco 25, 26, 124
Disasters of War 25
Graham, James, *Ink* 92–3, *92*
Grainger, Jenni 3, 32–4, 38–9, 50, 52, 73–4, 77–8, 80
Grant, Sebastian 43
Greek drama 88, 132
Greene, Graham
The End of the Affair 13–14, 15, 121–2
Travels with My Aunt 13
Greenwich Theatre, London 14, 63, 99, 131, 139
Grunpeter, Sacha 10, 31, 77
Guirgis, Stephen Adly
Jesus Hopped the 'A' Train 19, 34
The Last Days of Judas Iscariot 4, 34, 46–8, 79
Gulliver's Travels (Swift adaptation) 58, 66, 123
Guys and Dolls (musical) 9

Hamilton, Victoria 95, 103, 104, 130
Hamlet (Shakespeare)
Almeida 93
BBC TV film version 42
image *27*
Northampton 27–30
Shakespeare approaches 116, 118, 120
in *Six Characters in Search of an Author* 50, 51
Hampstead Theatre 9, 14, 139
Handy, Scott
in *Faustus* 24, 25
Goold's directing style 3, 96
Goold's work with actors 103, 104, 106–7
in *Macbeth* 116–17
in *The Merchant of Venice* 68, 70, 106
in *Richard III* 91
Shakespeare approaches 106, 116–20
in *Turandot* 134
Harders, Jake 50, 51
Harris, Jeremy O., *"Daddy"* 148 n.1, 151
Havergal, Giles 13, 23, 30
Haydon, Andrew 3, 54, 142
Headlong
American Psycho 83

artistic direction 136, 137, 138
Decade 70–6, 88
Earthquakes in London 66–8
The Effect 76–8
ENRON 58–63
Faustus 34, 38
Goold and British theatre 1
Goold early years (2005–2009) 31–54
Goold later years (2009–2013) 55–78
Goold departure 77–8, 79, 80
King Lear 51–4
The Last Days of Judas Iscariot 46–8
name change 33, 38
new writing 32, 125, 142
organization ethos 75, 86, 137, 138
overview 4, 31–4
Paradise Lost 33, 34, 35, 38
Restoration 37–9
Rough Crossings 44–6
Six Characters in Search of an Author 48–51
talent development 62, 141, 142, 143
as touring company 31–3, 38, 47, 77–8, 79
Hickling, Alfred 26
Hickson, Ella
as Almeida artist 87
Boys 75, 126
Decade 73
Goold and new writing 1, 126, 130, 152
Oil 84, 93, 125, 126, 149, 152
The Writer 126, 148–9
Hille, Anastasia 77
Hill-Gibbins, Joe 87
The Hollow Crown (BBC season) 70, 75
Holmes, Sean 47
Holt, Thelma 12
Homer
The Iliad 88
The Odyssey 88
Hopkins, Laura 19–20, 26, 27–8, 45, 55–7, 100
horror films 3, 40, 43, 119, 120
The Hothouse (Pinter) 9
The House of Shades (Steel) 148 n.1
The Hunt (Farr) 2 n.2, 4, 100, 108–14, 123, 150
Hunter, Sophie 61
Hytner, Nicholas 55, 79

Ibsen, Henrik 88
Little Eyolf 90
Icke, Robert
at Almeida 80, 81, 84, 87–8, 90, 93, 96
artistic direction 136, 137
Boys 75
Decade 71–3
emerging directors 15
The Fever 87
Goold and new writing 125

169

Index

Goold and talent development 1, 141, 143–4, 145, 152
Gulliver's Travels adaptation 123
Hamlet 93
Headlong 70–3, 75, 78
The Iliad 88
Mary Stuart 93, 118
Mr Burns 84
1984 78, 84
The Odyssey 88
Oresteia 88
Romeo and Juliet 143–4
Uncle Vanya 90, 93
The Wild Duck 152
The Iliad (Homer) 88
The Importance of Being Earnest (Wilde) 17
inclusivity 147, 148, 151
Ink (Graham) 92–3, *92*
Insignificance (Johnson) 23
Insult to Injury (Chapman Brothers artwork) 25

Jackson, Trevor 58
Jarecki, Andrew, *Capturing the Friedmans* 48–9
Jays, David 150
Jesus Hopped the 'A' Train (Guirgis) 19, 34
Johnson, Terry, *Insignificance* 23
Jones, Richard 49, 131
Jones, Ron Cephas 19, 46
Judy (film) 149–50

Katz, Richard 26, 64
Kaufman, Charlie 50
Kennedy, Laurence 11
Kidd, Ben 143
King Charles III (Bartlett) 84–8, *85*, 94, 126, 128, 152
King Johan (Bale) 121
King John (Shakespeare) 121
King Lear (Shakespeare) 47, 51–4, 55, 58, 118
Kingston, Jeremy 19
Kinnear, Rory 17
Kirkwood, Lucy, *Chimerica* 75, 78, 79, 80, 125
Kramer, Daniel 34
Kubrick, Stanley 26, 123
Kunuk, Zacharias, *Atanarjuat: The Fast Runner* 117
Kushner, Tony, *Angels in America* 34, 38

Lancaster, Sophie 64, 118
Landy, Michael, *Break Down* 82
Lange, Jessica 38
The Last Days of Judas Iscariot (Guirgis) 4, 34, 46–8, 79
Latif, Nadia 72
Ledwich, Anna, *Lulu* 142
Lennox, Amy *71*
Lepage, Robert 3
Lett, Ray 19

The Lion, The Witch and The Wardrobe (Goold adaptation/co-direction) 75–6
literary agents 144
Little Eyolf (Ibsen) 90
Little Revolution (Blythe) 87
Liverpool Everyman and Playhouse 51, 53
Lloyd, Jamie 66
Logan, Brian 14
London theatre 67, 88, 136, 146
Longhurst, Michael 87, 93
Lopez, Matthew 73
Love, Love, Love (Bartlett) 95
Lucas, Matt 91
Lukowski, Andrzej 83, 149
Lulu (Ledwich) 142
Lynch, Susan 46

Macbeth (Shakespeare)
 Chichester 3, 39–44, 51, 55, 118–19
 film version 42–4, 47, 61, 70, 86
 Goold imagination 1 n.1, 3, 69
 image *40*
 New York 47, 81
 Shakespeare approaches 116, 118–19
Macdonald, James 88
Machinal (Treadwell) 148
Macmillan, Duncan 78, 84
Malick, Terrence 70
Marlowe, Christopher
 adaptation 21, 123, 124
 Doctor Faustus 1 n.1, 23–4, 25, 37, 123, 124
 Tamburlaine the Great 23, 25
Marlowe, Sam 38
Marlowe Society, Cambridge 10, 20
Marmion, Steve 47, 143
Martin-Davis, Ashley 18
Mary Stuart (Icke) 93, 118
The Matrix (film) 56
Mayer, Louis B. 149, 150
McBurney, Simon 3, 44, 79, 152
McCurdy, Sam 43
McGuinness, Frank, *Speaking Like Magpies* 35
McIntyre, Blanche 78, 142–3, 148
McPherson, Conor, *The Weir* 18–19, 23, 103–4
Medea
 Bartlett adaptation 75
 Cusk adaptation 89–90
 Euripides 88
 image *89*
Medea Medea (Tighe) 142
Mendes, Sam 12, 15, 47
Menzies, Tobias
 in *Arcadia* 17, 18, 102
 in *Decade* 71–4, *71*
 in *The Fever* 87
 Goold's directing style 102, 104, 111, 112, 113

in *Hamlet* 27, 28, 29
in *The Hunt* 108, 111–13, 150
in *King Lear* 52
The Merchant of Venice (Shakespeare) 1 n.1, 68–70, 87, 102, 105, 106, 115, 117, 119
The Merry Wives of Windsor (Shakespeare) 115
#MeToo movement 148, 149, 150
Miéville, China 9
Miller, Dee 33
Miller, Jonathan 3, 99, 115, 118
Miller, Poppy 46, 112
Milton, John, *Paradise Lost* 33, 122–3
Mitchell, Katie 13, 152
Mnemonic (McBurney) 44
Morahan, Hattie 55, 56
Mr Burns (Washburn) 84, 151
Mud (Fornés) 11
Mullarkey, Rory 73
Munday, Donna 17
Murdoch, Rupert 147
music
   American Psycho 82, 83
   Decade 73
   The End of the Affair 13–14, 122
   ENRON 73, 101
   Goold on directing 100–1, 103, 109–11
   Hamlet 28
   The Hunt 109–11
   Macbeth 119
   opera 131–5
   Othello 20
   Paradise Lost 22
   Richard III 91
   Rough Crossings 45
   Six Characters in Search of an Author 101
   Travels with My Aunt 13
Muybridge, Eadweard 3 n.3, 56
The Myth of Sisyphus (Camus) 28

Napier Brown, Michael 16, 17
National Theatre (NT)
   Earthquakes in London 55, 66–8
   The Effect 75, 76–7
   Goold and Power meeting 20
   Goold's early years 9, 15
   Headlong 55, 56, 74, 76
   Hytner departure 79
   Power arrival 61
   Time and the Conways 3 n.3, 47, 55–8
Neilson, Anthony
   Edward Gant's Amazing Feats of Loneliness 47
   Orson Welles in the Land of the Peas 66
New Directions Award 141, 142
new writing 125–30
   developing new work 126–8
   directing new writing 128–30

Goold and British theatre 1, 152
Goold on 58, 62–3, 67
Headlong early years 32
overview 4, 125–6
talent development 142, 144
9/11 attacks 71, 72, 73, 74
1984 (Icke and Macmillan adaptation) 78, 84
No Man's Land (Pinter) 47–8
Norman (Lemieux Pilon 4D Art show) 57
Norman, Neil 74
Norris, Rufus 133
Northampton *see* Royal & Derngate, Northampton
Nottage, Lynn
   Decade 73
   Ruined 148
novel adaptations 121, 123
NT *see* National Theatre

The Odyssey (Homer) 88
Oil (Hickson) 84, 93, 125, 126, 149, 152
Okafor, Ben 45
Old Vic, London 115
Oliver! (Bart) 47, 58
Olivier Awards 42, 61, 80
O'Neill, Jonjo
   in *The Effect* 76–7
   in *Faustus* 24, 105
   Goold's directing style 3, 104, 105
   in *King Lear* 52, 52
   in *Paradise Lost* 21, 22
   in *Speaking Like Magpies* 35
On Thee We Feed (Chew and Norris opera) 133
opera 4, 68, 131–5
L'Opera seria (Gassman) 133
Oresteia (Aeschylus) 88, 93
Orr, Jake 75
Orson Welles in the Land of the Peas (Neilson) 66
OSC *see* Oxford Stage Company
Othello (Shakespeare) 3 n.3, 10, 11, 19–20, 26, 29, 51, 91, 115
Our Town (Wilder) 87
Oxford Stage Company (OSC) 31, 33, 38
   see also Headlong
Oxford University 12, 33

Paradise Lost (Milton) 33, 122–3
Paradise Lost (Power adaptation)
   Goold on 15, 29, 29, 85
   Goold's directing style 4, 101
   Headlong revival 34, 35, 38
   image *21*
   Northampton 20–3, 24, 29, 30
Parker, Freya 48, *49*, 50
Pattison, Lucy 88
Peele, George, *The Troublesome Reign of John, King of England* 121

Index

Pei, I. M. 30
Peter, John 28
Phillips, Caryl 44–6, 147
Pinter, Harold
   Betrayal 18, 23
   Goold on 58
   The Hothouse 9
   No Man's Land 47–8
Piper, Billie 76, 77
Pirandello, Luigi
   Goold on 58
   Six Characters in Search of an Author 2, 48–51, *49*, 76, 101, 123
poetic idiom 117–19
political theatre 146–7
Pollock, Adam 131, 132–3, 134
Il pomo d'oro (Cesti opera) 122, 131, 132
pop culture 102, 120
Postlethwaite, Pete 51, 52, 53
Powell, Michael 3 n.3, 19
Power, Ben
   arrival at National 79
   The Effect 77
   ENRON 58, 59
   Faustus 23–5, 30, 124
   Goold and new writing 125–6
   Goold and talent development 142, 145, 152
   on Goold influence 1, 2
   Gulliver's Travels 66
   Hamlet 27
   Headlong early years 32–4, 38, 44, 46–52, 53
   Headlong later years 55, 58, 59, 61, 66, 78
   Headlong departure 61, 66, 70–1
   King Lear 52, 53
   The Last Days of Judas Iscariot 46
   Northampton 20, 23–5, 27
   Paradise Lost 20, 21, 23, 85, 122
   Restoration 38
   Rough Crossings 44
   Six Characters in Search of an Author 48–51
Prebble, Lucy
   The Effect 75, 76–7, 80, 85, 96, 127–8
   ENRON (*see ENRON*)
   film and television interest 79
   Goold and new writing 1, 125, 127, 152
   The Sugar Syndrome 58
Pressburger, Emeric 3 n.3, 19
Priestley, J. B., *Time and the Conways* 3 n.3, 47, 55–8, *56*
programming 13, 87–8, 96, 138, 148
Puccini, Giacomo, *Turandot* 47, 61, 68, 133–4
Pugh, Aled *27*, 28

Quilter, Peter, *End of the Rainbow* 149

race issues 133, 147, 150, 151
Raggett, Daniel 88
Ramsden, Tim 18
Randle, Charlotte 52, 75, *89*
Reade, Simon 21
Ready, Paul 56, 57
Redgrave, Vanessa 91
regional theatre 16, 17, 29–30, 136, 142, 146
Regional Theatre Young Directors Scheme (RTYDS) 12, 139
rehearsals
   developing directors 141, 144
   directing new writing 129
   directing opera 135
   Goold directing style 3
   Goold on directing 102, 111–13
   Goold reputation 2
   The Hunt 111–13
   opera 132
   Time and the Conways 57–8
   working with actors 103–4, 105, 107
Renwick, Julie 39
research 101, 116, 128
Restoration (Bond) 34, 37–9
Richard II (Shakespeare) 70, 128
Richard III (Shakespeare) 90–2, 115, 120
Rickson, Ian 47
rights 144
Roberts, Clióna 33, 61
Romeo and Juliet (Shakespeare)
   developing directors 141, 143–4
   Goold on directing 4, 99
   Greenwich Theatre 14, 63, 99, 131, 139
   image 63
   influence on Prebble 127
   Northampton halls tour 20
   RSC 4, 61, 63–5, 118, 141
   Shakespeare approaches 116, 118
   stage design 64–5, 66
Rossini, Gioachino, *Le comte Ory* 133
Rough Crossings (Schama/Phillips adaptation) 34, 39, 44–6, 147
Royal & Derngate, Northampton 16–30
   Arcadia 17–18, 23, 25, 29, 102
   artistic direction 136–8
   Betrayal 18, 23
   Faustus 23–7
   Goold on 30, 31, 54
   Hamlet 27–30
   Insignificance 23
   organization ethos 137, 138
   Othello 19–20
   overview 4, 16–19
   Paradise Lost 20–3
   revivals 34
   Summer Lightning 23

Index

talent development 62
Waiting for Godot 18–19, 23, 29
The Weir 18–19, 23, 103–4
Royal Court 15, 61, 66, 78, 95, 125, 129
Royal Shakespeare Company (RSC)
   Complete Works Festival 88
   Goold early years 4, 38
   Goold tipped as artistic director 79
   Hamlet 42, 116
   The Merchant of Venice 68–70
   organizational messaging 137
   Richard II 70
   Richard III 115
   Romeo and Juliet 4, 61, 63–5, 118, 141
   Shakespeare approaches 53, 115–16
   Speaking Like Magpies 35
   style 85
   The Tempest 2, 35-37, 38, 115
   theatre mission 86
   Wood as producer 80
Royal Shakespeare Theatre (RST) 36, 115
Royal theatre, Northampton 16, 17, 18
   see also Royal & Derngate, Northampton
RSC *see* Royal Shakespeare Company
RST *see* Royal Shakespeare Theatre
RTYDS *see* Regional Theatre Young Directors Scheme
Ruined (Nottage) 148

Salinger, Justin 112
Salisbury Playhouse 12–15, 23, 139
   Bouncers 13
   The End of the Affair 13–14, 15, 121–2
   Summer Lightning 23
   Travels with My Aunt 13
Salome (Wilde) 66
Sater, Steven 81
Scaramouche Jones 51
Schama, Simon
   Landscape and Memory 44
   Rough Crossings 34, 44–6
Schechner, Richard 11
scripts 102, 105, 125
Scutt, Tom
   Almeida 85–6, 96
   Goold and talent development 1, 141
   Goold's directing style 3, 96, 100
   Gulliver's Travels 66
   Headlong 64–5, 68–9
   King Charles III 85–6
   The Merchant of Venice 68–9
   Romeo and Juliet 64–5, 141
The Seagull (Chekhov) 17, 78
Sellars, Peter 2
Seva, Botis 108, 110–11
   BLKDOG 110

Seymour, Lorna
   Almeida 83, 85
   Goold on directing 102
   Headlong early years 44, 50
   Headlong later years 60, 73, 90, 93
Shakespeare, William
   adaptation 123
   British traditions 62
   Goold approaches 4, 58, 106, 115–20
   Hamlet (*see Hamlet*)
   historical context 117
   influence on new writing 127–8
   King John 121
   King Lear 47, 51–4, 55, 58, 118
   Macbeth (*see Macbeth*)
   The Merchant of Venice (*see The Merchant of Venice*)
   The Merry Wives of Windsor 115
   Othello (*see Othello*)
   performance histories 116
   poetic idiom 117–19
   Richard II 70, 128
   Richard III 90–2, 115, 120
   Romeo and Juliet (*see Romeo and Juliet*)
   The Tempest (*see The Tempest*)
   Twelfth Night 10–11, 39, 120
   The Winter's Tale 120, 143
Shapiro, James 117
Shaw, Fiona 22
Shawn, Wallace, *The Fever* 87
Sheffield, Audrey 77
Sheibani, Bijan 148
Sheik, Duncan 75, 81, 82
Shelley, Paul *27*, 28, 41
Shepard, Sam, *Fool for Love* 10
Sher, Anthony 115
The Shining (film) 26
Shipwreck (Washburn) 100, 150–1
Sigur Rós 28
Simmons, Cat *71*
singers 131, 132, 135
. . .SISTERS (Goode) 47, 142
Six Characters in Search of an Author (Pirandello adaptation) 2, 48–51, *49*, 76, 101, 123
Smith, Chris 17
Smith, Matt 81, *82*
social media 75, 88
Speaking Like Magpies (McGuinness) 35
spectacle 1, 2, 4
Spencer, Charles 28, 29, 41, 46, 47, 65, 69
Spring Awakening (Wedekind) 81
staging 112–13, 121, 123, 135
Stalin, Joseph 39, 119
Stanislavski, Konstantin 106
Steel, Beth, *The House of Shades* 148 n.1
Stephens, Simon, *Carmen Disruption* 87

173

Index

Stewart, Patrick
    in *Macbeth* 39, 42, 43, 118
    in *The Merchant of Venice* 68
    in *Six Characters in Search of an Author* 51
    in *The Tempest* 36
Stones, Ben 22
Stoppard, Tom, *Arcadia* 17–18, 23, 25, 29, 102
Storace, Stephen, *Gli equivoci* 133
Styles, Richard 43
The Sugar Syndrome (Prebble) 58
Summer and Smoke (Williams) 145
Summer Lightning (Wodehouse) 23
Sunday Father (Pettle) 125
Supple, Ruth 18
Swift, Jonathan, *Gulliver's Travels* 123
Szalwinska, Maxie 74

talent development 1, 4, 139–45, 152
Tamburlaine the Great (Marlowe) 23, 25
Taylor, Paul 20, 22, 125
Taymor, Danya 148 n.1
The Tempest (Shakespeare) 1 n.1, 2, 35–7, 38, 69, 104, 115–18
Tennant, David 42
Tennyson, Alfred, *In Memoriam* 120
text work 105, 106, 128, 129
Thatcher, Margaret 52, 53
theatre
    accessibility 2, 81
    artistic direction 136–8
    and cinema 123
    current climate 146, 151
    finances and funding 31, 39, 78, 81, 136–8, 146
    Goold and British theatre 1, 4, 12, 151–2
    inclusivity 147, 151
    programming 87–8, 138
    ticket prices 81, 146
They Drink it in the Congo (Brace) 93
The Threepenny Opera (Brecht) 66
Tighe, Dylan, *Medea Medea* 142
Time and the Conways (Priestley) 3 n.3, 47, 55–8, 56
touring theatre
    artistic direction 136, 138
    emerging directors 142–3
    Goold and Godwin early years 18
    Headlong 31–3, 38, 47, 77–8, 79
Travels with My Aunt (Greene) 13
Treadwell, Sophie, *Machinal* 148
The Treatment (Crimp) 93
Trinity College, Cambridge 10–11
Troughton, Sam 63, 64
Trueman, Matt 152
True Story (film) 80, 89
Turandot (Puccini) 47, 61, 68, 133–4
Turksib (film) 43

Turner, Lyndsey 75, 93
Turner, Martin 40, *40*
Twelfth Night (Shakespeare) 10–11, 39, 120
Tynan, Kenneth 12

Uncle Vanya (Chekhov) 90, 93
Unitt, Chris 75
University College School (UCS) 9

verse speaking 106
Vinterberg, Thomas, *The Hunt* (film) 108, 109, 110
von Trier, Lars
    Breaking the Waves 24
    Dancer in the Dark 24, 134
    Dogville 24

Wachowski Sisters 3 n.3
Waite, Trevor 43
Waiting for Godot (Beckett) 18–19, 23, 29
Walston, Catherine 121–2
Ward, Anthony 60, 119
Wares, Sacha 87, 90, 93
Washburn, Anne
    as Almeida artist 87
    Mr Burns 84, 151
    Shipwreck 100, 150–1
Wedekind, Frank, *Spring Awakening* 81
Weinstein, Harvey 149
The Weir (McPherson) 18–19, 23, 103–4
West, Sam 60, 77
Whishaw, Ben 70, 88
The Wild Duck (Icke) 152
Wilde, Oscar
    The Importance of Being Earnest 17
    Salome 66
Wilder, Thornton, *Our Town* 87
Williams, Tennessee
    The Glass Menagerie 12, 38
    Summer and Smoke 145
The Winter's Tale (Shakespeare) 120, 143
The Wizard of Oz (film) 149
Wodehouse, P. G. 16, 21
    Summer Lightning 23
Wong Davies, Ava 150
Wood, Denise 80
Worton, Jenny 87
The Writer (Hickson) 126, 148–9
writers
    adaptation 124
    Decade writers 72
    and directors 80
    new writing 58, 125–30
    talent development 140, 152
Wyver, John 42, 43

Young Vic, London 1, 53